Social Issues in British Society

Social Issues in British Society

GERRY POPPLESTONE

HEINEMANN : LONDON

William Heinemann Ltd
10 Upper Grosvenor Street, London W1X 9PA
LONDON MELBOURNE TORONTO
JOHANNESBURG AUCKLAND

British Library Cataloguing in Publication Data
Popplestone, Gerry
  Social issues in British society.
  1. Great Britain – Social conditions – 1945–
  I. Title
  941.085'8   HN385.5

  ISBN 0-434-91579-3

Photoset by Rowland Phototypesetting Ltd
Bury St Edmunds, Suffolk
Printed in Great Britain by
Redwood Burn Limited,
Trowbridge

To Shunya, with love

'How I love my chocolate factory', said Mr Wonka . . . 'You see, my dear boy, I have decided to make you a present of the whole place. As soon as you become old enough to run it, the entire factory will become yours . . . I've got no children of my own. So who is going to run the factory when I get too old to do it myself? . . . Mind you, there are thousands of clever men who would give anything for the chance to come in and take over from me, but I don't want that sort of person . . . He will try to do things his own way'.

Charlie and the Chocolate Factory, by Roald Dahl, Puffin Books, 1973.

Contents

Preface

This book arose out of my experience in teaching day release students on professional courses. Through doing so, I realized that such students have very little time for extensive reading. They want to understand the gist of arguments usually laid out in books on the social structure of modern Britain.

Accordingly, this book aims to do three things. It aims to confront students who start off their professional work (especially in Housing or Social Services Departments of local authorities) with a series of prescriptions on how their customers should live their lives, based on the students' own understanding of the world. But therein lies a conflict. Students often come from social backgrounds quite different from the people they process in their work.

Students often assume, quite wrongly I believe, that their customers are free agents who can set their own goals and act appropriately. I have tried to focus on the constraints that people face in organizing their lives. People usually do not have much room for manoeuvre in how they live their lives. Everyone is caught up in a web of mutual obligations to others, as well as a set of constraints through lack of resources (especially time and money). To highlight these forces, I have adopted a simple Marxist framework. It has the advantage of showing how a person's position in the social structure is intimately connected with control of the means of production.

Most students do not readily make that connection. They usually assume that their own set of values has been arrived at rationally and fairly objectively. They often show surprise when teachers on such courses attempt to show how the students' own class position determines the way they view the world. I hope that my choice of explanatory framework will help to make students rather more clear about their own assumptions about the world.

People make their choices about how to live and what they want in life within their own set of constraints. The framework I have used focuses on some of these constraints before looking at the choices open to people at various points in the social structure. I think this helps students to distance themselves from their own set of values and see their customers more clearly in the context of their class position.

I have also tried to help students look at certain questions, not at personal problems encountered by some people but as public issues, to use C. Wright Mills' phrase. I have made passing reference to the way that such issues as race, poverty, unemployment, and divorce and family violence are often treated as personal problems. But I have treated these issues as public issues. This fits in neatly with a Marxist framework.

My overall concern in writing this book was to get students to think for themselves rather than learn answers to stock questions. I hope that the style I have adopted will encourage some students to take the issues further.

One

Demographic change

How rapidly does society change? And what are the most important changes that have happened in British society since the last war? My guess is that most people in their heart of hearts think that there have been few important changes that have significantly altered the lives of British people. We might all agree that the jet engine, the pill and now possibly the micro-chip are important innovations, and that unemployment and inflation are important economic issues. But we mostly believe that people are still basically the same as they always were. Human nature hardly changes. But is this really the case?

We shall map out the important social changes that have happened during this century, and discuss how they have affected us. Understanding how society changes may be quite difficult to conceptualize. It is important to see the changes in some concrete way and much social change is somewhat abstract. We shall start with some of the more obvious changes that have gone on within the family, and gradually move on to the less tangible changes later in the book. We shall first look at demography.

Demography is about populations and population change. It is about numbers of people and aims to highlight the underlying influences of population change. As such, it is a convenient place to begin an analysis of British society. We shall first of all describe the changes that have occurred in the size and composition of the population of Britain since the turn of the century. And we shall assess which of those changes have been the most important and what those changes imply for the structure of British society.

POPULATION

In 1971 the population of the United Kingdom (that is, England, Wales, Scotland and Northern Ireland) was 55.6 million. This was roughly double what it had been 100 years earlier. This dramatic increase was not even; the population grew in fits and starts. It was rapid at the beginning of the century but by the late 1960s the rate of increase had tailed off to half of what it had been. Indeed, at times the increase was so slight that demographers worried lest the population might begin to stagnate or even decline.

Table 1.1 shows the size of population of the United Kingdom at ten-yearly intervals from 1901 to 1981. It indicates the extent as well as the unevenness of the population growth. On the face of it, it is hard to think of an explanation for these rather erratic growth rates. But there are other changes in the population associated with

Table 1.1. Population in the UK

	000s	Average Annual Increase
1851	22,259	
1901	38,237	
1911	42,082	385
1921	44,027	195
1931	46,038	201
1951	50,290	212
1961	52,807	252
1971	55,907	47
1981	56,379	−44[1]

[1]Change between 1981 and 1982.

Source: CSO. Annual Abstract of Statistics.

growth that we may find hard to explain. For instance, between 1931 and 1974 the population of Great Britain grew by 9.6 million from 44.8 to 54.4 million. Of that increase 30 per cent were aged over 70; 43 per cent were over 65 and 56 per cent were over 60. By 1974 16.8 per cent of the population was over normal retirement age compared with only 9.4 per cent in 1931. And in the ten years from 1964 to 1974 the annual numbers of births in Great Britain fell from 980,000 to 710,000. In other words, as the population grew this century so the age structure of the population has noticeably changed. The two facts – an increase in the number of elderly and a decline in the number of births – were not peculiar to Britain alone but took place throughout most of Western Europe. It might seem surprising that, with the world as a whole concerned about population rising too fast, we should be worried about the reverse process.

A simple explanation is difficult to find. To explain these changes we need to analyse the figures in some detail and look at the separate processes of births, deaths and migration, since it is the interaction of these three processes that account for changes in the structure and composition of the population. While the overall changes may not appear terribly dramatic, the individual changes, especially the way the birth rate has dropped in the last fifty years, have been startling. Table 1.2 summarizes these changes and Figure 1.1 shows the up-and-down nature of births, compared with the rather more steady flow in the rate of deaths.

DEMOGRAPHIC TRANSITION

This sort of change is part of what is called the demographic transition, a concept that relates changes in births and deaths to broad changes in economic development. The notion provides a reasonably good description of what happened to population growth during the the course of the industrial revolution. According to this interpretation, population growth passes through a number of stages, each stage defined by a different balance between birth rates and death rates. For Britain (along with the rest of Europe) the slowly growing population of the pre-industrial stage was maintained by a balance between high fertility and (not quite so) high mortality.

As industrialization proceeded, the second stage, lasting from the late 18th century, saw a steady drop in mortality thanks to particular

Table 1.2. Population changes and projections, UK

| | Population at start of period | Average annual change | | | | |
		Live births	Deaths	Net natural change	Net civilian migration and other adjustments	Overall annual change
	000	000	000	000	000	000
Census enumerated						
1901–11	38,237	1,091	624	467	−82	385
1911–21	42,082	975	689	286	−92	194
1921–31	44,027	824	555	268	−67	201
1931–51	46,038	785	598	188	+25	213
Mid-year estimates						
1951–61	50,290	839	593	246	+6	252
1961–66	52,807	988	633	355	+12	367
1966–71	54,643	937	644	293	−40	253
1971–76	55,907	766	670	96	−37	60
1976–77	56,206	655	660	−5	−22	−26
1977–78	56,179	664	665	−	−12	−12
1978–79	56,167	720	672	48	+12	60
1979–80	56,227	744	659	86	−1	87
1980–81	56,314	741	656	85	−20	64
1981–82	56,379	722	669	53	−96	−44
1982–83	56,335	722	660	62	−21	41
	56,314	732	675	56	−34	22

Projections						
1983–86	56,382	786	686	100	−34	66
1986–91	56,715	823	689	134	−34	100
1991–96	57,215	793	685	107	−34	74
1996–2001						

1. Data for Northern Ireland prior to 1981 have been revised to the new population definition. Otherwise population estimates are as described in the Appendix, Part 1: Population and population projections.

2. Projections are based on mid-1983 estimates of home population for England, Wales, and Scotland, and mid-1981 for Northern Ireland.

Source: Office of Population Censuses and Surveys; Government Actuary's Department General Register Office (Scotland); General Register Office (Northern Ireland).

Figure 1.1. *Population changes and projections*

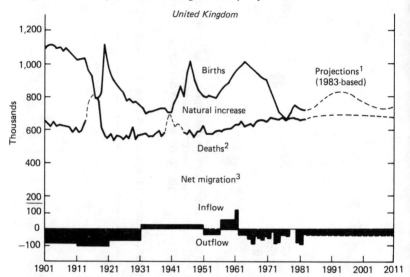

[1] Actual figures relate to calendar years. Projections relate to 12-month periods ending at 30 June in each year shown. They are based on mid-1983 estimates of home population for England, Wales, and Scotland, and mid-1981 for Northern Ireland.
[2] The dots on this line cover the periods 1914–1918 and 1939–1945 which include deaths of non-civilian and merchant seamen who died outside the country.
[3] Figures before 1961 show net civilian migration and other changes. Figures from 1961 show net civilian migration only.

Source: Office of Population Censuses and Surveys; Government Actuary's Department; General Register Office (Scotland); General Register Office (Northern Ireland)

improvements in public health standards in our towns as well as developments in medical science: while fertility remained high. This was the period of the population boom. It lasted in Britain until the early part of this century. The third stage, it was thought, should produce a new equilibrium once both birth and death rates found their new low levels, but this has not happened.

Demographic transition – either from a slow- to a fast-growing population, or vice versa – is usually associated with a marked change in the age structure of the population. So while some countries are faced with an explosion of births and the bulk of their population are under 21, we in Britain are faced with a shrinking birth rate and a rapidly-growing population of the elderly. Recently, demographers have pointed to a fourth stage where fertility rates are below death rates. The population fails to replace itself if average family size is less than 2.1; recently family size has dropped as low as 1.8 and there is little clear evidence that family size will rise in the near future. At this stage it seems that fertility, more than mortality or migration, is the key factor affecting population change. And at this stage, it is somewhat more difficult to relate the changes in fertility to any changes in industrialization.

Such processes as industrialization or urbanization are now so well advanced that their effects on fertility are minimal. Demographers argue (and it is fairly speculative) that, with reproduction now well under control, fertility is more likely to be sensitive to economic trends since families may plan the size of their families as an aspect of their consumption patterns.

The notion of demographic transition only roughly fits the facts. But it hardly *explains* anything. Fertility may be loosely related to levels of economic development but that does not explain why or how. Nor does it help us to understand how individual couples set about determining what size families they want. Also demographic transition theory does not explain how countries proceeded through the stages at different speeds, nor does it account for the variations in the relationship between the timing and speed of mortality decline and those of the fall in fertility. It ignores the important changes that have happened in fertility decline in different social classes and, lastly, recent falls in fertility have left the theory in a quandary about what will happen in the future.

At least the theory has highlighted the importance of the relationship between births and deaths for any balance in the population, and the realization that we are now in a fourth stage has sparked off once again a debate among demographers and policy makers about the likely seriousness of a stagnant or declining population.

FERTILITY

In order to understand the relationship behind this simple concep-
tualization about demographic changes we must unravel the strands
of the population equation more fully. We shall begin with fertility,
by which we mean the numbers of babies born to women in the
population. Table 1.3 shows the crude birth rates for the UK. These
have fallen from about 35 per thousand in the 1850s to a low of 15
per thousand in the 1930s. This was the third stage of Britain's
demographic transition.

But the birth rates have not remained at the level of the 1930s.
They peaked again in 1947 to 20.5 per thousand, fell in 1955 to 15
per thousand and rose to 18.4 per thousand in 1960. Since then the
rates have wobbled back to the 1930 rate of 15 per thousand in 1971

Table 1.3. Births in the UK

	Total	Rate[1]	Fertility Rate[2]
1900	1095	28.6	
1910	1035	24.6	
1920	1018	23.1	
1930	750	16.3	
1940	723	15.0	
1950	803	16.0	
1960	946	17.9	
1970	880	15.8	
1971	870	16.0	83.7
1976	649	11.9	60.6
1977	632	11.6	58.2
1978	661	12.1	60.1
1979	706	12.9	63.4
1980	725	13.2	64.2
1981	704	12.8	61.5
1982	692	12.6	59.9
1983	694	12.7	59.6

[1]Live births per thousand of all ages.
[2]Live births per thousand women
aged fifteen to forty-four.

CSO. Social Trends 15, 1985 Edition.

and they are still falling. In 1977 they fell to an all-time low of 11.8 per thousand and the evidence from Luxembourg and West Germany suggests that they could fall still further.

The post-war bulge of 1947 is easy to explain. The disruption of war-time life led many families to postpone starting a family until they could see the glimmer of stability. After the war the dominant trends in birth rates continued until 1955. But the period between 1955 and 1964 was anomalous.

The most striking changes in the birth rate this century occurred in the 1970s. In just over a decade the level of births fell from close to the upper end to close to the lower end of the range in the annual number of births recorded during the century – a rate of decline never previously experienced. The decade from 1955 to 1964 saw an average annual increase in births of 3 per cent reaching a peak figure of 876,000 in 1964 which was over 200,000 more births than in 1955. Since then the annual decline in births has averaged 2 per cent up until 1971 and has since shown a sharp annual decline of around 7 per cent for 1972 and 5 per cent in 1974. The Royal Commission on Population (1949) concluded that there would be 'a substantial decline in the annual number of births over the next fifteen years'. As it turned out those fifteen years culminated in fertility rates that were higher than they had been for over forty years. Even by the late 1950s the increase in fertility, now very much in evidence, was still seen as a short-term fluctuation. It was not until the increase persisted for ten years, with a rise of a third in the annual number of births, that people came to terms with a different level of fertility and demographers began to incorporate different assumptions about future family size into their population projections.

These remarkable changes in fertility during this century will need some explanation. A simple analysis of increases and decreases in annual births is not satisfactory for coming up with an understanding of the reproductive behaviour of the population. Nor is there a simple factor that will easily account for the changes. In investigating birth rates, we really want to know whether or not an increase in the rates implies a change in family size. Did the average British couple suddenly decide to have larger families in the late 1950s? We shall answer this later.

The crude birth rate is, in any case, rather misleading since it can be based on a population whose composition changes over time. As people live longer, that thousand of the population, used for calculating crude birth rates, will include more elderly people, well past childbearing age. Hence birth rates are best expressed as a proportion of the number of women of childbearing age (which is usually taken to be fifteen to forty-four) in the population. This gives us a better idea of the size of population of women 'at risk' of child-bearing. We also need to sort out the relationship between the timing of family building over the reproductive life span of a woman and the ultimate size of any family. Fertility rates over an age span of fifteen to forty-four years mask a host of different fertility patterns among women of different ages as well as changes in marriage patterns, duration of marriages, and the timing and spacing of child-bearing within marriages. The job of a demographer is to sort out these rather complex relationships.

Stocks and Flows

To understand fertility we need to distinguish between *stock* data and *flow* data, to borrow two terms from accounting procedures. Any warehouseman will know that the turnover of any item can be calculated by measuring not only the stock existing in the warehouse at any particular time, but also by the flow of that stock item through the warehouse during any particular period. Similarly, we can think of fertility as partly a function of the stock of women in the childbearing age in the population at any one time, and the flow of women (see Figure 1.2).

If we look at the number of births to fifteen to nineteen year-old women in the population, we find a startling increase between 1951

Figure 1.2: Increases in fertility

STOCK FACTORS:

- increase in number of women of childbearing age
- increase in number of women who marry
- decrease in childless marriages
- increase in births outside marriage

FLOW FACTORS:

→ women marrying earlier
→ compression of family formation period
→ earlier age of beginning a family

and 1964 of two-and-a-half times the number of births compared with the previous period. There appears at first sight to have been a rise in promiscuity among the young (the permissive society?) In fact half the increase was attributable to the rise in the number of (or stock) of female teenagers, born during the post-war bulge. As well as that, the marriage rate (a flow factor) for this age group increased from forty-two to seventy per thousand between 1951 and 1964. Similarly, half the increase of births to twenty to twenty-four year-old women was due to the numbers of women (stock factor) of that age group in the population and an increase in their marriage rates (a flow factor).

Marriage rates have risen throughout this century. In 1900 only a third of the total population was married, whereas by 1960 the proportion had increased to a half (in spite of the fact that the population now contains a higher proportion of elderly widows: which would tend to depress marriage rates). Marriage rates of the young particularly are rising. In the 1930s only one in four of 20–24 year-old women married whereas in the 1970s almost two in three of that age group married. These increasing marriage rates are partly accounted for by an increase in the numbers of men relative to women from the 1950s onwards. By 1971 there were almost 1.4 times as many single men in the population as there were single women and this helped to increase marriage rates among women. The change in the sex ratio may also have contributed to the rise in the (largely male) gay movement in the late 1960s, the surplus of men made the possibility of some of them not being heterosexual more feasible. But also, greater competition among men to find marriage partners may have been a factor in bringing down the age of marriage. The average age of both bride and groom fell steadily from 1945 till the late 1960s. In 1971 the mean age for first marriages was 24 for men and 22 for women (24 and 25 respectively at the end of the War).

An important flow factor in fertility is any change in the timing of births within marriage. Some age groups have their children in the early years of marriage; others postpone their families until later. These changes are difficult to unravel using data on total births. Demographers analyse these changes in fertility patterns using cohort analysis.

A cohort is a group of people with a common reference point. Thus all women born in 1930, or all women married for the first time in 1970 when aged twenty to twenty-four are cohorts. Cohort analysis is a way of following through time the family-building histories of a group of women, born or married in a particular year, and then comparing their experiences with groups of women born or married at a different time. Cohort analysis can be used in different ways. It can shed light on different patterns of fertility behaviour among women born or married at different times. It can be applied to all aspects of marriage patterns, family formation and marriage dissolution to understand the changes that have taken place in the population.

Thus we can look at women born in the 1930s and examine in what ways they behaved differently from women born in the 1940s. If we do, we discover that those born in the 1930s reached their peak fertility when aged twenty to twenty-nine. But those born in the 1940s reached theirs earlier when aged twenty to twenty-four. This meant that the flow of births of some of the mothers born in the 1930s coincided with the flow of births of some of the mothers born in the 1940s. And this bunching of births caused by the change of timing of family formation is now known to be the prime contributor to the rise in births in the years between 1955 and 1964.

We can only speculate as to why this was so. Demographers are coming round to the belief that people's decisions about the timing and size of their families may be related to short-term economic or social considerations. Women born during the depressed period of the 1930s were at school during the war and started work in the post-war austerity period. They were subject to some important experiences. Their attitudes were moulded by parents who had survived the depression. Women born in the 1940s may have been subject to war-time scarcities but they probably viewed the late 1950s and early 1960s as a time when they had never had it so good. Expectations about the future were high and this might account for the earlier building up of their families.

So the strange increase in crude birth rates in the late 1950s and early 1960s is due neither to a sudden new found promiscuity among post-war teenagers, nor to an impulse of couples to have a larger family in that period. Nor even is it due to some strange failure in the quality of contraception devices sold, nor even a sudden loss of electric light. Demographers, with cohort analysis, can provide more plausible accounts!

By contrast with this period of increasing birth rates, annual births in the period since 1964 fell by an average of two per cent each year to 1970, with a further sharp annual decline of around 7 per cent in 1972 and 1973 and 5 per cent in 1974. They kept falling to 1977, the year with fewest births this century. So the country experienced a fall in births from a peak in 1964 of almost the highest this century, to a trough in 1976 which is the lowest this century, the greatest recorded change in the numbers of births in just twelve years. How can we explain this? It is not just a question of a change in family size. The average number of children born for different generations of women has shown more stability than the average fertility rates.

When we look at the different cohorts, we see that there was little change in the percentage who had married by ages twenty and twenty-five as between women born in 1940 (whose main childbearing ages of twenty to thirty occurred in the 1960s) and women born in 1950 (whose main childbearing ages occurred in the 1970s). For women born in 1955 there has been some increase in the proportion married by age twenty, a reflection in part of the 1969 Family Law Reform Act which reduced the age of majority to eighteen. This new tendency to earlier marriage is shown by the marriage rates in the sixteen to nineteen age group, rates which rose from an average of seventy-six per thousand for the period 1961–5 to ninety-three per thousand for the period 1970–3.

If other things were equal we would expect some increase in births among young married women as a result of earlier marriages. Instead the number of births to married women aged under twenty fell from 60,000 in 1969 to 53,000 in 1973. This indicates that newly married couples are remaining childless for longer in the early stages of marriage. For instance, the proportion of women married in 1970 aged twenty to twenty-four who were childless after three years of marriage is virtually the same as the proportion of women married in 1961 at the same ages who were childless after two years of marriage. In other words, the 'centre of gravity' for family formation within marriage has shifted to the third and fourth years of marriage.

But this is what we would have expected. The cohort having their babies in the early 1960s had started families considerably earlier than the cohort having their babies in the late 1950s. The next cohort was returning to family formation patterns similar to the earlier cohort; not very surprising when we think about it. Since

1977 births began to rise again. It peaked between 1979 and 1980 (see Figure 1.1 and Table 1.3). Since then it has shown signs of falling again. As yet, there are no signs that demographic life will be as dramatic as it was in the 1960s and 1970s.

We now seem to experience peaks and troughs in the numbers of births, which are explainable mainly in terms of the timing of families. These short-term changes in family formation patterns appear to be related to social and economic changes in ways we are not really clear about. Perhaps decisions to invest in babies now compete with decisions to invest in housing.

However it happens marriage begins earlier, and fertility sometimes begins quite soon (two years) or people wait a while (three or four years). And fertility now seems to end earlier. We cannot yet be sure. It takes up to fifteen years, using cohort analysis, to get a complete picture of how a particular cohort responded in any particular period of history. So the family-building patterns of couples married in the mid-1960s will only be clear in the 1980s. But the broad changes are clear. For example, women who married in 1889 eventually had 5.13 children each, and they had 60 per cent of these children by the time they have been married ten years. Women who married in 1948 also had 82 per cent of all the children they were going to have in their first ten years of marriage. And in 1966, 58.6 per cent of all births occurred to women who had been married less than five years. By 1974, the proportion had risen to 63 per cent. Also, although the number of women aged thirty to forty-four decreased by 8.4 per cent between 1964 and 1971, the number of births to women in this range went down by 33.5 per cent. We can be fairly certain that this compression in the period has since increased. We also know that there is a decline in the proportion of families going on to have four or more children, a marked decline in childless and one-child families and an increase in the proportion of two-children families. Between 1951 and 1964 the proportion of families with one child fell dramatically from 27 to 17 per cent, and the proportion of families with four or more fell (after a rise) from 8 to 7 per cent. But the proportion of two-children families rose steadily from 35 to 48 per cent and the proportion of three-children families rose from 16 to 19 per cent.

Hence, in spite of the short-term fluctuations in births owing to changes in the timing of family formations with different cohorts of couples, we can also detect a secular decline in fertility attributable to a steady drop in family size.

So, in the last twenty years we can identify four important influences on birth rates. First, there has been a change in the age at which women are likely to have children. The childbearing stage happens earlier, and especially happens to women under twenty. This has continued with increasing emphasis in succeeding age groups. Second, we can detect the impact of a particular historical generation passing through their childbearing years, whose high fertility at first increased the age cycle change to produce the rising trend in births in the late 1950s and early 1960s. Third, there is evidence of a subsequent compression in the period taken in family building, with the consequence of a more recent falling off in crude birth rates. Fourth, the change of most interest to us has been the universal drop in family size. In the past, the first social group to limit family size was the entrepreneurial class. Banks and Banks (1964) discuss the attempts of this class to limit their families. Faced by a fall in profits at the end of the last century, they needed to cut their consumption patterns in order to maintain their levels of capital accumulation. Hence the only way they could do this and still provide their children with the sort of privileged backgrounds they wanted, was to have fewer children. Family limitation was later practised by other social classes for other reasons. First, as we shall see later, infant mortality was brought under control. Couples could be more confident of planning their families in the knowledge that some of the children would not immediately die. Second, rising incomes for working-class families made it possible for couples to limit family size with the intention of providing a better standard of life for the few children they proposed to have. Third, the greater diffusion of birth control methods in the 1960s made this possible.

Since 1970, births have declined for all social classes. Between 1970 and 1975 they fell by 24 per cent. But for manual workers they fell by 30 per cent, and for clerical workers they fell by 25 per cent. This move to smaller families is a widely accepted phenomenon. We may still believe that the lower classes have large families but evidence shows that this is not so any longer. Reproduction is now something that is under complete control for all kinds of families. Family size in the future is more likely to be related to economic conditions and changes in government policies affecting families. These are topics we shall discuss in Chapter 5.

MORTALITY

The second component of the stages of demographic transition is mortality. Death rates are less important than birth rates, at least in this century and especially since the 1960s. The widespread use of the 'pill' and IUD had enabled individuals to determine their reproductive decisions more fully.

Mortality cannot be controlled in the same way. It is determined by a different set of influences. Fertility now seems to be related to short-term economic and social conditions. Mortality is less sensitive to short-term variations but, instead, follows well defined trends associated with health and environmental improvements. This can easily be seen in Figure 1.1 which shows a steady improvement in death rates over time compared with the ups and downs of fertility. And the trends in fertility and mortality have been quite different this century. Birth rates have fallen dramatically especially in the last two decades. Death rates fell rapidly in the early part but have since declined more slowly. Between 1880 and 1910 they fell by a third. Since then they dropped slowly up to the 1930s to reach a level of about ten to twelve deaths per thousand of the population.

Baldly stated, fertility is about a stock of women of childbearing ages and their decisions whether and, if so, when to build a family. By contrast, mortality is basically about a flow of the population, going through a set of experiences that exposes them to different rates of risk of mortality. Thus babies catch influenza and can die; young men buy motor bikes and increase their risk of death, older people smoke heavily or eat too many steaks that may bring on a coronary. These selective events that different age groups experience can cause deaths directly or may influence a person's general state of health. Selective events in demography include joining the army, joining any occupation, marriage, migration or whatever.

Infant Mortality
The separation of fertility and mortality is a somewhat artificial distinction. As soon as a baby is born its risk of death is high. In fact death rates at the beginning of the life span are as high as the death rates of seventy-year-olds in the population. The death rates of babies on their first day of birth are high. They exceed those in the rest of the first week and, together, these exceed later infant mortality.

The term, infant mortality, is a general one that covers all babies who die in the first year of life. It is an important indicator of the social, environmental and health conditions of any country, and is often used as a comparative measure of any country's well-being. The different types of infant mortality are shown below in Figure 1.3. The most important is peri-natal mortality (those born dead and those who die in the first week) and neo-natal mortality (those who die in the first four weeks of birth). Peri-natal deaths are most likely to be caused by something associated directly with birth (such as congenital diseases or some genetic defect in the child giving it little chance of survival). Neo-natal mortality is associated with external conditions such as infectious diseases or accidents.

The other type of death associated with childbirth is, of course, the death of women in pregnancy or childbirth. The rate has always been surprisingly high although it is falling rapidly. It was twenty-six times more frequent in the 1930s and five times more frequent in the 1950s than in 1971. But, even in 1971, the number of women who died in childbirth was 0.17 for every 1,000 births.

Table 1.4 shows the improvement in death rates in England and Wales between the nineteenth and twentieth century. In a hundred years, infant mortality has been reduced sevenfold, childhood mortality fourteenfold, and mortality in the reproductive years fivefold.

The drop in infant mortality is dramatic. Up to the beginning of

Figure 1.3 Rates for infant mortality

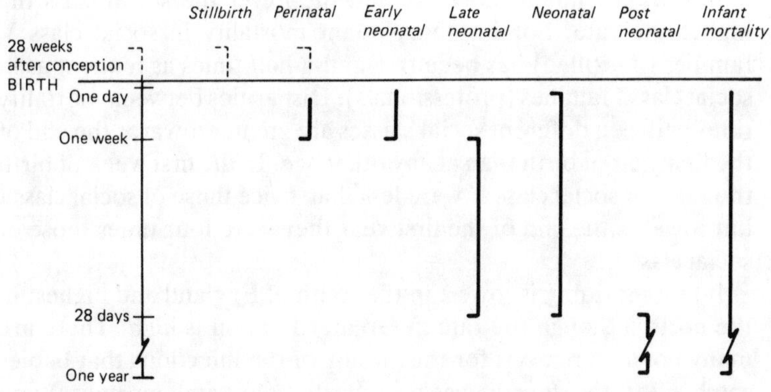

Source: Lambert, 1976.

Table 1.4. Mortality by age groups per thousand

Age		1860	1960
Prenatal	Prenatal	250	180
0 –1	Infancy	150	19
1 –14	Childhood	70	5
15–44	Reproductive	150	30
45–65	Middle Age	140	124
65	Old age	240	642
	Life expectancy	43	72

Source: Llewellyn-Jones, 1974.

the twentieth century it had remained constant at about 150 deaths for every 1,000 live births, for about fifty years. But the first three decades of the twentieth century saw a real breakthrough in improving these high rates. By the outbreak of the Second World War infant mortality had fallen to fewer than 53 for every 1,000 live births. This improvement can be attributed largely to better maternal nutrition as well as the greater availability of protective innoculations. Infant mortality fell again to 32 per 1,000 live births by the late 1940s thanks largely to the introduction of penicillin. In the 1950s it fell to about 23, in the 1960s it was about 19 and by 1978 it had fallen to 14 for every 1,000 births. But stillbirths are still significantly more common among working-class than among middle-class families. In fact social class and location are both sensitive indicators for infant mortality and the lower the social class the higher the rate. For instance, infant mortality in social class V families (unskilled) has been two-and-a-half times as fequent as in social class I families (professionals). Disparities between mortality rates between different social classes are greater towards the end of the first year of birth than at any other age. In the first week of birth the rates of social class V were less than twice those of social class I but towards the end of the first year they were four times those of social class I.

Infant mortality is lowest in the south of England and highest in the north although the rate in Greater London is high. There are many possible reasons for this. Many of the infections that babies catch after the fourth week of birth (neo-natal mortality) are associated with the damp or over-crowded living conditions, more likely to be found in the North and in London. While children of all social classes are likely to contract some of the typical childhood infections, those living in overcrowded houses are likely to do so early in life when the risk of fatality is greatest.

Adult Mortality
Although death rates have not fallen suddenly this century in the way that birth rates have changed, they have fallen slowly and steadily. For age groups above fifty-five years death rates in 1971 were four-fifths what they were forty years earlier. And for those age groups under thirty-five, death rates are now between a fifth and a quarter what they were forty years earlier.

The improvement in death rates (especially for men) since the middle of the nineteenth century is striking. At that time half of all males born died before they were forty. Even by 1900 still less than half survived until their fiftieth birthday and it was not until the 1950s that half of all males were likely to live a full working life. But it now seems likely that, of all males born in 1971, two-thirds will survive until retirement. Death rates for women are lower than for men at all ages. In fact the sex differential for life expectancy has widened from two years to six, giving women a longer life expectancy than men.

While sex is an important indicator of differential mortality, age is of course more so. Mortality variations by age are not only due to the passage of time and to the development and decay of the body. People also pursue their lives in different surroundings and the environment undoubtedly plays a part. This is particularly so with respect to accidents. Table 1.5 shows the high rates of accidents that males in the population face, particularly in their late teens and twenties. Differential death rates by sex are also partly accounted for by differences in occupational mortality. Death rates for men aged twenty-five to twenty-nine and social class V are more than three times those of similar aged men of social class I. A recent study of occupational mortality in 1970 showed that non-manual social classes had 14 per cent fewer deaths and manual classes 12 per cent more deaths, compared with the national average. And the relative difference between unskilled and semi-skilled occupations compared with national rates was highest for younger men. Social class differences are particularly marked for deaths from infective and parasitic diseases as well as respiratory complaints and accidents.

Table 1.5. Deaths from traffic accidents, by age and sex 1974

	All ages	1	1–4	5–14	15–24	25–34	35–44
Male	178	12	52	73	367	163	112
Female	80	3	41	46	90	47	43

	45–54	55–64	65–74	75–84	85+
Male	119	188	254	509	658
Female	45	82	157	265	201

Death rates presented per million population.

Source: OPCS, *Mortality Statistics: Cause,* 1974.

Age differences occur more with deaths from lung cancer or certain heart complaints.

It is important to note that a death may not be as clearly defined an 'event' and may not be greeted with as much happiness as some births. The exact timing of a death and its principle cause may not be clear. And families may have their own reasons for wanting to hide the reasons for death (as in the case of suicide for example). Although an international list of causes of death was compiled as early as 1893, the 'cause' that eventually gets written on the death certificate may possibly be the result of some subtle negotiations between interested parties as to why the person died. For this reason mortality statistics by cause of death may be suspect, although they are widely used in demography.

The decline in fertility at the third stage of the demographic transition, coupled as it was with an extension of life expectancy led basically to a transformation of the age structure. Not only were fewer babies born; more adults survived their childhood into adulthood, thereby swelling the population. And subsequently the population of the aged has begun to grow.

The broad age distribution of the population generated by births but subsequently modified by deaths and migration can be encapsulated in two demographic indicators – an index of ageing showing whether the population is getting younger or older and a demographically defined dependency ratio. The ageing ratio is the ratio of elderly people in the population to the number of young people. Since both the young and the old are dependent on those aged between fifteen and retirement age, we simply add them together and divide by the total population, to calculate the dependency ratio. Table 1.6 shows the change in the dependency ratio between 1951 and 1971.

Table 1.6. Dependency ratio, 1851–1971, England and Wales

Year	0–14 (%)	Elderly (%)	Ratio
1851	35.6	5.9	415
1901	32.5	6.2	387
1951	23.3	16.5	398
1971	23.9	16.4	403

Source: Moroney, 1976.

During the nineteenth century dependents were largely children. As the birth rate fell and life expectancy increased more of the population moved into old age. The dependent population took on a new shape. In 1851 the elderly made up 14 per cent of the dependent population; by 1951 they constituted 41 per cent of the dependent population. In 1931 there were 51 people dependent on every 100 people in the working age groups; by 1974 every 100 workers had to support 68 dependents. The recent sharp fall in fertility compensates for the further increase in the next few years in the number and proportion of elderly people. Another striking way of summarising the changes happening to the age structure is to look at the changing proportion of very elderly in the population. Thus between 1901 and 1951 the population grew by 34 per cent, but the population over sixty-five years grew by 215 per cent and the population over eighty-five years by 29 per cent. Even more striking, between 1901 and 2001 the population is expected to increase by 70 per cent, the population aged over sixty-five years by 372 per cent and even more dramatically, the population aged over eighty-five years by 1212 per cent! We shall consider how this affects social policy in Chapter 5.

MIGRATION

The third part of the demographic equation is migration, the flow of people into and out of a country. As with births and deaths, migration can be regarded as a population flow that speeds up and slows down from time to time, or a stock that can be compared with the total share of population. Migration is an integral part of any dynamic society and this has always been so for Britain. Merchants came to ply their trade in medieval time; artisans arrived to sell their labour. A high level of migration has always been a measure of the degree to which any country is urbanised and Britain urbanised early in the industrial revolution. As the towns expanded and grew into cities, it was not only the peasants and landless labourers who flocked to them in search of work: Europeans also entered the country looking for the stimulus of the new industrial growth.

Britain had a second reason for expecting high rates of migration, and that was its colonial past. From the beginning of the nineteenth century until the 1930s Britain experienced a considerable outflow of people, moving especially to the new opportunities being generated in the empire. People were moving particularly to the Commonwealth and the USA. The size of the outflow exceeded 20 million throughout the period. And, while British people moved overseas, Europeans moved into Britain. But there was a net outflow. Between 1871 and 1931 the UK lost 4 million of its population through net out-migration. Given that fertility was falling rapidly and people were beginning to live longer we can hazard a guess about the effect of this migration on the age structure. The out-migrants were likely to be young and able bodied families and we can presume the elderly relatives were left at home.

Even before this century Britain has had a long history of immigrants arriving at its shores. At the turn of the century, they were Jews and East Europeans, there have always been immigrants from Ireland, (many of them did not necessarily settle but remained as transients), as well as Britons who had spent their lives in the Commonwealth and had returned to Britain to retire. More recently, especially in the 1950s and 1960s we have had a wave of immigration from the New Commonwealth countries – Caribbean, Asian and African.

We have already mentioned that there was a net population loss from Britain up until 1931. During the depression years this loss turned into a substantial net gain as many former emigrants returned to Britain after finding life in Canada, Australia or the United States even harder for the unsuccessful than they had known it here. But this influx was also exacerbated by a large scale immigration from Europe to escape repression, and included a quarter of a million unemployed. Post-War Britain soon became a net exporter of population as people began to move to Canada, South Africa, Rhodesia and the USA again. These out-migration streams to the Commonwealth reached a peak of 200,000 in 1952 and 1957.

It was not until the early 1960s that Britain became a net population importing country. This was largely as a result of the activities of industrialists and government officials, anxious to attract unskilled labour in times of acute labour shortages, in recruiting labour in the West Indies and Asia. Britain had a net inflow of 170,000 a year in the early 1960s. As a result of the 1962 Commonwealth Immigration Act this inflow was cut back sharply and in every year since 1965 (except one) there has been a net outflow of population.

In spite of this, immigration has been a widely discussed and explosive issue since the 1950s. In fact the figures come as a surprise to many people not acquainted with them. Table 1.7 below shows the rate of the net inflow.

Note the sudden jump in 1961. The increase in numbers of immigrants from Pakistan increased tenfold between 1960 and 1961. The jump partly caused, and partly was, the product of, the 1962 Act, which limited numbers from Commonwealth countries for the first time in history. The passing of the Act was accompanied by last minute flooding and this accounts for the high numbers entering Britain in the first six months of 1962. Since the mid-1960s, immigrants have been mainly dependents of earlier immigrants and the steady net out-flow has continued. But net migration masks much larger gross flows in both directions. Between 1964 and 1974 2.8 millions left the UK and 2.3 millions entered, giving a rough outflow of 50,000 each year.

Table 1.7. Net immigration

1958	45,000
1959	44,000
1960	82,000
1961	172,000
1962	136,000
1963	10,000

Two further immigration Acts extended controls: the 1968 Act obliged New Commonwealth migrants to obtain employment vouchers before entry: and the 1971 Act made Britain's entry requirements consistent with EEC policy and also created the 'patrial clause' (giving right of entry to potential immigrants with parents or grandparents born in the UK). These controls have brought about two major changes. Since the 1960s immigration from India and Pakistan has been almost exclusively of wives, husbands and dependents of men and women who had already settled here. (The only exception to this was the sudden arrival of some 26,000 Ugandan Asians in 1972–3.) This means that immigration from New Commonwealth countries will tail off as all the dependents eligible to join their families, do so. This is the second major change. Immigration from New Commonwealth countries has fallen off, especially since the early 1970s. In the first half of 1979, only 19,000 New Commonwealth migrants were accepted for settlement. In fact the level of migration, out of Britain as well as into Britain, had fallen off in the 1970s compared with the 1960s. The overall position during the 1970s was in line with Britain's traditional role as a net exporter of people to the rest of the world and in contrast to the exceptional experience in the late 1950s and early 1960s when, mainly due to the large influx from the New Commonwealth, especially the West Indies, the country was a net importer. Figure 1.4 shows the destination of British emigrants and the country of origin of Britain's immigrants for the period 1964 to 1973.

The important questions for the purposes of this chapter are how big is the flow of immigrants expressed as a proportion of the stock of the country's population, and what impact does net migration make on the age structure? The black population is widely discussed as a 'problem' and a component of this is often the size of the country's population. Much of this discussion is emotionally loaded and sometimes merely reflects the propaganda of racist groups. It was noticeable that, in the late 1960s, Enoch Powell was given to making periodic statements showing how black immigrants would have a devastating impact on the country's welfare services. Many of the figures he used were regularly refuted by the various organizations that collate information on immigration. Nevertheless the statements that stuck in the minds of the general public were the inaccurate slogans of Powell. Thus many people believe that there

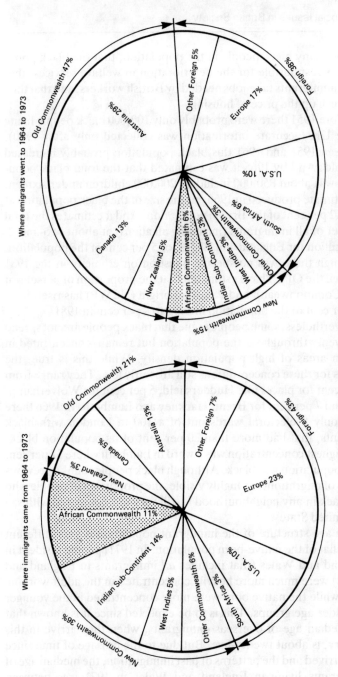

Figure 1.4. Origins and destinations of immigrants, 1964–73

Where emigrants went to 1964 to 1973

Old Commonwealth 47%
- Australia 29%
- Canada 13%
- New Zealand 5%

New Commonwealth 15%
- African Commonwealth 6%
- Indian Sub-Continent 3%
- West Indies 3%
- Other Commonwealth 3%
- South Africa 6%

Foreign 38%
- Other Foreign 5%
- Europe 17%
- U.S.A. 10%

Where immigrants came from 1964 to 1973

Old Commonwealth 21%
- Australia 13%
- Canada 5%
- New Zealand 3%

New Commonwealth 36%
- African Commonwealth 11%
- Indian Sub-Continent 14%
- West Indies 5%
- Other Commonwealth 6%
- South Africa 3%

Foreign 43%
- Other Foreign 7%
- Europe 23%
- U.S.A. 10%

are too many black people in the population, that the black population is responsible for the deterioration in welfare services, that black immigrants take jobs needed by British workers, and that they also push up the price of housing.

Before 1951 there were probably only 100,000 black people living in the UK (accurate information was collected only after 1960). Between 1951 and 1961 this black population probably increased fourfold. And by 1965 it was estimated that the total black population was about 850,000 including 200,000 children under sixteen. An estimate produced in 1966 put the size of the black population at about 2 per cent of the British population. And it estimates the total number of all immigrants (including all aliens) at about two-and-a-half million for England and Wales, or 5 per cent of the population. Although there was no specific question on ethnicity in the 1981 Census, the OPCS have estimated that the proportion of persons of New Commonwealth and Pakistani origin (NCWP) has risen from 2.5 per cent of the population in 1971 to 4 per cent in 1981.

Nevertheless, some people argue that black people are not spread out evenly throughout the population but remain concentrated in certain areas of high population density. While this is true, the figures for these concentrations still are fairly low. They range from 4 per cent for places like Huddersfield, 5 per cent for Wolverhampton, and 7 per cent for Brent, Hackney and Lambeth. In 1966 there were only 8 electoral wards out of a 100 in London with black residents, that had more than 20 per cent of its population black. The highest concentration was a ward in Lambeth where 31 per cent of its population was black. Although black people, unlike previous waves of migration, are highly visible, the proportion of people who are black in any neighbourhood is still very low compared with say the United States.

The age structure of the immigrant population is very different from that of the native-born population. In 1971, people resident in England and Wales (that includes *all* immigrants in England and Wales) were much more heavily concentrated in the adult working ages, while the native born were more concentrated in the younger and older age groups. This is to be expected since it is known that the median age of overseas immigrants, when they arrive in this country, is about twenty-five. But due to the passage of time since they arrived and the patterns of past immigration, the median age of immigrants living in England and Wales in 1971 was between thirty-six and thirty-seven years – some two years older than the native born. This leads to the somewhat paradoxical conclusion that immigration tends to increase (slightly) the age of the population as a whole.

In order to study the full demographic effect that migration has on the population of a country it is necessary also to look at the extent to which migration causes the number of births and deaths to differ from what would have occurred without any migration.

For our purposes, the leading question is, was the level of immigration so large in the 1950s and 1960s that it had an explosive effect on the country's birth rate or put intolerable stress on the country's welfare services? This is difficult to establish since it is only from 1969 that parent's countries of birth have been recorded on birth certificates. The indirect effect of net migration between 1951 and 1976 was to make the natural increase (i.e. births less deaths) some 350,000 greater than it would have been in the absence of migration. These figures are small in relation to the total level and change in population (in fact births were 2 per cent higher than they would have been with no migration). Although many of the children born to immigrants who came here in the late 1950s and early 1960s are still under twenty years, their numbers have been more than offset by some reduction in births, due to the net emigration of more recent years and the recent net emigration of people in this age group. Similarly, the population aged twenty-five to sixty-four is over 400,000 higher solely because of the net amount of people into and out of the country in this period 1951–76. And because of the age of migrants (both in and out) only a few will have reached retirement age.

CONCLUSIONS

It is easy for demographers to lose sight of the wood (the overall structure of the population) for the trees (births, deaths, migrants and such esoteric indices as proportion of fertile women in the population, proportion of the population who marry, childless couples, age of marriage, and tempo of fertility). For those who do not see the wood and get confused by the trees we shall summarize the important changes this century.

Up until the 1930s the population was firmly in the third stage of demographic transition, with birth rates down to a low of fifteen per thousand and a fairly dramatic drop in death rates thanks to modern medicine. But the population was not to continue to decline at such a steady rate. The war disrupted family life and many people postponed starting families until they saw signs of an end of hostilities. Consequently births were bunched together in the mid-1940s and babies born up until 1947 have ever since been known as part of the baby boom (will they still be known as such when they retire?). But by 1949 with the birth rate back on an even keel it looked as if the rate would decline so much that Britain's population might even decline. But this was not to be.

The period 1955 to 1964 saw the biggest rise in births ever in this century. It took a long time to reach the consciousness of demographers. It had very little to do with family size or promiscuity. In fact it was little more than a change in the patterns of family formation. Marriage rates were increasing, the age at which couples married was falling and one generation of women began having babies earlier, thus overlapping with the births of an earlier generation. We need to remember in all this that these variables (age of marriage, etc.) had previously been pretty stable. Thus demographers had not needed to take them into account before. Added to all this confusion was the increase in the population owing to a net inward migration to Britain for the first time this century. In fact the figure for 1961-2 for England and Wales (147,000) amounted to half the natural increase in the population. In this period of confusion it was difficult for demographers to sort out exactly what was happening.

The period after 1964 was just as confusing. Annual births began to fall and this fall reached a trough in 1972-3 but kept falling until by 1975-6 deaths were greater than births. The population was in decline.

While in the late 1950s and early 1960s women were having babies earlier and compressing the period during which they had them, in the late 1960s and early 1970s women began having their families later in their marriages. By 1978 they were waiting on average for 31 months before starting families. And for women who married when they were older, the interval between marriage and first birth was even greater.

In between all these changes in demographic variables we can discern an important and long-term change that is having far-reaching implications. That is the widespread adoption of the small family pattern. And no longer is it a pattern adopted merely by the upper classes. Working class families, too, could choose what size family they wanted and they, too, opted for the small family. We shall consider the impact of a changing age structure, the other important change this century, later when we consider how population change affects Britain's health, welfare and education services. It is a salutary thought that official forecasts of Britain's population have always been subject to some of the highest errors in Europe.

QUESTIONS

1. Why has the population of Britain increased since 1900? Describe and account for the major changes that have contributed to this.
2. The fall in the birth rate between the late nineteenth and twentieth centuries has been the most important single cause of changes in family life in the last 100 years. Discuss.
3. What are the most important concepts in demographic analysis that can be used to describe change in a country's population?
4. The theory of demographic transition is more useful for the questions it raises than for those it answers. But it does focus on changes in the place of the family in society. Explain.
5. Enoch Powell in 1968 talked of 'rivers of blood' flowing in our cities as a result of racial conflict. Do you think his prediction is accurate? Explain your answer.
6. The numbers of births in Britain between 1975-7 fell below the number of deaths. Should this be cause for concern?

FURTHER READING

Changes in Britain's population this century are lucidly summarized in A. H. Halsey's *Changes in British Society*, OUP, 1978.

The classic introductory text is R. K. Kelsall's *Population* (fourth edition), Longman 1979.

The most useful analytical book on demography is P. K. Cox's *Demographic Analysis*.

For the most up-to-date information on population changes in Britain and their impact on the population structure, the reader should consult *Population Trends*, published quarterly by the Office of Population Censuses and Surveys.

A readable account of the relationship between population dynamics, birth control, and obstetrics is to be found in D. Llewellyn-Jones' *Human Reproduction and Society*, Faber and Faber, 1974.

Detailed information about population statistics and sources of data can be found in the Open University second level course *Statistical Sources* especially Unit 2: *Population* and Unit 3: *Vital Statistics*.

Two

The family and its functions

In the next three chapters we shall look at the small nuclear family in more detail. There are many different ways of looking at the family. People tend to hold very strong views about the importance of the family in society. Some people want to protect it from the harmful aspects of urban society. Others want to attack it, even to destroy it. They regard the family as a repressive institution that does harm to its members. There are many aspects of the family that cause heated arguments – battered wives, battered children, one-parent families, new expressions of sexuality and sexual orientation, pornography, abortion – to name but a few. These viewpoints are mainly concerned about what the family *ought* to be like and what *should* be done to protect the family. These moral judgments need not concern us. We want to analyse the family and the functions it serves, mainly because we want to ask whether it is the case that the family is changing and possibly becoming weaker. Readers can take their own moral positions but we do not want moral judgment to cloud our initial analysis.

So what is a family? Are all groups of wives, husbands and children families? How about groups where some of those persons are missing? Is a man living with his son actually a family? Basically we want to define the family as a small face-to-face group that gives special recognition to the relationship between a man and a woman, usually involving the sex act, and children. This is a western conception of a nuclear family. It by no means covers all families. Our definition is too narrow. It would be difficult to find a definition covering all forms of the family. A good description of the variability of family forms is given by Gans (1972). He describes black families in Washington with their much looser sexual liaisons between men and women and with children from different parents living together. And that sort of complex pattern of relations has been typical of some communities in Britain, notably the fishing communities in places like Hull. We need not bother too much about the particular form of the family before analysing it. In fact the purposes of the family may be more important and universal than its particular form. We also need to remember that most of us have two families – the family we were born into and the family we ourselves form. And we often jump from one to the other when talking about them. Just think how many different meanings can be given to the statement: 'I didn't take the family with me'. Aunt Agatha, just the wife and kids, or does it include little Johnny's friend down the road, and what about Cousin Isobel? Exactly who is included in such a statement can only be inferred from the context.

FUNCTIONS

A sociologist's first question about any social institution is often, what functions does it fulfil? This is actually quite a sophisticated question. We have to understand a lot about any institution and its relations with the outside world, in order to answer it. But it does help us to look beneath the surface of things that we all usually take for granted.

The traditional answer to our question is that it fulfils four basic functions: the satisfaction of sexual needs; an economic or productive function; a caring function for the young, old, and maybe disabled; and a socializing or educative function. At least this is the answer that Murdoch (1948) arrived at in his analysis and it has been repeated ever since. These four functions are carried out by families for society. The family is a useful way of bringing children into the world, nurturing them, educating them in how society expects them to behave, and generally 'finishing them off' so that they are useful members of society. We will consider each of the functions in turn.

Sexual

Families are an acceptable organization in which to regulate sexual relationships and cope with any offspring that are born. People have come to accept whatever sexual activity goes on within marriage without much question. Any sexual activity outside marriage is more likely to be questioned. This is even more the case where any extra-marital activity results in pregnancies. The establishment of sexual rights within marriage is a widely established value in our society. But it is only one of a very large number of controls on sexual intercourse in society.

Fidelity in marriage is still supposed to be an ideal that many families adhere to. But it is widely broken. And in many ways an industrialized society makes the ideal very difficult to follow. There are many developments that threaten this ideal. Consider, for example, the dilemma of the travelling salesman. His job is made necessary by the level of industrialization. He is obliged to be away from his wife for maybe long periods. What is he to do? If it is necessary for spouses to be separated for long periods because of their work, what is the meaning of the vows of fidelity they made to each other?

Consider also the technical developments in our society that have made sexual encounters very possible. Zip fasteners, easy public transport, the ready availability of places where two people can be alone with no questions asked – all these have provided opportunities for sexual encounters among young people, outside any marriage relationship. This has considerably weakened the argument that sexual activity is located within the family.

Reproductive

This function is concerned both with the biological and the social aspects of reproduction. The family is the unit for producing and nurturing offspring. In fact the nurturing of children is the usual expectation of nuclear families. Children have a right to expect the parents to take care of them. As such, families have been described as institutions concerned with dependancy. The obligations between family members are as near to unlimited liability as any social relationships in society (Rustin, 1979). The emotional aspects of this are of increasing importance. Talcott Parsons (1952) argues that there are two sorts of relationships in modern societies. There are the intimate, personal, face-to-face relations that go on in the family, and there are the increasingly impersonal instrumental, contractual relationships that go on in the economic and political spheres of life. He argues that, as the latter become more widespread, so there is a need for the family to offer the former type of relationship. Many commentators idealize this aspect somewhat. They give the impression that family relationships are generally harmonious and that the emotional life of members of any family are warm, positive and conflict-free. We all know how fraught relations can be in most families. Some writers, notably the psychiatrists R. D. Laing (1970) and David Cooper (1971) and the anthropologist Edmund Leach (1968) argue that the family has a very destructive effect on its members. 'Far from being the basis of the good society, the family with its narrow privacy and tawdry secrets is the source of all our discontents' (Leach, 1968).

In any case what may be functional for society may not be quite so cosy from an individual's point of view. An additional pregnancy may be an intolerable burden for a particular mother. For the society with a low birth rate it may be functional in helping to replace the population.

Economic
The family was in the past an economic unit, producing many of the goods needed by society. And, apart from producing babies, women produce goods and services for the family. This is not necessarily true of families today. Few families are productive units in the sense that a family bakery or a family farm once used to be. And many wives go out to work and produce very few clothes or meals, compared with wives in former times. The rapid expansion of fast-food chains and many other innovations has minimized the amount of work many women do within their families. Nevertheless, the state still regards the family as an economic unit, as we shall discuss later.

Socialization
All groups have at least one problem in common. New members to the group need to be taught acceptable forms of behaviour. This is still an important function of the family. In fact socialization is very far reaching. It is within the family that children are taught many important lessons about how to survive in the world at large. It is

within the family that they get their first experience of power relationships and begin to learn how to deal with and react to powerful people. They can also acquire a lot of useful information about permissible gender roles, within the family. In fact some people argue that it is the family that passes on to children much of the sexism inherent in our society. Boys learn that men can assert themselves at the expense of women. Children learn a division of labour that precludes their displaying similar qualities. Girls learn to be pretty as a way of communicating, boys learn to be argumentative. Westergaard & Resler (1975) point out that, because so much learning in the family happens within a power relationship, it is extremely difficult to unlearn these patterns of behaviour in later life.

Does the listing of these functions that the family carries out for society tell us very much? It is easy to make the list longer and longer, the more we think about it. No one would dispute that the sexual, reproductive, economic and socialization functions are necessary conditions for the continued existence of society. But does this really amount to an explanation of the family and its continued importance in spite of widespread changes within society? Maybe not, but one way of looking at them is to look at how these functions have changed. We can then ask what this implies for families.

THE DEVELOPMENT OF FAMILIES

The notion that the family fulfils certain important functions for society is a useful analytical tool for looking at changes that have been going on within families as society has become more industrialized. We can formulate three important stages in the development of families. The boundaries between each of the stages are a bit rough and ready but the formulation is useful. In order to clarify them, we can call them the Production Stage, the Disruption Stage and the Consumption Stage. These three stages are best discussed in Young and Willmott's book, *The Symmetrical Family*.

The Production Stage

This stage was associated with pre-industrial stages. Families and work units were one and the same. Men and women and children worked together producing the necessary items of consumption. Or they worked together as a team producing for the market (a form of production known as the 'domestic system'). Industrialists supplied them with the raw materials and took back the finished product. In both cases, although there was a division of labour, the family was presided over by the husband. He was husband, master, patriarch, and boss of the servants. The wife and children were his legal property: they were regarded as chattels. Nevertheless, the wife was important. She had a great deal of authority in spite of the authority of her husband. Children too were a useful source of labour.

The production stage coincided with the form of family unit commonly known as the extended family. It consisted of more than two generations living together under one roof, usually including grandparents and adult sons and daughters not yet married, as well as other single people working for the family. Families consisted of three generations because people tended to marry at a much later age. This was partly as a form of birth control. But it was mainly that each family's livelihood was tied up with a family business or land. Sons were obliged to wait for their fathers to retire and pass on the farm before they could be in a position to marry and start a family. Individuals within the family were subordinated to the interests of the family as a whole, particularly the family as a productive enterprise. Hence marriage at this stage was always considered from the point of view of what any potential spouse would contribute to the future prosperity of the family.

The Disruption Stage

With the development of the factory system, the family as it had operated previously, came under attack. The family changed. Gradually it lost its production functions to the factory. The domestic system survived for a while but under the threat of competition. This often meant that husbands pushed their wives and children harder in order to eke out a living. Eventually the home and the workplace became separated. This meant that families spent less time with each other. All of them may have been employed by the factories but they were taken on to do different jobs. People were no longer employed together as members of a family. Instead they were employed as individuals, for an individual wage.

This was stage two of the demographic transition described in Chapter 1. Fertility was high and mortality was beginning to fall. It is easy to see why families had many children. With wage rates as low as they were, one way of increasing family income was to have large families in the hope that the babies would survive infancy and become young wage earners.

This was the stage at which the division of labour between husbands and wives was greatest. There was a man's sphere and a woman's sphere. The home was usually quite spartan and not very inviting. The man would tend to spend much of his time outside it in the company of his workmates. The woman, for her part, was left to manage as best she could, keeping the house and caring for the children when she was not at work, and making do on whatever housekeeping money she got from her husband. The strain of poverty was such that women relied on their own kin (mothers, sisters, grandmothers) to help out in time of trouble.

Although the extended family tended to break down with the rise of the factory system, there was a sense in which the extended family still operated. Young and Willmott (1978) describe it as a sort of informal trade union. It created a protective device against the insecurities, for women, of families at the stage where its members were individual wage earners. Since husbands could rarely be relied on to support their families adequately, women tended to build up an organization for their defence and in defence of their children. The only kin relationship they could stress was that between mother and married daughter. This relationship had always been close, with the men away from home all day. Thus this kind of extended family was largely mother-centred. In their account of life in Bethnal Green, Young and Willmott show how the mother would usually have a word with the rent collector in the hope of his agreeing to find a nearby property for her daughter to rent when she married. The link between mother and daughters could then be sustained. Mothers could give their daughters and grandchildren a feeling of security. Not only could they look after the children if any married daughter got a job, but they could also pass on money and gifts in their capacity as co-ordinator for the extended family.

The more people belonged to it, the more effective was the large family in providing insurance for its members against hard times. When one person had money problems, someone else in the family might be in the opposite position and able to contribute directly or through the grandmother to the welfare of the family. The family helped its members to weather the poverty that comes at particular stages of the family cycle. Thus child rearing and old age were stages that were coped with. The elderly were available to help out with child care for parents who were out working and earning. Pahl (1970) points out that the family was for working class people what mortgages and financial assets are for middle class people, a source of security to tide people over in bad times.

The Consumption Stage

Eventually, with greater prosperity, men got paid a family wage, enabling them to keep their families without their wives having to go out to work. And rising incomes have brought the family into the third stage of development. Wives are no longer merely their husbands' chattels. And their legal rights have been extended this century, so that, in many ways, they can now expect to receive equal treatment with men. Since the War they now have the option of taking jobs outside the home. This means that a financial partnership is now more possible within marriage. And with the development of effective methods of birth control, wives can now determine how fertile they will be. 'A woman's right to choose' became the slogan of the abortion lobby in the 1970s, but it could equally well apply to fertility generally.

These changes have signalled changes in the relationship between husbands and wives within marriage, and they have also heralded important changes within the home. Marriage relationships are more likely to be partnerships of equality. But part of the reason for this is that the nuclear family, as it has become smaller, has at the same time become more isolated and more home-centred. The significant point is that it has turned into a consumption unit. In fact consumption is now a function it fulfils for capitalism. If families stopped being centres of consumption then, other things being equal, capitalism would fall apart.

Home is now an attractive place to be, for husbands as well as wives. And it is a place where chores are carried out with the use of a high level of sophisticated equipment, ranging from electric toasters, vacuum cleaners and automatic dishwashers to deep freezers, washing machines, spin dryers and even microwave ovens. Families are encouraged to spend time together at home. Families who own their houses spend time improving them. Do-it-yourself is a major growth industry. And families are offered a range of leisure and sports activities that they can participate in together.

Rising living standards and increased security saw the demise of the extended family described in the previous section. Michael Anderson (1971) points out that the 'critical life situations' declined with improvements in health, the introduction of full employment and better social security provision. People are now better able to meet any crises they encounter with the entitlements the Welfare State provides as of right. The extended family was to a large extent bound together by the economic adversities of the past.

The increased emphasis demanded by industrialism on geographic mobility, has also weakened the bond between relatives in large extended families. By 1971 about 8 per cent of the population moved every year and, in any five years, more than a third of the population moved. And public housing policy also exacerbates the difficulty of keeping extended families living nearby. Very few council house units are large enough to permit a family to have their aged parents to live with them.

Greater affluence, while enabling the family to consume more durables, has brought about the demise of the extended family. But the family as a consumption unit has seen the rise of a new type of family relationship – the symmetrical family. At least that is the conclusion that Young and Willmott came to in their analysis of the new functions of the family. Not everyone agrees with that conclusion as we shall see in the next chapter. But at least everyone is agreed that the family today is a unit of consumption.

Thus as industrialization has become more developed, so the family has changed in the functions it fulfils. The family as a production unit is not now very important. This has stripped it of some of its power in the economy. It no longer allocated the jobs of one generation to the next. That is now done through the education system – largely a State function. As its production function has withered away, so its function as a unit of consumption for capitalist enterprises has greatly expanded. This function gives it less power in society (consumers as such have little power in the economy). But it has not necessarily weakened its importance as a vital institution in society.

CRITICISMS

In some ways the analysis we have presented is vague. As a conceptual tool, this analysis is quite helpful. It gives us a framework for looking at the ways in which the family is changing. We merely have to elaborate how the few functions have changed through time to have at hand quite a detailed analysis of families. We only have to consider much of what is said by moralists on the family to realize that they lack any real analysis of how families change through time. Without some analysis that relates changes in the family to industrial change, it is easy to conclude that any change within families is bad and should be opposed.

This analysis helps us to understand how the role of the family is changing. Its loss of some functions has not thereby weakened it, since it apparently takes on new functions. As these functions change to fit the needs of industrialization, so too do the relationships between members of the family change. An analysis of the division of labour within families is important. It helps us to assess how strong is the case put forward by the Women's Movement that women are still widely oppressed.

Our analysis in terms of functions may not take us very far. And the criticisms of the approach are rather more substantial than the insights the approach provides. The sociology of the family had always been the Cinderella of sociology when it comes to theoretical developments. It is only recently that a more rigorous and incisive analysis of the family from a sociological point of view has developed. This came mainly from the Women's Movement as well as from a Marxist analysis of housework. We shall elaborate these approaches in the next chapter.

One of the weaknesses of a functional approach to the family is that it is possible to add to the list of functions as many new functions as anyone likes, *ad infinitum*. No authority on the family necessarily agrees with any other authority exactly how many functions the family fulfils. This is not surprising. The definition of each function is vague and some of them overlap. While it is clear that the family no longer has a production function, it would be difficult to get much agreement on what other functions it fulfils.

Young and Willmott (1973) argue that the consumption function is now the significant and defining function. Feminists argue that the production function is still there but in a different form (families produce labour power for capitalism). In fact a functional analysis of the family permits anyone to say anything they want to about the role and importance of the family in society. The main criticisms centre around the following five points.

1. The analysis gives the appearance of more theoretical weight than it can deliver. For instance, few people would deny that there is a close overlap between the family as an institution and the activities of sexual intercourse, reproduction and socialization. A functional approach does not provide any further clarification.
2. All the activities carried out by the family are also carried on outside the family. The State has taken on more and more responsibility for socialization, production, and has the technology to carry out the family's reproduction functions. People have sex outside the family. It could be argued that many people have children and bring them up outside conventional families. This point is debatable: we now have a special category for adults who bring up children by themselves (single-parent families) and we also prohibit single people from adopting other people's children.
3. The functions present a somewhat passive account of these activities. This is true for instance of socialization. In Chapter 4, when we discuss adolescents and their relationships in the family, we shall present a conflicting view of family relationships. But functional analysis provides no place for analysing conflict either between members of the family or between families and the wider society. The account is also somewhat static. It does not happily take account of change. Our analysis of change in the three stages is very superficial. And it is not very clear what exactly are the important factors that change in each stage.
4. Functional analysis is pretty insensitive to the rich variations in family life of different kinds of family. Talcott Parsons' analysis (which we have not really gone into) presents a picture of family life that is a somewhat idealized middle-class account and probably accords very little with other kinds of family. It is only really possible with functional analysis to enumerate all the issues that all families carry out. Thus any differences in how particular families behave have to be ignored. To take an obvious illustration, in socializing children for society, some families adopt a very authoritarian approach, others a permissive approach and many others a number of variations between authoritarian and permissive. What does this mean in terms of the function of socializing the child? They presumably both enter the same society (this is not quite true as we need to consider different

class positions too) but with very different kinds of socialization.
5. The overall emphasis of functional analysis is on harmony and equilibrium. The family is supposed to adapt to change by finding a new equilibrium. But this is really a conservative ideology suggesting that things ought to be kept the way they are. In fact any change is seen as weakening the family and therefore not good enough for the general health and well-being of the family.

FAMILIES AND THE STATE

Families in fact have generally carried out their functions in co-operation with other institutions. The degree with which the four basic family functions are shared with other institutions changes over time. It may be true that families are more capable of achieving the survival needs of its individual members than they could on their own. But this statement could also be made of many other institutions in society and the individual's needs they cater for. Perhaps the best description of the incomplete way the family carried out its functions is given in the following quote. The functions of the family are 'developing their (members') capacities to socialize children, enhancing the competence of their members to cope with the demands of other organizations in which they must function, utilizing these organizations, and providing the satisfactions and a healthy environment to the well-being of a family.'

This definition makes us delineate each of the functions more accurately and define how much responsibility the family takes for carrying out the function and how much other institutions take. Moroney (1976) argues that it is important to decide which functions it is appropriate for the family to undertake, which are best dealt with by other institutions, and which could be shared. Unfortunately the analysis presented in the past that the family had been pressured into surrendering many of its functions to other institutions, he believes, is erroneous. Instead he maintains that families now share their functions with other institutions.

With the demise of the extended family, the nuclear family gradually evolved. This new unit, husband, wife and children, independent from their kin-related families, was viewed as ideal for meeting the demands of geographical and occupational mobility which was an important requirement of modern industrial society.

The nuclear family may be efficient for the purposes of the economic system. But it entails casualties. It is difficult, in mobile nuclear families, to care for the aged, the infirm, and the disabled members of any family. Some of these are cared for by the State. In any case the State had already developed its health system to ensure the delivery of healthy babies. This meant that families were left with minimal socialization and recreation functions.

A further point that we shall pursue in the next chapter, concerns the nature of the socialization and caring functions. Although functionalists might argue that these are family functions, in reality they are usually the responsibility of women. When we take into account more fully exactly who does what within the family, it is difficult to sustain the argument that families as such have important functions to fulfil.

We began this chapter by listing some of the emotive issues that surround any debate on the role of the family in modern society. And we have ended on a sceptical note, arguing that functional analysis tells us very little substantively about the family and how it is changing. Nevertheless, it would be foolish to throw out the baby with the bath water.

Even though functional analysis is simplistic, it has enabled us to think systematically about the family, to look at some of the ways in which the family has changed with the development of industrialization, and to wonder in what ways the family shares its functions with other institutions.

The analysis may not be very scientific. Certainly it leads different theorists to make radically different conclusions. But, like the theory of demographic transition we discussed in Chapter 1, it does raise a number of important questions. And that is part of what analysing British society is all about.

QUESTIONS

1. Many sociology textbooks refer to the 'functions' of the family. Discuss the deficiencies of this approach for an understanding of the family.
2. The Welfare State had stripped the family of its functions and thus hastened its demise. Discuss.
3. Families are still important agents for socialization. In what ways is this the case, and how else are children socialized?
4. As the family has become a unit for consumption, so family relationships have become more symmetrical. Summarize the arguments put forward by Young and Willmott.

5. The development of industrialization has destroyed the extended family. How has this happened? Is there any evidence for the continued existence of extended families?

FURTHER READING

A very readable study of the family is Mary Farmer, *The Family*, Longmans, 1975, but she does not spend a great deal of time on the functions of the family.

A better book from the point of view of this chapter is C. C. Harris, *The Family*, Allen & Unwin, 1969, but it is somewhat heavier to read.

The best analysis of the way in which the functions of the family have changed and the argument that relationships between husband and wife are now symmetrical, is set out in Young and Willmott, *The Symmetrical Family*, Routledge and Kegan Paul, 1973.

A critical account of family functions that brings together writers on the family from different disciplines is found in D. H. Morgan, *Social Theory and the Family*, Routledge and Kegan Paul, 1977.

An incisive analysis of the functions of the family and the relations with the functions carried out by the State is contained in R. M. Moroney, *The Family and the State, Considerations for social policy*. Longman, 1976.

Three

The structure of the family

We have argued so far that the family changed as Britain industrialized. Firstly it shrank in size. Families are smaller than they used to be, not only because parents have fewer children. Fewer generations now live together under one roof; children leave home at an earlier age; grandparents usually live independently; and few unmarried adults remain living with their parents. People marry earlier, live longer and form their own family units in the process. There are more as well as smaller families now. More generations of the family co-exist at any point in time.

Secondly, the family shrank in the functions it fulfils. It has lost its economic functions. No longer does it produce goods and services. And the children each family produces are no longer a necessary requirement for the survival of any family. State support and affluence have changed the significance of family rearing in the family. The family is now more important as a consumption unit.

In this chapter we shall look at how these changes have affected the internal organization of the family. It is said that the family now experiences freedoms previously undreamt of. Titmuss (1958) argued that a woman at the beginning of the century could expect to live to her mid-sixties and devote a third of her life to bearing and caring for children. A woman today can expect to live at least ten years longer and to spend only 7 per cent of her life dealing with children. A reduction of such magnitude in just two generations represents a radical enlargement of freedom for women.

Young and Willmott (1975) argue that the power of women to control their own fertility has changed their position within the family. They point out that, ever since women first got the vote in 1928, the status of women has gradually improved. Rising living standards have transformed homes from the somewhat drab, uninviting places they were in Victorian times into attractive places where families can positively enjoy being together and sharing activities. Husbands spend time working in the home and playing with their children. Wives make the most of their new-found independence, gained through having a job outside the home. Marriages can now be said to be partnerships with spouses making joint decisions over their more ample family budgets. Children also benefit from having parents less caught up with a concern to survive, and more able to offer their children a rich and more fulfilling family background.

Halsey (1978) encapsulates these changes when he argues that the demographic trend towards the small nuclear family has resulted in three benefits: the emancipation of women, the domestication of men, and an enrichment of childhood. We shall explore each of these in turn to see in what ways roles within the family have changed.

EMANCIPATION OF WOMEN

Much of family sociology in the 1950s looked at the roles each spouse played and what respective tasks each had assigned to them. Bott (1957) looked at the relationship between marital roles and the social environment. By social environment, Bott meant that 'network of friends, neighbours, relatives and particular social institution's. She categorized family networks as either close-knit (typical of working-class families living in traditional communities where friends, neighbours and relatives often know each other) or loose-knit (typical of geographically mobile families where there is little overlap between friends, neighbours and relatives).

Families with close-knit social networks were likely to have a clearly defined division of labour between spouses and to spend much of their leisure time separately. Families with loose-knit networks made family decisions jointly, spent more of their leisure time in shared activities, and carried out household and childcare tasks either jointly or interchangeably. This research sparked off an enormous amount of interest on how different couples allocate tasks within the family, providing us with an enormous amount of information on families living in different kinds of community in Britain. It is probably the most widely known part of British sociology (see Frankenberg, 1966).

This work has come under considerable criticism from feminists. They dismiss much of it, complaining that it focuses unduly on the minutiae of family roles while ignoring the wider industrial forces of capitalism that shape the relationships between men and women inside as well as outside the family. Sociology has been dominated in the past by men who had their own blinkered view of society; they made an unreal distinction between home and work. 'Real' work, they argued, is done mainly by men in factories and offices and is best studied by industrial sociologists. Thus workplace studies tended to focus on men in coal mines, steel mills, car assembly lines and other male occupations, thereby ignoring women in the work-force. Studies of women were left to family sociologists who were meant to look simply at women's unpaid labour in the home.

To understand women's roles adequately it is important to recog-nize their dual existence, in the home and at work. This existence has changed dramatically with each stage of industrial develop-ment. We shall look at four stages – the pre-industrial stage when work was organized under a domestic system, the early industrial stage of wage labour, a later stage when a woman's place was said to be in the home, and the most recent stage when women have had two separate roles.

The Domestic System

In pre-industrial society household and work chores were not differentiated. The home was primarily an economic unit, formed at marriage in which a family was the unit for production, of goods intended for consumption and sale. A woman's role in adult life was always the role of a productive worker, in the home and outside it, on the land or in the urban workplace. Laws relating to labour did not differentiate between the sexes. Women, engaged in any trade, had the same rights and responsibilities as men doing the same work. They lived arduous lives and were subject to the authority of their husbands, but were regarded as important and influential members of the household. This was a period of strength for women when they lived diversified lives doing activities they could control themselves. The industrial revolution was to change that and, with it, the notions of womanhood changed.

Wage Labour
The essential change in family life brought about by the industrial revolution was that people, instead of being paid for their products, were paid for their labour. The change seriously undermined family life. Gradually the family was displaced as industrialists harnessed the new sources of power in a system of production that made it possible to increase output substantially at lower costs. Labour costs were thereby lowered, as was the demand for labour.

The factory system had two disastrous effects on family labour. First, wages were depressed as the supply of labour in the towns increased. People were employed solely for the muscle power they had, in exchange for a wage. The majority of factory workers were at first children, often paupers from the workhouses since they were a source of cheap labour. As steam developed, factories needed stronger labour. Textile factories wanted healthy girls valued according to their output at a particular (labour) price. Workers were employed solely as individuals and this affected family life. If wages were good, the family would stay intact, if wages were low the family often broke up.

It was easy for husbands also to regard their wives as so much labour power. Unless the wife was able-bodied, healthy and physically unaffected by child-bearing, she needed her husband more than he needed her. Families could easily fragment if wages were insufficient. Husbands would leave their wives to fend for themselves and the children who could end up on the streets as orphans.

Second, the factory system removed the economic ties that held families together. Home and workplace were now physically separated. As a result husbands and wives spent most of their work lives apart. For men, industrialization often enlarged their world, expanding the range of occupations available. For women it increased the difficulties, imposing a new problem – childcare when they were at work – on them. Thus the early part of the industrial revolution set the foundation for modern women's situation. The workplace was separated from the home, the tradition of family labour and a family income was lost, and women had increasingly to be concerned with childcare as a problem.

'A Woman's Place'

Towards the second half of the industrial revolution the roles of working-class and middle-class women began to differentiate. For the middle-class factory owners and the professionals who serviced their transactions, the end of the century was a time of unprecedented accumulation of wealth and one of the ways in which this wealth could be displayed was in the home. Middle-class homes became a symbol of gracious living; they had all the accoutrements of wealth – furniture, dinner parties, servants, and the 'lady of leisure'. The mark of prosperity was that a husband could afford to have his wife and daughters living a life of ease and elegance, pursuing beauty in all its forms. It was ironic that this idealized picture of a woman's role in life was possible only at the expense of working-class women. As middle-class women withdrew from domestic work to the leisured drawing rooms, their places were taken in the kitchens of Britain by working-class women. In 1851 a quarter of the female population were domestic servants.

The upper-class ideal that a woman's place was in the home was to spread to affect the position of working women. This happened mainly as a result of the legislation of the Victorian social reformers who had earlier excluded children from working in many industries and now turned their attention to women. In 1842 women were excluded from the coal mines. In 1844 they were classed with children as 'protected persons'. Their working day was reduced and women's shift systems abolished. They were in fact gradually banished from the factories.

This protective legislation lay at the heart of the creation of the role of the modern housewife. Between 1841 and 1914 the greatest change in women's occupations was the increasing evidence of the full-time housewife. In 1818 one in four married women worked. By 1911 only one in ten did so. This transformation was due to the increasing prosperity, a prosperity that owed much to the earlier trade union struggles when men fought for a decent family wage. Families could now exist on a man's wage alone.

The retreat of working-class women into lives of domesticity was paralleled by a return of middle-class women to their kitchens. Domestic servants were becoming more expensive as alternative occupations (shop, clerical, and teaching work) expanded. Hence the combination of the maternal role and the housewife role, previously a feature of working-class existence, now became the norm for both classes.

Women's Two Roles

This retreat of women into full-time housework was reversed at the turn of the century. Women went back to factory work. It began with the First World War. In 1914, 1.7 million women were drawn into industry, increasing the percentage of women employed to 22.5. The First World War had the effect of establishing employment as a normal practice for unmarried women from all social backgrounds. Between 1939 and 1945 this percentage doubled; by the time of the Second World War married women were the only ones not already working. Between 1939 and 1945 an additional two million women took jobs outside the home. This trend continued. Female workers made up 27 per cent of the labour force in 1939, 39 per cent in 1945, fell to 35 per cent in 1951 but has continued to rise throughout the 1970s. By 1971 they made up 43 per cent of the labour force. Married women in the female workforce rose between 1951 and 1971 from 40 to 64 per cent.

This was made possible by technological changes which affected domestic life. New products (tinned foods, biscuits and jams and many more recent ones) mushroomed. Young and Willmott point out that the miniaturization of machines now provides the housewife with as much mechanical assistance as was displayed by the industrial workers in 1914. Domestic capital has harnessed housework into a profitable enterprise and turned families into important consumption units. Women were also needed to fill the labour shortages in the 1950s and early 1960s. Like black people, they were a cheap source of labour able to do boring repetitive work. Because of their family commitments, they were in a poor bargaining position.

Women's participation in the labour force is precarious. It depends on the needs of industry. As a result, the notion of where a woman's 'natural' place in society is to be found – in the home or in the factory and office – has a habit of changing to fit the needs of the economy. Consequently the permanent features of a woman's life are usually found in the home, as a mother and housewife, unlike a man whose activity is defined as outside the home.

Women's Equality

What of the position of women today? Women's liberation was arguably the most important political movement in the western world during the 1970s. How liberated are some women allowed to be in this age of emancipation? How permanent were the gains made by women in the earlier period of labour shortages? We need to look at four aspects that together determine the freedom each woman has in society.

Legal rights: The status of women has undergone some important changes during the twentieth century. Women have more legal rights. The right to vote, to be elected to Parliament, to higher education, to hold professional jobs, to retain one's legal personal identity in marriage, to pass on property separate from a man . . . these rights have culminated in the right to equal pay with men for doing comparable work. But legal rights provide only a theoretical basis for emancipation. Oakley (1976) argues that the rights conferred on women during the course of their emancipation were privileges held by men. They are rights based on a male norm of achievements and ignored the constraints of family life. To claim these rights women often have to compete with men on male terms, left to cope with their family commitments as best they can. Free childcare facilities outside the home are still not regarded as important rights for families. Education does not provide children with equal access to vocational courses regardless of gender. Girls are still expected to prepare for typically female jobs while technical, scientific and mechanical jobs are still male preserves. The right of women to pursue their careers in spite of maternity has only been partly acceded to. Women may take pregnancy leave and expect to return to their former jobs. But if they leave for a period to look after small children, these commitments are not taken into account.

Women at work: Women's participation in the labour force shows a similar ambivalence towards their family responsibilities. Their work rights are not protected. They are frequently not unionized. Six times as many women as men work part-time and their need for part-time work is only a concession. The cost of this is seen both in the level of wages and the kinds of jobs they do. In spite of the 1970 Equal Pay Act and the 1975 Sex Discrimination Act, women's pay on average is behind that of men. They still have fewer comparable opportunities. The labour market still has a clear division of labour, with women working by and large in the low and men in the high paid sector. The bulk of women's work is overwhelmingly concerned with servicing the needs of children and men. Even professional jobs have more direct contact with 'clients' in teaching, medical and social work. Few women are employed in the occupations traditionally reserved for men, such as dentistry, engineering, medicine, and the law.

Investment decisions in large companies, senior management posts, directing posts in television, bishoprics in the church, judges, surgeons, and other major posts with power and influence are still masculine preserves. Because the labour market still gives precedence to men, any clash of interest between men and women over their obligations are likely to be resolved in favour of men. Men are still considered the bread winners.

State support: The state buttresses the subservient role of women in the way it treats female claimants within marriage; the role of female is assumed to be financially a dependent one. No exceptions are made. Outside marriage the interpretation of dependence on a man is imposed. Social security benefits to a woman are cut if she is found to be cohabiting with a male. Women are thus trapped into relationships of dependence by the regulations.

Although women have rights protected by law, those rights are conceived within a context of a gender-differentiated society in which women are expected to be dependant on men, and to give precedence to their domestic role. The state still discriminates against any life style that attempts to achieve relationships based on material independence of men.

Women at home: As industrialization has stripped the family of its production function, so it has left it bereft of any function of political or social importance. Yet industrialization has also been responsible for creating the small mobile nuclear family, isolated from its wider kinship network and detached from the wider community. Greater importance is now attached to the very function that binds women to the family – the reproduction of the labour force. By attaching greater importance to childhood, motherhood itself has more importance. The emotional development of children and the fulfilment of their aspirations is now a central theme in many families.

Women are not free to go out to work and forget their family responsibilities. Many go out to work partly in order to fulfil their increased aspirations towards their children. With rising living standards and increased educational goals, children are now costly forms of investment.

Marriage still defines a woman's place in society. Marriage rates are rising and a woman is defined as such within the home. Both maternity and domesticity are important components of femininity and it is the interaction of these two which distinguishes the situation of the housewife-wife-mother from the husband-father. Men continue to look outside the home for success, achievement and social acceptance. Children also have their own expectations of a life outside the family. Both come home to a private place where they can find emotional support which the housewife-wife-mother is expected to provide. How much of this support is provided by men, we shall consider in the next section.

DOMESTICATION OF MEN

How are men affected by the changes within the family? How have they been affected by the change in the legal status of women? Some changes that have happened have improved the lot of both husbands and wives. Many of the examples that Young and Willmott provide show how this is so. Families have acquired more spending power and are entitled to longer holidays than before. Parents are now free to enjoy themselves and to spend more time with their children. Men are more prepared to spend time with their families and less with their workmates. More money has made these conflicts less acute. Fathers can now do both. And this in turn may mean that fathers are more willing to take some responsibilities for domestic work such as childcare. But how far does this apparent equal sharing of chores really go? 'Are husbands good housewives?' asks Ann Oakley.

Things are changing. The notion that men should help out in the home is probably more widely accepted than before. Fathers may want to be more involved with what happens at home. Some workplaces have begun to give men paternity leave. Gavron (1966) found that 54 per cent of working-class husbands of women she interviewed spent more time sharing household tasks than they had done before. Young and Willmott give a good deal of evidence that husbands help out at home and spend time with their families. The move to greater equality is indisputable, but what is the extent of the apparent equality?

Young and Willmott suggest that families are becoming symmetrical. By this they mean that both husbands and wives have two jobs – one in the home and one outside; one unpaid, the other paid. They tend to assume all four roles are qualitatively equal. Can we therefore assume that it is a matter of time before these roles between home and work and men and women are interchangeable? Will it soon be a matter of indifference to people who is the chief breadwinner and who the main domestic person?

The situation is more fluid than it used to be. Husbands and wives may be freer within the limits of their own relationship to allocate responsibilities in their families. It is possible to switch the responsibility for washing the dishes and playing with the children, to ensure that husbands take on more work. We shall look at four aspects: housework, childcare, family budget decision-making, and leisure activities.

Housework: Men make a distinction between housework and childcare. Although they help out in housework, men are cautious about taking full responsibility. It seems that one factor responsible is the continuing belief in 'natural' differences between the sexes. Some husbands will not go into shops, others will shop but not carry the shopping bag, for fear of being labelled effeminate. Other husbands may refuse to push prams or change nappies. Men are still at best only aids to the housewife who still retains full responsibility for what is done in the home.

The effect of this is that women are under pressure to remain psychologically involved with housework. Women still set the standards and establish the appropriate routines. Oakley argues that these routines are learnt by women in long apprenticeships beginning at birth. Mothers are still the female child's role model for feminine as well as for housework behaviour. Housewives can still seek satisfaction in housework comparable to the work satisfaction their husbands may get out of their jobs. A housewife's role is part of her self image. This negates the assertion of Young and Willmott that families are becoming symmetrical. A husband's outside job tends to be equated with the wife's job in the home.

Husbands are still regarded as not domestic creatures, and

domestication is not set up as an ideal for them. In the light of this, Oakley argues that any help the employed wife gets from her husband is a response that is due purely to the fact that she is employed. It signals no necessary or direct change in the concept of the male role. Housewives generally do not question their primary duty as being that of looking after the home and the physical needs of the family.

Young and Willmott found an increasing interest in shared tasks carried out within the home. But their study was mainly about leisure activity: little of it was concerned with housework, Oakley looked particularly at housework – cleaning, shopping, cooking, washing, ironing and washing-up. She found that 15 per cent of the husbands in her study participated in these chores to a high level. Also, 60 per cent of couples had clearly defined segregated roles. In these the husbands carried out their tasks about the house separately from the wives who had their own tasks. The distinctions that men make have changed very little with the increase in male unemployment. Beatrice Campbell tells of one man she interviewed for her book, *Wigan Pier Revisited*. He sat, unemployed, in the kitchen in front of the washing machine, with the weekly wash on the floor beside him. He was unable to make the move of putting the clothes in the machine. The role change it entailed was too threatening for him.

Childcare: Husbands usually share in childcare tasks more than they do in housework. Oakley provided a telling example of one couple where the husband was one of the most participating fathers in the study. He helped a great deal with childcare: he regularly got the two-year-old up in the morning, dressed him and put both children to bed. During the interview she conducted with the family, the father came into the room and asked the two-year-old whether he would like to go to the lavatory. The child acquiesced and the father bore him off, and came back, reporting no success. 'It's a great problem, that', he said and proceeded to launch into a monologue on the problems of toilet training this child. He seemed to be emotionally involved in it, in a way more typical of mothers than fathers in our society.

In many couples, the notion of how good a father a man is revolves around the issue of whether or not the father plays with the children. To play with the children in the evenings and weekends; to take them off the mother's hands on a Sunday morning; to be interested in their welfare; and to act as mother substitute in times of illness or childbirth – this defines a father's role for many men. Some men even refrain from an active role with their children until they are grown sufficiently to be involved in sports.

It has become acceptable for fathers to help out. The concept of help is a political one for husbands and wives. Because they help, fathers do not take the main responsibility for childcare. Helping with baby is an index of a man's involvement with his children. Birth produces the peak of masculine domesticity. Many fathers may be quite heavily involved in the early days but this level of participation falls off as babies become older. Life then becomes more routine-like and the reality of fatherhood is eroded by time and the number of sleepless nights.

Domestic politics are important. 'Pram pushing is a highly public act . . . a policy statement in the sexual politics of baby-care, a delicate demarcation line between two countries: his and hers' (Oakley, 1978). The division of labour between husbands and wives begins to change when the woman gives up work in late pregnancy. From this point in time the two roles become much more clearly divided: housewife at home, husband-father at work. And because housework is not 'work', all the work that has to be done might as well be done by the mother. Although the baby is the reason why the mother is not out at work full-time the walls of the home close in on her, as washing the floor becomes indistinguishable from washing the nappies, buying baby food no different from buying husband food. For women the distinction that men usually make between housework and childcare is not important. 'Although having the first baby permanently alters the emotional interior of a couple's relationship, it is the social division in parental roles that most threatens it. Husbands and wives can pretend to be equal; mothers and fathers know they are not' (Oakley, 1978).

Family budgeting: Money is one aspect of the power relationship between husbands and wives. How it is distributed within the family reflects the inequalities between spouses. When wives are not working, the husband's power is at its peak. Symmetrical families need equal access to financial resources if the relationship is to remain equal. Pahl (1980) suggests that there are three ways in which a wage packet gets distributed between couples. Low-income households give the whole wage packet to the wife. The wife manages all the financial affairs, giving the husband a certain amount of pocket money. When money is short, having one person in complete control makes budgeting easier. Budget management is a chore rather than a source of power. Middle-income families usually have an allowance system. The wife gets a specific amount of money each pay-day and some wives are not told how much the husband earns. A study carried out by *Woman's Own* in 1975 showed that one-fifth had received no increase in housekeeping during the previous year, in a period of inflation. And the lower the husband's earnings, the less likely it was that the wife had received an increase.

Households with higher incomes (especially those with two earners) seem more likely to adopt a pooling system. This may reflect the more egalitarian pattern of marital relationships or it may be a consequence of greater affluence. But even under this system the wife's earnings were more often used for the payment of household expenses, the wife not having the same economic independence as the husband. Pahl indicates that money disputes play a significant part in relationship problems between spouses. Money is one form of power in our society as well as a measure of worth. And the relative economic situations of husband and wife must reflect the relative power in their relationship. It reveals something of the extent to which husbands are still free to determine the limits of equality within their married lives.

Leisure pursuits: Young and Willmott found that, with the increased money and leisure families now had, nearly all families were more home-centred than previously, even when families do things together wherever they are. In the home the most important activity on the part of husbands is watching television. After that came gardening, listening to music, repair work, car cleaning and reading – much as we would expect. When husbands were not at home, they were likely to be out with their children, visiting friends, or relatives, or eating out. Middle-class families played more sport and went out to eat or to places of entertainment more than working-class families. The proportion of the time spent outside the home was the same; the nature of the engagement was different. Most people did not think their families constrained them in what they wanted to do, except in their time spent out as a couple. Most people spent a great deal of time at home and seemed to be content with it.

We can sum up these sections by noting that men are sometimes more domesticated than they used to be. The situation is fluid: they can help out if they choose to. The phrase – 'help out' – is apt. It is rare to see a husband accepting complete responsibility for domestic work. Husbands have the power to determine their level of involvement in domestic activities. That power is determined partly through economic power; partly buttressed by cultural prescriptions of what is masculine and permissible for men to be seen doing around the home; partly by sheer muscle power. After all, traditional prescriptions of the male role contain a lot of male privilege!

ENRICHMENT OF CHILDHOOD

The small nuclear family was a product not only of changes in industrialization; it was partly a conscious choice on the part of parents no longer faced with the need to struggle against poverty. The adoption of birth control allowed a concentration of resources – emotional, cultural, and material – on the smaller number of children in any family. No longer was it necessary to have children as an insurance against old age. The whole purpose of children within working-class marriages has changed: children could for the first time be seen as an end in themselves (Oakley, 1976).

This change is called 'familism': a style of life decisively centred on the small nuclear family, which makes a major emotional investment in family relationships, which are for all members their chief source of social and psychological support. This social unit is frequently sentimentalized by the media. Beautiful, unharrassed mum goes about her task caring for the family, knowing just how to convert the latest quick food into a tasty, nourishing meal. Contented, active dad, full of fun, is playing with the kids or mending the car. The bright kids, always full of energy, are appreciative of what their parents do for them. An oppressive stereotype that has been used by the media to sell consumer products but also an ideal that many families strive towards.

This new-found familism is child-centred. Childhood has now been prolonged past puberty; there are striking differences between child and adult roles and during their years of dependency, children are treated as if they are innocent precious creatures.

Part of this change can be explained by the growing importance of child psychology. Spock (1945) has sold 30 million copies. His book is described as a substitute grandmother, when she is not there; and that was the point of it. Millions of families were no longer in close touch with their mothers or grandmothers who used to advise them what to do when baby was ill. Spock and the child psychologists took over the job, improving on grandmother's advice, upgrading the information to suit the needs of a modern, more technological society.

Much of the new advice came from the new experts in childcare who often based their help on the writing of Bowlby (1953). He argued strongly for traditional roles in the family and claimed a special importance for the relationship between the mother and child. His initial claim that the child needed to experience a warm and continuous relationship with the mother (a view he later modified) was to prove influential in keeping young mothers at home with their children. Oakley calls this notion the most subversive part of the myth of motherhood. Child neglect was to become a highly emotive phrase, implying that mothers who went to work were being selfish and callous. Bowlby's work also allowed the State to quietly drop many of the nurseries opened during the Second World War. Day-care, it was argued, was no substitute for a strong attachment between mother and child. Rutter (1972) pointed out that warmth is an essential ingredient in all family relationships and that there was nothing special about the mother-child relationship.

Nevertheless the damage was done. Popular opinion had firmly taken hold of the myth that all children need their mothers and experts were happy to promulgate this myth. The ideal gave childhood a prominence as never before. This was partly brought about by the growing awareness of educationalists of the extent of provision that was necessary to cope with the post-war baby boom. New schools had to be built and many reports (from Plowden to Robbins) argued for better and increased provision. The post-war economic growth provided many working-class couples with an awareness that free education together with adequate family support could give their children opportunities that the parents had never dreamed of themselves. Working-class families could plan not only the size of their families but also their expectations of the sort of life they wanted their children to experience.

EQUALITY IN THE MODERN FAMILY

Many of the changes happening within the family are beneficial. The nuclear family makes fewer physical and emotional demands on women: in Victorian times a woman was often worn out by excessive childbirth. She could not conceive of a life of her choosing outside the confines of the home. Homes are very different today from what they used to be. Working-class men, before the wars, had their clubs and pubs as sheltering places from the deprivations of work. That place has now been taken by the modern family. Family life within the home is something to be enjoyed and shared with one's spouse.

Nevertheless optimists like Fletcher (1966) and Young and Willmott (1973) have come in for a good deal of criticism for their somewhat bland analysis of family life. They have been accused of ignoring the wider influences (particularly the ideological forces of sexism) on family relationships. The glaring error of Young and Willmott, according to many feminists, is that they have failed to understand the importance of the reproductive function of the family for society. The family is still required to produce the future labour force needed by society. No other unit of society can ever do this as cheaply as it is done by the family where childcare and housework are unpaid activities.

In order to ensure that this is carried out, alternative female employment is badly paid; women are subjected to a great deal of ideological pressure to convince them of the importance of their primary roles – motherhood and housework. Even within the home, women are obliged to take the responsibility for servicing their husbands and children. A husband's source of power, derived outside the home from better career prospects and higher wages, and buttressed within the home by superior physical strength and ideological support, will always ensure that gender relationships are assymetrical.

It may not be true that a woman's natural place is in the home: nor is it true that the relationship between men and women is fast becoming symmetrical. In spite of legal improvements to the status of women, legal definitions still tie the status of wife to the role of unpaid domestic worker. A husband is still entitled to unpaid domestic service from his wife; a right that courts still uphold.

In one way the situation is fluid. The greater freedom of women has come about, not at the expense of men, but as a result of the improvements to family life. It is this that gives the members of a family the scope to exercise choice about family roles. Husbands can, if they want, spend more energy and do more within the home. Husbands and wives can negotiate new ways of allocating domestic chores. But they are not free to live their family lives unaffected by the constraints of social and economic pressures from outside the family. Husbands are still predominantly the breadwinners and the concerns of work and promotion prospects still impinge on family life. They still need to give priority to the concerns of their jobs when they conflict with the family. Their source of financial sustenance still comes from their participation in the labour market, where they continue to get advantages over women in spite of the Equal Pay Act. Equal pay and equal career prospects for women are a *sine qua non* for equality with the family.

Our brief review of the studies of the amount of housework and childcare that husbands are prepared to undertake reveal the traditional attitudes which husbands and wives still hold. Those ideologies do not come out of the blue: they reflect the dominant ideologies of industrial capitalism. Things may be changing. Readers of this chapter must make up their own minds how much emphasis to give to each part of the argument.

QUESTIONS

1. What notions would you use to assess the amount of equality within the family?
2. When Harold Macmillan said: 'You've never had it so good', he could have been talking about the position of women in society. Discuss.
3. A woman's place is in the home.
   Do you agree? Give your reasons.
4. The separation between home and work, together with the responsibility of women for housework and childcare, serves to perpetuate inequality between the sexes.
   How accurate is this statement in the light of legislative and economic changes which have taken place in the twentieth century?
5. Husbands and wives can pretend to be equal: mothers and fathers know they are not.
   In what ways is this the case?

6. Children need their mothers.
How true is this and how does it fit in with the greater emphasis on familism and the enrichment of childhood?
7. Domestic politics are about the respective power relationships of husbands and wives. What are the sources of power in marital relationships?
8. Equal pay and equal career prospects are a *sine qua non* for equality within the family. Say why you agree or disagree.

FURTHER READING

An excellent series of feminist writings is appearing in paperbacks published by Tavistock. Called the Tavistock Women's Studies, so far two have appeared:

Mackie, L. and Pattullo, P., *Women at Work*, Tavistock, 1977.
Wilson, E., *Women and the Welfare State*, Tavistock, 1977.

A novel that quickly became an international bestseller provides a good understanding of the feminist perspective, and has the warning on its front cover: 'This Novel Changes Lives!' French, M., *The Women's Room*, Sphere Paperbacks, 1978.
Ann Oakley has produced five books to date. The Penguin is particularly recommended. They are:

The Sociology of Housework, Martin Robertson, 1974
Housewife, Penguin, 1976
Becoming a Mother, Oxford, 1978
Subject Women, Martin Robertson, 1980
From Here to Maternity, Penguin, 1981

Two good books on childhood are:

Aries, P. *Centuries of Childhood*, Jonathan Cape, 1962
Slater P. *The Pursuit of Loneliness*, Penguin, 1975

Three rather more detailed feminist books:

Barker, D. L. and Allen, S., *Sexual Divisions and Society: Process and Change*, Tavistock, 1976
Barker, D. L. and Allen, S., *Dependence and Exploitation: Work and Marriage*, Longman, 1976
Malos, E., *The Politics of Housework*, Allison & Busby, 1980

Four

Conflicts within the family

The functions of the family have changed as the family itself has changed. There is no evidence that these changes have weakened the family as an institution. Nor has the increased involvement of the state in some of the functions which the family traditionally carried out for the wider society, impaired the family's capacity to function. It has simply changed it.

But the family has been criticized for what goes on within it. As each family develops along the course of its life cycle, it meets various crises. Some families find these too much and break up. Others become locked in persistent conflict. If we add all these crises together, the sum total makes it appear that the family as an institution is falling apart under the strain of modern life. Divorce, adolescent rebellion, wife and child abuse, and the failure of some families to look after their aged members, are all cited as an indication that this is so. The family would appear to have lost its way.

How do people assess the success of their own families in achieving the goals they have set for them? How do they determine whether their own family, as it has developed in the course of its own history, has fulfilled their dreams of what family life should be about? Institutions such as the church and schools as well as the media all have stereotypes of what ideal families are like. Yet the reality is often very different. People may harbour fears that their own families have failed in some way to match up to what a good family should be like.

How far are people's hopes and expectations about family life realistic? We have already pointed out that the family is not the free floating, malleable institution that some people think it is. Couples are not free to choose the kind of relationships they want to create within their families, outside of the constraints of the wider society. They live within a network of social and economic forces.

We shall relate the crises that families have to face to a framework of change that goes on as they develop from marriage to dissolution. These changes alter the locus of power within families and provide an insight on the struggles that some members of a family have in maintaining their own positions within its structure.

FAMILY CYCLES

The family is both a biological and a social unit. It goes through a series of stages as it matures biologically. As the family grows up, so individual family members pass through a series of events some of which may assume significance within the family. Families change as their members grow older. To sociologists, the events associated with these changes can be regarded as marking off points in the family life cycle. The birth of the first child launches the family into a new stage – a family-building stage. Similarly when the last child leaves home the family enters another stage in its life cycle.

All families go through similar stages. Families are born at marriage and reach a peak as the period of procreation is passed and the children grow up and mature. Families then decline as the children marry and leave home to form families of their own. The original family finally disintegrates with the death of one of the original partners. Families have a natural rhythm like the seasons: there is an endless process of families moving from stage to stage.

We can divide up the family cycle in many ways: it all depends on what aspect of change we wish to focus on. Donnison (1967) divided up the family cycle into five stages to indicate its housing needs at various points in its development. Abrams (1978), in analysing the family's economic structure, divided the family into seven stages. He highlighted the demands made on a family's financial resources through the family cycle. Rosser and Harris (1965), in their study of families in Swansea, divided family spans into four stages – homemaking, procreational, dispersal, and final (Table 4.1). This simple division is useful. Its advantage is that each stage represents easily identified and distinct milestones in the progress of the family through its cycle. On average the first phase, with marriage happening about the age of twenty-three, will last about two years. The second will last about twenty-three years (from the birth to the marriage of the first child). The third phase will be quite short like the first; depending on the number and spacing of the children, it will last four or five years. The last phase is one that has extended, as life expectancies grow.

Each phase has its own characteristic patterns of household composition, of family behaviour, and of participation of family members in outside activities. The homemaking phase entails considerable adjustments for the newly-weds, not only in having to adapt to each other, but having to relate to a new set of relatives (the in-laws) as well as preparing for another new, unknown relationship at the end of the phase – the new baby.

The procreation stage is what most people regard as family life. 47 per cent of the Swansea families were at this stage (the proportion now would be less). For some families it is a stage of conflict and dramatic change. Children grow up and challenge their parents. Some are determined that their own families (when they form them) will be differently organized. Relationships between the spouses change. The family may even be dissolved at this stage because of the inability of members to adapt to change.

Table 4.1. The family cycle

Phase		From	To	% of total
I	Homemaking	Marriage	Birth of first child	17
II	Procreation	Birth of first child	Marriage of first child	47
III	Dispersion	Marriage of first child	Marriage of last child	16
IV	Final	Marriage of last child	Death of original partners	20

Source: Rosser and Harris (1965).

The dispersal stage may appear relatively peaceful. Parents have to adapt to losing their children and to living with each other again. And it is the obverse of stage one, with parents acquiring relationships in the marriages their children make. The final stage, when all the children have left home, covers two important changes that families have to adapt to. They are the time when the mother is free to go back to work, if she has not already done so, and the time of retirement. It is also a stage when some parents are required to make arrangements for caring for their own aged parents.

POWER AND CONFLICT

All families operate with a particular distribution of power and authority, between their members (see Goode, 1971). The distribution of power is likely to change as the family develops and the children grow up. At birth a child may be almost completely subject to the power of its parents. (Some babies soon learn how to disrupt and get what they want from parents.) In adolescence children are more capable of challenging their parents' authority. As the family matures and parents grow older, so the power positions may get reversed and the children may take control, making decisions on behalf of elderly parents.

While this is a simplified picture, it is easy to see that conflicts are likely to emerge as power changes hands. It changes both between parents and children and between spouses. At the time of marriage both spouses may regard themselves as equal. Money may be scarce, requiring sacrifices to be made. And time (another resource) may be plentiful. Couples make sacrifices and disagreements may get resolved easily.

As the couple moves into the procreation stage, these conflicts of interest assume greater importance. First, the distribution of power changes dramatically as the wife gives up employment and becomes financially dependent. The husband's power is increased. This change may assume a degree of permanence as, faced with a drop in income, families alter their goals and attach greater weight to the husband's career prospects. Second, the transition to the family-building stage with the arrival of the child, can be stressful.

With the onset of parenthood and the changes in the distribution of power, both parties may develop a new sense of their own interests, where previously they had common interests. Oakley

(1979) points out in her discussion of domestic politics that sleep, peace, and money are all highly valued resources, with the arrival of new children in the family. If babies make demands, it is easy for the wife to feel obliged to sacrifice her sleep or free time, in the interests of the demands a husband's job has on him. His work interests take precedence because of his breadwinning responsibilities. Blood and Wolfe (1960) point out that the typical bride, marrying in her early twenties and bearing children a couple of years later, never really has time to work out an egalitarian relationship before the children begin to arrive.

Family sociologists highlight the importance of the negotiations between spouses as the way in which both parties contain the conflicts and thereby strengthen the relationship. But husbands have distinct advantages: they are usually stronger, they are the breadwinners and can claim the constraints of work override any other considerations, and they are usually supported by the ideology about gender relations in our society.

Men are supposed to be dominant in our society: they are given more training in the skills of argument. They are usually more skilled at defending their own positions. Women may be trained to defer. This often means that men take the responsibility for conflict regulation within the family. The justice or otherwise of a man's doing this is a matter a wife may passively ascribe to. She may eventually give up airing grievances, knowing that her husband has a different stake in these conflicts.

FAMILY VIOLENCE

Physical violence within a family is usually associated with times when the family is under stress. This is typically the time of peak family formation. At this stage, patience, personal space and money are in short supply. Family size itself is not an important predictor of family violence. It appears that low income families are used to living with stress and that high income families can use their resources to minimize their conflicts. Middle income families suffer the greatest incidence of violence.

The findings on family violence are dismal. Violence is closely associated with unequal power relations. Wife abuse is more common in homes where power is concentrated and least in democratic households. Violence may be used by the most powerful member to legitimate that position. High rates of violence occur when families are subject to more than average amounts of stress, when they have to cope with children, and when one spouse dominates decision making.

But there is hope. Families now have fewer children, making for less stress, and spouses are working towards more equal relationships. That violence is endemic in families should not surprise us. We tend to regard the family as a private haven of peace. But that does not mean that it is shielded from what goes on in the wider society. Urban societies are violent and some of this violence happens inside families.

The family is violence-prone for other reasons (Marsden, 1978). It demands a high commitment of its members from which it is difficult to withdraw. Families meet each other at close quarters at bad times and may often be involved with issues that cannot be resolved in everyone's favour. Authority is unequally distributed and disputes may be settled by those in authority, partial to their own interests. There is no outside institution for settling family disputes. And little formal training is available to family members in acquiring negotiating skills for this task. Compared to other institutions, the family is backward in dealing with its own industrial (domestic) relations.

Physical abuse, family disputes and individual depression may all be connected. It is difficult to generalize over such complex issues but there are patterns in the outcomes. When men are more powerful in the interactions between spouses, they are likely to win. Married women may feel trapped, helpless and unable to change their situation. Accepting this may leave many wives feeling powerless and depressed. Women are locked into any marriage more than men (Marsden, 1978): they are bound by economic and social constraints and are less likely to find alternatives to being physically or psychologically abused by husbands. For example, *Good Housekeeping* (September, 1977) reported that nine in ten men with alcoholic wives, compared with one in ten wives with alcoholic husbands, eventually leave their spouses.

The extent of depression in marriage is well documented. The extent of physical abuse is only beginning to surface. Since it was socially unacceptable, very little abuse came to light. It was a self-fulfilling prophecy. Neither men nor women are very eager to acknowledge the significance that force or its threat can play in the daily drama of family life. Male violence towards women has surfaced at three points in history. In the late nineteenth century, a debate on matrimonial violence led eventually to a change in matrimonial law (Young, 1976). It surfaced again in the suffragette movement and the recent women's movement has supported it as an issue (Hanmer, 1978).

The rise of women's refuges (safe places for women away from a violent spouse), supported by the women's movement, has encouraged some women to regard marital violence as a public rather than a private issue. When violence is covert, it is easy to interpret it in personal terms. Institutions are still reluctant to support women in bringing violence to the attention of the authorities. Social workers may still try to keep couples together and social security officers may raise obstacles for unsupported women.

> Whether or not a woman is free to leave a violent and stressful marriage will depend on her emotional involvement in the ideals of marriage and motherhood, contrasting with the alternative identities available to her as a lone mother or worker; her social status in the circle of her friends and how this depends on her marriage; her financial investment in the marriage, that is, the standard of living and financial protection it brings compared with alternative resources for living alone . . . This means that the behaviour of battered wives who keep going back to violent men, and even say they miss them, need not be explained as sado-masochism or immaturity. In our society, it may be explicable . . . for the security and status which a man, any man, tends to confer upon a woman in marriage (Marsden, 1973).

The actual incidence of physical abuse is greater than the observed incidence. An American study points out (Strauss, 1980) that three parents in five regularly hit their children. Every other household is the scene of family violence at least once a year. These are American national averages. Some households are more violent. Two million children and women are battered and beaten by family members each year and that is only the tip of the iceberg.

Women have been raped, choked, stabbed, beaten, shot, had their jaws and limbs broken, and been struck with horse whips, pokers, bats and bicycle chains (Davidson, 1978), all within the family. Three parents in a hundred kicked, bit, or punched their children in 1976 (Strauss, 1980). One child in every hundred faced a parent who threatened to use a gun or a knife, in 1975!

There are no comparable figures for the extent of physical abuse in the UK but it is unlikely to be very different. Violence in some form is widespread within marriage, so widespread that many incidents go unnoticed. A woman is far more likely to be attacked within the family than she is outside it. Husbands are legally entitled to insist on their conjugal 'rights' regardless of the inclination of their wives, in all countries except Australia and Norway.

Dobash and Dobash (1980) is one of the few British studies that emphasizes the routine nature of violence. It is not that all marriages are violent. The preconditions for marital violence exist in most marriages and, given certain stresses, it is likely to occur. The Dobash study highlights the connection between a man feeling possessive over his wife and becoming violent if she did anything that made him jealous. In many of the marriages they investigated, violence became an index of how jealous and (by inference) how loving, the husband was. A certain level of violence, within that framework of meaning, thus became an acceptable sanction for the husband to use.

ADOLESCENCE

Adolescence represents a peak in the power struggle between parents and children, when children are most likely to challenge their parents' remaining authority over them. Adolescence is that period of enforced dependency imposed on children (with economic sanctions) in spite of their emotional and physical readiness for independence. This enforced dependence has become necessary because of the greater goals parents have for their children, for better education, better job opportunities, better housing: whatever the parents have decided (Smith, 1968).

Parent-child relationships have always been rooted in conflict. Children have always been able to disrupt their parents in order to get what they want in varying degrees. As children participate increasingly in activities outside the home, so family authority runs the risk of being challenged. The intensification of childhood within nuclear families has clouded the specific rights and duties that children have at each age. It is now much more a question of individual bargaining between individual parents and their children. Confusion about these rights is of critical importance during adolescence. Also, this conflict of interests between the short-term goals of the child (in being freer) and the long-term interests of the parents (in getting something better for their children by postponing the point of independence) has been exacerbated by the increased affluence of many parents. Parents now have more choice to decide on goals for their children. Sometimes these goals may be unrealistic, judged by the capabilities of the child, and may reflect more the frustrated ambitions of the parents when they were young, rather than realistic goals for the children.

Education is an important source for social mobility in our society. But to some teenagers the aspirations that they should remain at school long enough to acquire qualifications is unrealistic and does not take into account their position within their school classes. Education forces many working-class children into a system of middle-class values that may exclude them (especially the average ability working-class teenagers) from the very success it supposedly offers. School may have little impact on their future occupations. They may be destined to jobs with no future or even to no jobs at all. Parents may find this difficult to accept. They see the sacrifices they have made so far being wasted by their children being apparently indifferent to educational goals. It is not difficult to see why many teenagers, with few chances of getting anywhere in the economic system, give up so easily. To parents this may prove difficult to understand.

Another important source of social mobility (at least for women) is marriage. Marriage is still an important goal for a woman in our society: the implicit bargaining that goes on over marriage partners is often highly complex. Few parents are likely to oppose their children's marriages. Few parents may have very clear ideas about the kind of husband they would like their daughters to choose but they may know what kind of a partner they would not like for them.

For working-class girls, pregnancy may be the only avenue to gaining independence from an impossible (conflict-full) home life. Middle-class children can often gain their independence through going to college. Victorian upper-class parents used to lock up their daughters and provide brothels for their sons, staffed by working-class women. Controlling the sexual proclivities of children may be inordinately difficult. While sexual experience is now much more permissible, couples are still expected to have their children within marriage. Smith (1968) points out that child-bearing is more strictly controlled than sexual experience. The significant stage of transition from adolescence to maturity is not when the young gain access to sexual satisfaction, nor even when they marry, but when they set up a family unit of their own and have their own children.

YOUTH CULTURES

Adolescent peer group activity is a usual framework for teenagers, especially working-class ones. In all their spheres of activity – educational, work, sexual, marital and civic roles – their statuses are subordinate. They are subject to rules determined by social relationships based on age.

The social meaning of adolescence is a world apart from the world of adults. Youth cultures are systems of support that help adolescents to deal with the difficulty of being treated as dependent while being sexually and physically mature. Lacking an identity in such a contradiction, adolescents gain their identity from their subculture. They turn to their peers for support and, together, they develop collective identities to give meaning to their lives. Young people have few avenues in which to express themselves. Working-class teenagers may regard their job opportunities as poor and may look elsewhere for modes of expression.

These modes are often found in four outlets – dress, records, transport and leisure activities. It is almost as if youth cultures are a way for young people to provide answers to questions they know are intractable. Destined for dead-end jobs, frustrated by the kind of class struggle of their parents' generation, they displace this struggle from the arena of work and politics into leisure-time pursuits even if it is only temporary and symbolic (Brake, 1980). Thus victory is achieved partly in the shock value of youth cultures, as well as in the intense feeling of community that peer group solidarity can create. The peer group is important to all subcultures not just to youth ones. But for young people peer group support is important since they are barred admission to so many adult roles and statuses.

Adolescence is important for parents today when they have invested so heavily in their children. Parents may find it difficult to say what precisely their goals are for their children but they may have a sense of not achieving what they set out to achieve for their children. It is rare for parents to admit to a sense of failure about the bringing up of their children but their goals for their children may be misplaced or unattainable. 'Look what we have sacrificed for you,

and you throw it in our faces'. If children choose goals for themselves that are at variance with what their parents wanted, it must be
easy for parents to feel that their sacrifices have been wasted.

FAMILY DISSOLUTION

The family unit traditionally came to an end at the death of one of
the spouses. It can also be terminated along the course of the family
cycle by the separation or divorce of the couple. There is no doubt
that many more people are choosing to dissolve their marriages in
preference to waiting for the eventual death of one of the partners.
In Britain today there is one divorce for every three marriages in any
one year and the rate of dissolution is moving steadily towards the
American rate of one divorce for every two marriages each year.

The divorce rate has increased rapidly in recent years. Between
the late 1950s and early 1960s, it increased four-fold. The rate in
1971 was three times as high as the rate in 1961. Table 4.2 shows the
rapid increase: it also shows a slight steadying of the figures since
1980. Many people assume that these figures indicate a falling in
moral standards to do with the significance attached to the sanctity
of marriage. But we must be careful in our interpretations.

In the first place the overall increase in the figures tells us very
little. They may merely reflect other changes connected to mar-

*Table 4.2. Divorce in England and Wales –
petitions filed*

Date	By husband 000	By wife 000	Total 000	Rate 000
1961	14	18	32	2.1
1971	44	67	111	6.0
1976	43	101	145	10.1
1978	47	116	164	11.6
1979	46	118	164	11.2
1980	49	123	172	12.0
1981	47	123	170	11.9
1982	47	128	174	12.0
1983	45	124	169	12.2

Source: CSO, *Social Trends 15*, 1985 edition.

riage. The numbers of people marrying throughout this century has increased dramatically. Before the last war, people married later in life and more people remained unmarried. In 1931 roughly a quarter of females aged twenty to twenty-four were married; by 1961 the rate was almost 60 per cent. The proportion of females who were unmarried at the age of forty-five to forty-nine fell from 17 per cent in 1931 to 7 per cent in 1974.

In order to calculate the risk of divorce, we need to compare the number of divorces (usually expressed annually) with the number of marriages. Currently the rate is running at one in ten of all marriages (a stock figure). If we wish to ascertain recent changes in this trend, we need to express divorce ratios as flow figures – the flow of people into and out of marriages at one point in time (usually expressed as divorces in one year compared with marriages in the same year). The flow divorce statistics is one in three.

In the second place, access to divorce has changed. At the beginning of the century it was an option available only to a very small élite. Marriage was an institution still controlled by the church, held to be sacrosanct and indissoluble. Marriages could be annulled under certain circumstances, or the couples could separate. Divorce was available only through a private act of Parliament, a costly procedure. Up to the 1930s, fluctuations in the divorce rate occurred only when there were changes either over the legal grounds for divorce or relating to the financial assistance to would-be litigants. Before the last war, the number of divorces granted never exceeded 10,000 a year. It is only since 1945 that divorce has become a major factor in the legal termination of marriages.

A dramatic change-about followed a report of the Law Commissioners in 1966 which argued three things. There was no evidence that the proportion of broken marriages had increased this century; a good divorce law would seek to buttress rather than undermine the stability of marriage; and it attached great importance to providing a decent burial for dead marriages. Easier divorce would legitimate about 180,000 illegitimate children. The 1969 Divorce Reform Act put the sole grounds of divorce as the irretrievable breakdown of marriage, or a separation of five years or two years of living apart and the consent of both parties. Since 1971 when the act became operative, the increase in divorce rates reflects this change in the grounds for divorce as well as a backlog of dead marriages.

DIVORCE AND SOCIAL CHANGE

So what do divorce rates tell us about marriages and the family? Probably very little. Changes in divorce can at least remind us that people use very different criteria for establishing the success of their marriage.

In other societies marriages may be judged more successful and family dissolution may be less frequent, simply because overt conflict between the couple is dealt with differently. For instance, in some societies there may be a lower expectation about what individuals may expect from marriage. Personal happiness may not be a high priority.

The success of such a marriage would be rated, not so much by the intimate harmony of the husband and wife, as by the contribution of the couple to the extended kin. Elders would direct the affairs of the family, arrange the marriages and intervene in quarrels between husband and wife.

Public opinion during the nineteenth century took for granted that spouses who no longer loved each other and who found life together distasteful, should at least remain together for the sake of the children. People's expectations about the family and marriage have changed. Taken together there would probably be less consensus today than there used to be about what people may expect from the family. Some people still regard marriage as sacred and indissoluble, others regard marriage as something based on the quality of the relationship between the spouses. If the relationship were good, commitment could be added to the relationship; if the relationship deteriorated, then both parties should have the freedom to dissolve the relationship and to seek others. Between these views there is a whole spectrum of variations.

The view of most commentators on divorce is that the rates by themselves tell us very little. A major study conducted by McGregor (1967) concluded that the historical increase in divorce does not represent a genuine increase in marriage breakdown. Rather it is due to the movement from separations to divorce and is mainly the result of easier financial access, through legal aid. The Law Commissioners in the 1966 report also agreed with this conclusion, as did Finer (1974). McGregor and Finer further argue that we must attribute the rise in divorce simply to easier access to divorce. Changes in the law may have greatly eased the possibility of dissolving a marriage. But we must also bear in mind the enormous changes that have occurred in the institution of marriage, what Finer calls the silent revolution in marriage habits over the last two generations.

In the past many women could not marry: wars and large-scale emigration reduced the number of potential husbands. Today marriage is a near universal institution. Finer hints that so many people now marry that some of them make unsuitable spouses. People marry at an earlier age, and the potential life of marriages is longer. Divorce must reflect these changes. Finally, we also need to bear in mind that the goals of marriage have changed. The notions of romantic and exclusive love mean that couples emphasize the significance of the marital relationship. It is little wonder that the conjugal family unit is often dissolved. The high expectations currently placed on marriage that the partners will fulfill each other's emotional needs places a strain on the relationship previously unknown.

In any case we cannot conclude that the rise in divorce rates indicates a dissatisfaction with marriage *per se*, since re-marriage rates are so high. In the USA three-quarters of all divorced women and five-sixths of all divorced men remarry. In Britain, Leake (1978) has estimated that remarriage rates are high and rising. About half the people divorcing in any year remarry within five years. If remarriage rates remain at current levels, then about one in five men and women born around 1950 will have entered a second marriage by the time they are 50.

Divorce rates, far from suggesting that marriage is breaking down, point to the increasing expectations that people have (Chester, 1973). Delphy (1976) argues that marriage and divorce are intertwined. Divorce is only really necessary if marriage continues to exist. She does not conclude that divorce is an indication (along with falling age of first marriage) of the increased popularity of marriage. Instead she implies that women remarry after divorce because of their exploitation. Generally, women can expect to do relatively worse in the labour market as they get older: men can expect to do better. Many women who divorce will be obliged to remarry. They are confronted by a paradox; marriage is an institution that exploits them (by requiring unpaid work) and still offers them the best career economically. From a woman's standpoint, marriage often creates the conditions for its own confirmation.

This situation is clear in the case of children. Their custody is usually entrusted to the mother in any dispute. But the woman's income after divorce is usually lower than her former husband's, and her contribution to the cost of children that much higher. As a result her sacrifices are relatively greater. It is easy to make what one wants to from the divorce figures. But it makes little sense to argue that rising divorce rates are an indication of the breakdown of marriage.

LONE-PARENT FAMILIES

Lone-parent families are the by-product partly of increasing divorce. One estimate (Finer, 1974) has suggested that as many as one family in eight has only one parent at any time in Britain. Few people choose to become single parents as a way of life. Such families arise in the main through increased family dissolutions. Many single parents are as committed to the two-parent family as are other married couples. Many families whose marriages have been dissolved produce orthodox two-parent families in due course. Thus the status of single parenthood is generally one of transition between the dissolution of a former family and its eventual reconstitution into a new two-parent family. This transitional stage is usually sufficiently lengthy to ensure that it forms a significant part of the lives of its members.

It is impossible to know for certain how many single parents there are. It is a distinctive domestic situation, rather than a legal status, and is therefore not accounted for in official statistics. Many marriages are dissolved without recourse to formal separation and many lone parents eventually form new two-parent families without necessarily formalizing the status by marriage. Figure 4.1 shows how one-parent families are formed and how they change. We have only partial measures of the flow of people into the status, the stock of one-parent families at any time, and the flow of people out again.

It now seems that Finer's estimate of nearly two-thirds of a million mothers and fathers looking after one million children was too high. A more recent estimate (Leete, 1978) puts the figure for 1971 at 570,000 lone parents, rising to about 750,000 by 1976 and to 920,000 by 1980. Table 4.3 shows the composition for this group of lone parents by sex and marital status. Divorced and separated mothers constitute the two largest groups, accounting for over half,

Figure 4.1. Formation and ending of one-parent families

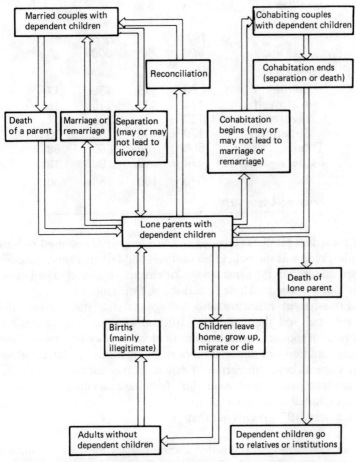

A dependent child in this context is a person aged under sixteen, or
between sixteen and nineteen and undergoing full-time education.

followed by single and widowed mothers. There are seven times as
many fatherless as motherless families, although other studies put
the ratio at around four to one. We have no information about how
long lone-parent families remain as such (that is, the speed of the
flow) nor do we know the total number of families in the population
who have passed through lone parenthood.

One-parent families face many problems and prejudices. A study

Table 4.3. Estimated numbers of one-parent families

	1971 000	%	1976 000	%
Mothers:				
Single	90	16	130	17
Widowed	120	21	115	15
Divorced	120	21	230	31
Separated	170	30	185	25
Total:	500	88	660	88
Fathers – total	70	12	90	12
	570	100	750	100

Source: Leete 1978.

of fatherless families (George and Wilding, 1972) pointed to how widespread was the belief that mothers and fathers cannot care for their children in the same way. Mothers are supposed to be best at the emotional side. These beliefs are still widespread.

Lone-parent roles are also ambiguous: the status is socially depricated and there is little institutional regulation of the behaviour of spouses during the time of break up. Few lone parents get much emotional or material support. Being formerly married is not the same as being unmarried. Because of this normative haziness, many lone parents feel unsure how to behave and may withdraw or feel excluded from social situations.

Chester (1977) points out that

adult social life . . . is oriented towards couples. Patterns of invitation and response, topics of conversation, and systems of cooperation revolve around couples and their concerns, and there is little place for the unaccompanied in the structure of sociability . . . lone parents find special difficulty in getting out socially because of burdensome obligations . . . problems of childcare, and lack of finance . . . contemporary mores place more restrictions on public social ventures for unaccompanied women than for men. . . . The most straightforward way of countering all this exclusion is to find a permanent partner, and thus an entry ticket back to orthodox society and sociability.

The third problem that lone parents have to cope with is lack of money. Hunt (1973) shows a range of incomes among families, running down from two-parent through mother-absent to father-absent families. After adjusting for family size, the mean incomes of mother-absent families run at about a third less than two-parent families, probably reflecting the absence of a wife's wage. The incomes of father-absent families average two-thirds of those of lone fathers. The Finer Committee made it clear that female-headed families are likely to be poor. There is also a hierarchy: widowed mothers have more income than divorced mothers who have more than unmarried mothers. Economic deprivation is normal for female-headed one-parent families and this undermines its viability as a family form.

Their low incomes are exacerbated by the treatment they get from the state. On the face of it, their treatment is no different from other claimants. They get what they are entitled to, according to criteria set down, providing an allowance for the parent, each child and special payments to cover certain other needs. But they are subject to certain restrictions that limit their life style. First, their relationships with men have been policed in the past in an offensive way. The state cannot afford to allow them to live as single people and gain the benefits of being dependent on another adult (like a married couple). So it has closely questioned lone parents in the past to ascertain that they are not cohabiting. Since lone mothers are often vulnerable, state officials may have overstepped the bounds of propriety in the past. This has been changed after considerable protest by pressure groups. Nevertheless, the state continues to monitor this group more closely than other groups who evade state regulations.

Second, lone parents are restricted by being precluded from supplementing their benefits by working part-time without loss of benefit (only a small part of the benefit is disregarded if they work). This is particularly burdensome for lone mothers. Again, on the face of it they are treated in the same way as other groups assisted by the state. They are permitted to earn only up to £4 weekly before having their benefit cut. But this is precisely the problem: their needs are different. Unlike most other claimants of working age, single parents can continue to need state support for as long as it takes to raise a child. Lone parents often have lower reserves than other claimants. Lone mothers are the only group of mothers who are prevented from supplementing their incomes by part-time work (a common enough activity for married mothers with children). Finer recognized the financial needs of mothers and proposed a guaranteed maintenance allowance, but in spite of widespread support, his proposals have never been implemented.

Rimmer and Rossiter (1982) argue that one-parent families have two poor choices: they can claim state benefits and remain in poverty for some years or they can go out to work, in which case they will be severely disadvantaged. Of those who do work, they are more likely (23 per cent compared with 15 per cent of two-parent families) to need to work full-time to earn sufficient money. Lone mothers with pre-school children are twice as likely to be working full-time as their two-parent counterparts. Nixon (1979) found a higher proportion of lone mothers who worked were low paid, compared with other mothers. This is because they are in no position to bargain for reasonably paid work but must take whatever they can find.

It is in these ways that lone parents are a social problem. They have arisen without warning, as the regulation surrounding divorce have been liberalized. And the needs they have generated have simply not been met. Hence it is more accurate to say that society poses heavy problems for them, rather than to label lone parents as social problems. The problems posed reflect the widespread attachment to the norm of the two-parent family and the treatment of any variant on this as deviant.

It is hardly surprising that most lone parents appear not to remain as such for very long. This is the paradox of the absence of structured provision for the consequences of family dissolution. Lone parents are pressed towards remarriage as the only viable alternative for their (socially induced) problems. At least two-thirds of those whose marriages break up eventually remarry.

As Chester points out, the penalties and deprivations visited upon families which are dissolved pressurize lone parents into wanting to remarry. But the isolation they experience while lone parents makes it extremely difficult for them to find eventual partners to remarry. Our arrangements for lone parents force them to rely on ingenuity and luck rather than planning and frequent chance encounters through which to meet possible marriage partners.

It is not necessarily the case that the high rates of remarriage of divorced people is a measure of the popularity of marriage. It would be more accurate to argue for the persistence of the norm of the nuclear two-parent family and to conclude that any deviation from that is likely to experience such penalties as to be driven back towards the norm. There is in fact no evidence that lone parents freely choose to be so in the face of such overwhelming societal support for the two-parent family.

AGED MEMBERS OF FAMILIES

A further crisis for many families occurs over the care of aged members. Average life expectancies this century have almost doubled from forty to seventy years: the proportion of the aged in the population has increased two and a half times. This is partly because of increased numbers. It is also a result of the dramatic drop in births. The dependancy ratio, while it has changed little over the last 120 years, has taken on a new shape. In 1851 the aged made up 14 per cent of the dependent population: by 1951 they made up 41 per cent. And this trend will continue. Table 4.4 shows the growth of the aged population this century, and highlights the dramatic growth between 1951 and 1971. The increase is expected to decline slowly after 1981 although the average age of the elderly will increase considerably over the next four decades. Table 4.5 shows how this growth will be among the very aged – those over seventy-five. Those over eighty-five will increase by 1200 per cent by the end of the century.

This has posed a serious dilemma for many families. On the one hand, women are freed from childcare earlier in their life span, and are available to join the labour market full-time. But on the other hand, aged people live longer and will at some stage need care and attention. Moroney (1976) points out that it is not simply a matter of transferring from the care of children to that of the aged. There is often enough of a time gap for some women to establish themselves in a full-time job.

The pool of potential caretakers has shrunk considerably over the past fifty years. Table 4.6 shows the caretaker ratio and its decrease since 1901. The ratio includes both married and single women between forty-five and sixty. In 1901 for every 100 aged people there were 83 women between forty-five and sixty, of whom 13 were single. By 1971 the ratio had fallen to 49 of whom only 5 were single. And the problem is aggravated through geographical mobility:

Table 4.4. Elderly population, England and Wales

Year	Total population 000	Over 65 %	Over 75 %	Over 85 %
1901	32,528	4.7	25.9	3.3
1911	36,070	5.2	24.3	3.4
1921	37,887	6.0	25.1	3.3
1931	39,952	7.4	24.6	3.2
1951	43,758	11.0	28.4	4.1
1961	46,105	11.9	30.5	5.5
1971	48,750	13.3	28.6	6.6
1981[1]	50,817	14.3	31.6	6.4
1991[1]	53,025	14.0	33.6	8.0
2001[1]	55,473	13.0	34.6	9.1

[1] Projected figures

Source: Moroney, 1976.

a third of all families move every five years and a tenth every year.

Does this confirm the popular myth that aged people are abandoned by their families and taken care of by the state? Or are aged people destined to living isolated lives on their own? It is widely believed that institutions for the aged are overfull and incapable of catering adequately for the increased numbers. Certainly the cost of state support for the elderly has risen. A person over seventy-five costs roughly eight times as much as any working aged adult in

Table 4.5. Elderly population over seventy-five years, England and Wales

Population	Percentage increase		
	1901–51	1951–2001	1901–2001
Total population	34	27	70
Population 65 plus	215	50	372
Population 75 plus	245	82	530
Population 85 plus	294	233	1,212

Source: Moroney, 1976.

Table 4.6. Caretakers 1901–71 – United Kingdom.

Year	% Elderly population	% women 45–59	Rate per 1000 elderly	% single women 45–59	Rate per 1000 elderly
1901	7.6	6.3	830	0.8	130
1911	8.1	6.9	850	1.1	160
1921	9.8	8.2	840	1.3	160
1931	11.3	9.1	810	1.5	160
1951	17.0	9.5	640	1.5	110
1961	18.7	9.3	610	1.3	90
1971	19.0	8.1	490	0.8	50

Source: Moroney (1976)

health and social services. Since 1963 almost half of key social welfare expenditure has been allocated to the aged even though they account for only 16 per cent of the population. Given a projected increased of an additional million aged people in the next two decades, it will be impossible to sustain this level of expenditure.

Aged people do have higher rates of disability than the general population. Three studies – Townsend (1979), Harris (1967) and OPCS (1973) – measured the extent of physical impairment. Each study measured this in different ways. Townsend asked respondents whether they could perform minimal caring tasks; Harris looked at physical impediment (a defective limb or organ that limited the person in some way); and OPCS measured any limitation caused by a chronic illness.

The two studies of incapacity show that 55 per cent of the aged have no limitation. The studies of serious incapacity show that 2–6 per cent of the aged are as defined, and this group will have increased by a further quarter by 2001. Also, over a third of the severely disabled are either bedridden or chair-ridden. Three-quarters of these are women and the majority are over seventy-four.

There are two ways in which the state can provide help for the aged: institutional care and community-based services. Institutional care represents a complete transfer of the caring function to the state, in providing an array of residential-based services that substitute for the family. The aged population in institutional care amounts to only a fraction of the aged population. 97 per cent of the aged do not live in long-term care institutions.

The majority of non-institutionalized aged live elsewhere: with their spouses (40 per cent), alone (26 per cent), with their children (19 per cent) or with other people (15 per cent). Those who live in the community can in theory make use of a range of services the state provides with the aim of preventing or delaying admission into care. Community-based services are provided as a cheaper alternative to institutional care and one in the best interests of both the aged and the family. The family is still regarded as the social institution most suited to carry the major caring function.

Since the 1950s, community-based social services have been increased considerably, faster than the rise in the aged population. But the services are spread very thinly, especially among the disabled aged. 37 per cent of the very severely disabled and 56 per cent of the severely disabled have not been receiving any of the community-based services. Those who live with their spouses are more likely to get help. Services to aged people living with families are withheld (even when the family will not or cannot provide care) on the assumption that provision is not necessary. What this does to the caring partnership between family and state we shall discuss in the next chapter.

The vast majority of the aged, then, still live in the community. Only 3 per cent are institutionalized and this has remained so throughout this century. Although the long-term institutionalized population doubled between 1952 (when the state did away with the Poor Law institutions) and 1973, this was still a lower proportion than at the turn of the century.

Care for the elderly has changed, but it is not true to say that families have abandoned them. The Royal Commission (1909) pointed out that care at that time was more instrumental. Women were looked after by families as long as they were useful; men were more likely to be sent to workhouses since they were a trouble to keep at home. In any case families could simply not afford to care for their aged parents at the time. It was state pensions that enabled families to offer non-calculative and emotional support (WHO, 1959).

Many elderly people now live alone through choice and because they can afford to do so. They often prefer to live near, but not with, their families.

The great majority of old people are in regular contact with their children, relatives or friends . . . where distance permits, the generations continue to shoulder their traditional obligations, of elders towards their children, and the children to the aged (Shanas, 1968)

The state now provides a high priority to income maintenance, a support that enables families to offer other forms of support. Nuclear families often function in an extended network with interaction between and among generations, offering mutual support. We shall look more closely at the assumptions on which state provision is made, in the next chapter.

FAMILY GOALS

The family has changed. It is not a stable institution where people always have the same kind of relationship with each other. Nor is it completely fluid where people can work out exactly how they want to relate to each other. The family is moulded by forces from within and without.

We have looked at some of the issues that families may face as they move through their life cycles. Many of the topics discussed – the distribution of power in families, physical abuse, adolescent rebellion, divorce and single parenthood, and the dilemmas of caring for the aged – may appear to be the negative side of family life. They may be the issues that families least wish to deal with. These are not the issues people raise in discussing the improvements in family life brought about by social changes in the twentieth century. In fact some of the issues are the ones raised by people who argue that the family has been weakened by contemporary change.

We have argued that there is little evidence for this thesis. Some may want to argue that the family is alive and well: others that it is dead and needs to be buried. But others want to argue that it is currently dying.

As affluence has become more widespread and families have come to think about what sort of life they would like to create, so couples have been encouraged to define their goals for family life only in very general terms. Political parties emphasize the importance of family life and commit themselves to the well-being of the family, knowing that such terms are little more than shibboleths. Families may themselves decide that they want a better life for their children than the parents had themslves. Beyond that they find it difficult to articulate their goals.

One of the interesting aspects of the developmental cycle of the family is that various events impose on the family a need to rethink what is happening. These crises, often an integral part of the family developing, implicitly make families re-assess their goals. 'Where did we go wrong?' ponder parents with a difficult teenager, a homosexual son or a pregnant daughter. 'Why is my marriage in such a mess?', asks a husband whose wife is asking for a divorce. 'Why should we have to look after grandma?', asks a young married couple, or 'how did this mess happen?', asks a battered wife. Families may see these crises as personal failures. We see them as part of family power struggles, connected to outside forces.

Part of the confusion lies in the myths we have of family life. We regards families as isolated, private units of warm, caring relationships: a haven from the storms of life. We presume from this that what goes on in the privacy of the family home is that family's choice, that they are in control of it and can determine it. We think of idealized parents and ideal children, drawn from the images often presented to us of what families should be like.

It is difficult to realize that we are not in control of the wider economic and ideological forces that mould the nature of any family's existence, and that determine the roles they play and the power conflicts they negotiate over. The good and the bad is all part of the nuclear family as it has developed in the twentieth century.

QUESTIONS

1. Far from disintegrating, the modern family is in some ways in a stronger position that it has been at any period in our history of which we have knowledge.
   Would the Church of England have regretted making this judgment in 1958 if it could have predicted the future course of the divorce rate in Britain?
2. Increasing divorce rates, together with the high rates of remarriage, are in indication, not of breakdown in the institution but of a change towards a new, serial form of marriage. Discuss.
3. The elderly and battered wives have both been defined as 'social problems' in recent years. Explain why.
4. The caring functions of the family have changed dramatically since the beginning of this century. Explain how.

5. Examine the validity of divorce statistics as an indicator of social change.
6. Parent-child relationships are rooted in conflict. Explain.
7. Examine the role of youth cultures in dealing with the central dilemmas faced by teenagers in twentieth-century Britain.
8. Examine the issue of loneliness facing single-parent spouses and the aged. In what ways are they different?
9. In what ways are physically abused wives, adolescents, lone parents and the aged all stigmatized?
10. Youth culture 'arise as attempts to resolve collectively-experienced problems arising from contradictions in the social structure'. Explain.

FURTHER READING

A number of modern books on the family deal with the issues of power, conflict and negotiations between family members:

Dreitzel, H. P., *Family, Marriage and the Struggle of the Sexes*, Macmillan, 197.
Burr, W. R., *Theory Construction and the Sociology of the Family*, Wiley, 1973.
Scanzoni, J., *Sex Roles, Women's Work and Marital Conflict*, Lexington Books, 1978.
Tilley, L. A. and Scott, J. W., *Women, Work and Family*, 1978.
Cromwell, R. E. and Olson, D. H. (eds), *Power in Families*, Wiley, 1975.
Barker, D. L. and Allen, S. (eds), *Dependence and Exploitation in Work and Marriage*, Longman, 1976.

Two readable and different books on the aged (the first a series of interviews with aged people as well as an insightful long essay by the author and the second a book with data on the major issues):

Blythe, R., *The View in Winter*, Allen Lane, 1979.
Bosanquet, N., *A Future for Old Age*, Temple Smith, 1978.

A readable overview of divorce and lone parenthood is contained in the introduction to Finer, M., *Report of the Committee on One Parent Families*, HMSO, 1974.

On family violence see:

Tutt, N. (ed), *Violence*, DHSS, 1976.

Select Committee on Violence in the Family, First Report, *Violence to Children*, HMSO, 1976–77.

Five

Demography, the family and social policy

Social policy is about the planning of the public welfare services provided by the state to take account of the social and economic changes going on. In this chapter we shall use our understanding of the changes in the demographic structure as well as our analysis of the salient changes that have happened to the family, to ask how this has been taken into account by British social policy. After all, if the provision of services such as education, housing, or social services is to be adequate, it has to take these two changes into account.

DEMOGRAPHIC CHANGE

First, what has the government done to make itself aware of the demographic changes that we outlined in Chapter One? 1976 was the year in which the birth rate fell below the death rate for the first time in recorded history. Throughout the early 1970s, most of the discussion on social policy focussed on the problems of over-population, in the wake of the peaking of births between 1955 and 1964. In response to the dramatic fall in births subsequently, the government commissioned a report by the Central Policy Review Staff (CPRS, 1977). We shall summarize its findings.

The report examined the implications of the likely changes in the size and structure of the population over the next twenty years. It identified the main demographic and social issues for the proper planning of social expenditure. This was only the second time such an exercise had ever been done: the first time, in 1949, was also a time of population decline. When the report was published it was immediately shelved as the birth rate subsequently soared.

Population projections are difficult exercises. Projections for the country up to the end of the century have varied from 50 million to 72 million and births have been estimated at anything between 650,000 and 1½ million a year. Of the three significant variables, only mortality is at all stable, although migration rates since 1972 have been very low. Fertility is the most difficult to predict, although some useful predictions can be made for the future. In any case, demographic variables are more important in services such as education and regional planning than they are in, say, public housing policy where concepts such as household fission (the formation of new households out of existing ones) are more important.

The future population is expected to change. The CPRS predicted that births would fall until sometime in the 1980s and then rise as a result of the bulge in babies born in the early 1960s. After that they will decline. For children under five the pattern will be five years later, with a peak at the beginning of the 1990s followed by a falling-off. The school population will fall, with a rise towards the end of the century. Young people between sixteen and twenty-four will increase by a million by 1985 and this peak will have fallen by 1992. The working age population is expected to increase as a result of the decline in the numbers reaching retirement, although it is difficult to estimate the size of the labour force since it depends also on the rate of participation of women in the labour market.

SOCIAL POLICY

The four social welfare services (social security, health and personal social services, education, and housing) taken together, account for over half of government expenditure. Their share of government spending has been rising since the 1950s when they accounted for only 36 per cent of total expenditure.

But the distribution of money between the four services is not very even. The health service spends six times, education seven times and social security nine times what is spent by the personal social services (Glennester, 1979). The apportionment of spending between them does not depend simply on demographic change. An obvious example is the maternity service. When he was Minister for Health, David Owen used to point out that there was at least one clear anomaly in the allocation of resources in the health service. While the birth rate had been falling steadily since 1964, spending on maternity services had risen!

The reason for this growth is easy to find: medical provision in any speciality grows with a momentum of its own, regardless of the number of customers requiring the service. This is very easy: all that has to happen is for doctors to insist on lengthening the average hospital stay for each pregnant mother, or to insist that more mothers be hospitalized, in the interests of improving the quality of service.

Resource allocation is insensitive to client populations in other ways. Long-life assets cannot be shed quickly or easily redeployed. This is true of buildings and training resources. In any case hospital planning is more sensitive to regional movements in population. Growth areas are more likely to attract young families than to experience any change in the local birth rate.

The provision of services for children under five – health visiting, day care and nursery education – has always been the cinderella of children's services. It is easy to see why. Maternity services and education provision have a long history of acceptance as important services. Both are now backed by fairly powerful lobbies defending them. Child services both lack this political muscle and the ideology supporting such services for working mothers waxes and wanes depending on the need for women in the workforce.

Health visiting is severely understaffed: there is a shortfall of a third in the number of pre-school nursery places and the targets that Margaret Thatcher laid down, as Minister of Education in 1972, now look ridiculously optimistic. The customers for these services are politically powerless to get any change.

Expenditure Cuts

Expenditure on social provision in the four social services rose more rapidly in the 1960s and early 1970s than the corresponding increases in the populations of the users. The direct connection between demographic trends and the change in provision was lost around 1976. This was the year that marked the beginning of massive cuts in services, cuts that have continued ever since.

Previously the allocation of extra resources depended on how much support a particular minister could muster with his colleagues. Now the reverse happens: cuts can only be resisted if a minister can find enough support. The climate of opinion has changed. In the 1950s social provision was regarded as complementary to economic growth. It is now regarded as detrimental, taking away resources from the investment needed to sustain Britain's competitive position.

Social welfare is relatively easy to provide for in times of growth: it becomes more difficult in recessions. In any period policies are shaped by economic factors and practical needs. They are more likely to emerge from compromise and negotiation than they are from objective analysis of demographic changes. There appears to be little agreement about where the cuts should be made. As a basic principle, resources need to be allocated in line with the growth of any service's client groups. But there are other considerations in social policy. A dependency ratio may be a useful way of looking at demographic change: it is hardly an adequate conceptual tool for allocating social welfare resources.

All sorts of important priorities get established in a seemingly haphazard way as a result of various outcries. The non-accidental injury of children and the treatment of patients in mental hospitals became issues of concern in the late 1970s after various scandals were raised in the press. The personal social services are often expected to respond to issues that the 'public' think ought to be high priorities.

FAMILY NEEDS

So much for demography. But how do social policies respond to changes in the structure of family life? After all, the family is a social unit and social policy is dispersed according to individual need, whether that need is for dentures, remedial education, aids or adaptations to housing, institutionalized care, income support, or any other of the plethora of services provided by the Welfare State. It is easy to predict the given need for particular resources in the future, based on an assumption of individual need. For instance, we have a good deal of data on the physically disabled, on their capacities and incapacities, the degree of impairment, their socio-economic status and their housing conditions. They can easily be grouped by age, sex and the severity of their social condition. We know which physical functions a group of disabled people are capable of, and can soon translate this data into specific service plans. This is possible precisely because we are computing individuals in need, focusing on their particular pathologies and grouping them together by similarities. The whole procedure, while complex, is based on simple principles that relate directly to age population projections.

Such a procedure ignores any understanding of the role the family plays in the needs of the disabled. Families have changed dramatically not only in the functions they carry out and the social connections between individual nuclear families and their extended kin networks, but also in the problems they pose for social policy. It is more difficult for central government to have an appreciation of such changes.

There are three views about the relationship between the family and social policy. One is that the expansion of social welfare has adversely affected the family's willingness to provide care for its needy members. This view argues that the provision of social welfare has weakened the family as a caring institution. Another view presents the argument the other way around. The important changes that have gone on within the family have themselves rendered it less capable of functioning as a major caring institution.

In other words family changes came first. The extended family was gradually replaced by the nuclear family which was obliged to be more mobile than extended families could be. And the state was required to step in to take over the functions previously catered for quite adequately in the family. The third view puts the blame on family members themselves, arguing that people are less willing than they were to take on the responsibility of looking after needy members in the family.

These statements somewhat oversimplify the argument. Three different changes have been going on simultaneously, all of them connected with the argument. The composition of the elderly, the structure and function of families, and the nature of state provision have all changed. It is neither true to say that families have repudiated their responsibilities and dumped their weak members on an unwilling state nor is it true to say that families take all the burden. Families and the state share the caring function. But this inter-dependent role of caring assumes that the state has an intelligent understanding of how families deal on a day-to-day basis with the members who need care.

In fact, the state has little understanding of the part played by families in the lives of some people. Moroney (1976) gives the example of elderly people. It is easy for the state to count the number of aged people who are without any family to support them and need institutional care. It is also easy to assess the extent of community-based welfare services required by aged people living alone or with spouses. For the rest, the state simply assumes that their families will take responsibility – completely. No assessment is made of the particular ways any family can or cannot cope with its aged relatives. Moroney argues that this is simplistic.

In order to take family circumstances into account in a way that is useful for the quantitative planning of services, it would be necessary to develop more detailed sets of categories, not about individuals and their particular needs, but about family circumstances. This would provide information of quite a different sort, that measured relative need and relative family support. The myth that the family has been weakened through the unwillingness of families to care for their elderly, infirm and disabled members can be explained partly by the inadequacies of information. Some families may be very willing to support their aged members provided the state takes part of the responsibility. Some aged members might need to be offered institutional care, say, in the winters because the family could not cope adequately with any extra illness through cold weather. Other families may need a regular commitment from the state to providing temporary institutional care, merely to reduce the strain of looking after aged parents. Other families where the couple work full-time could cope with looking after the elderly parents provided the state undertook some help in partnership with them.

Ironically many of the welfare services have been based on fine sounding sentiments about the importance of family life. The 1959 Mental Health Act recognized the need to provide supportive services to help families look after their mentally ill members if possible, outside the confines of mental hospitals. The Ingleby Report on children and youth emphasized that the state's principal duty was to assist the family in carrying out its proper functions. In fact many of the reports emanating from committees set up by the government in the 1960s (Plowden, Seebohm, and Court for instance) all recognized the powerful influence that any family had on the performance of any individual family member, and advocated the importance of the state's working with and through the family, in any professional intervention. This sort of partnership is not impossible between any particular local authority and families, but it does require a better measure of what help any family can give and what needs to be provided by the state.

The Seebohm Report (1968) advocated a family focus for personal social services to assess needs and mobilize the necessary services. The primary objective of the newly created social work departments was to strengthen the capacity of the family to care for its members. Moroney argues that this has not been achieved in respect of the aged, the mentally ill or the physically disabled. There are a number of anomalies in the present system of support for families. Income support is given to families in need on the assumption that the family is a normal unit to live in for most people. But this means that a great deal of confusion exists around particular families' entitlement to invalidity benefits or attendance allowance. Another anomaly is the divergence of tax policy and supplementary benefits policy towards unmarried women living in a stable relationship with a man. The Supplementary Benefits Commissioners can refuse benefit to a woman on the grounds that she is cohabiting, while the Inland Revenue will at the same time refuse the man a married man's tax allowance on the grounds that the couple are not legally married.

Local authorities do little to help working mothers look after their children. The facilities that exist seldom match conventional hours of work or school holidays. In 1978 in Britain, out of 3.4 million children under five, about 800,000 had mothers with a paid job. About half of these get some form of day care. The other half either go to the 34,000 places in day nurseries, or are looked after by child minders (Moss and Sharpe, 1979). Some are looked after by relatives. No one knows how many. And it is known that many child minders are unsatisfactory (Jackson and Jackson, 1979).

The Meade Committee on tax reforms suggested a Home Responsibility Payment. This would help families with dependents (children, the disabled and ill as well as the aged) to carry out their responsibilities with less stress. Some families have to make very costly arrangements to care for their dependents while they are absent at work.

Governments pay only lip service to the importance of the family as a caring institution. The family was recognized as a vote catcher in the late 1970s: the two main parties committed themselves to something called Family Policy. We must be quite sceptical about what political parties mean when they rally round the notion of family policy. Each party has a different ideological perspective on the family. To the Conservative Party it signifies the traditional values of self-help, discipline, individualism, and initiative (the sorts of values that families are traditionally supposed to instil). To the Labour Party the family is an important buttress against the deprivations of industrialism. Co-operative living within the family is supposed to be the beginning of a more co-operative society that socialism will bring about. But we need to be quite cynical of what political parties say about the family. We have already pointed out that the family's prime function in post-industrial society is to reproduce the labour force as efficiently and cheaply as possible. Thus it is unlikely that any government will put a large financial commitment into helping the family do something which families are already committed to doing.

At a general level, the importance of the family is something we can all agree about: on any specific level disagreements are rife. Some people believe that the traditional family is under attack and that old values need to be reasserted. Others believe that some family break-up is inevitable and that laws need to be liberalized to make this possible when families want it.

Unlike some European countries, Britain has never had an explicit family policy. Some commentators argue that it is time such a policy was introduced. Margaret Wynn (1970) argued that, even though the family is acknowledged as a caring institution, it does not get parity of treatment with other groups in society.

She argued that the value of all benefits received by families (including the cost of education, family allowances, the health service and social security benefits) was at the time substantially less than the same families as a whole paid into taxation including insurance contributions. She also argued that the average income of parents with children was substantially lower than couples without children and reminded us that adolescent children cost more to keep than any other age group. In fact, families lost out considerably ever since the Second World War and especially since the 1960s. Parity of treatment, she argued, is an important principle that has received considerable support from the family poverty lobby. Her call for a family policy that assesses the impact of any social policy on the family, has since been reiterated by the Study Commission on the Family (1980), which called for a family perspective in policy making.

This means three things. The state needs to be better informed of changing family patterns in Britain; it needs to understand more effectively what sort of partnership it has with particular types of family in providing adequate care facilities; and it needs to evaluate the effect or impact of its policies on families of different types.

A major difficulty is the current lack of available data. Few government officials are interested in a family policy and they provide little information that is useful for formulating family policies or at present, even for identifying the number of families at different phases of the family cycle. The Central Statistical Office does not analyse households by numbers of children making it impossible to assess the redistributive effects of welfare benefits on families of different size.

The Illusions of the State

In the absence of any explicit policy we have a family policy implicitly by default. This is all the more oppressive since the assumptions on which it is based are not spelt out. They are there if we take the trouble to investigate them. They are based on particular assumptions about the pattern of responsibilities and dependencies within the family as well as the duties of parents for their children.

Land (1979) argues that the State's assumptions about what is typical is inappropriate, given the scale and pace of change in family life. In the first place, she argues that the State continues to preserve the illusion that the family is a private domain. Law enforcement agencies are reluctant to intervene in family disputes: it is regarded as a fragile institution in which the State should not intervene. This is somewhat contradictory. The State has certain powers to intrude on certain measures quite ruthlessly. Lone mothers can tell of undignified examples when their sex life has been open to detailed investigation by state officials. The behaviour of parents to their children is also open to investigation, even if neighbours make anonymous complaints.

In the second place, the State has one set of standards for women and another set for men. This is so in spite of the increased participation of women in the labour market, bringing about a certain measure of equality between both sexes. It is now largely the case that couples share the economic support of their families and some may wish to share responsibility for domestic work. But according to the State, breadwinners are still male and women care for the children, the sick and the aged. If women have paid employment, the State assumes it will take second place compared with women's prime duty for housekeeping and domestic duties. People still do not have a choice of making their own domestic arrangements fitted to their own desires. There are many examples of discrimination still being exercised. Aged parents of sons are more likely to be offered institutional care than the aged parents of daughters. Three times as many old people live with daughters as with sons (Hunt, 1973). Women, if they claim sickness benefit, have to show that they are too sick to do housework; men are not expected to prove the same with regard to gardening. The State still shows considerable ambivalence about nursery and childcare facilities for women who go out to work. Even female lone parents may find nursery or day care provision is scarce. Lone fathers, on the other hand, will be encouraged to go back to work in order to provide materially for their children.

In the third place, employment statistics severely underrepresent female unemployment. Only women registered for work are counted. According to the State, women who would like to work are not considered part of the workforce. The State's assumptions about the typical family (consisting of a man in full-time employment, with a woman as a full-time housewife and two dependent children) is obsolete. In 1971 this kind of family accounted for only 10 per cent of all families. One in six of families rely almost entirely on a woman's income for support and the majority of these have children (Land, 1979).

Land suggests that the ambiguities arise from a fear by the State that too much support for families might erode their functions. As H. G. Wells once observed, many are fearful that, in seeking to save the family, they should seem to threaten its existence (Wells, 1966). Too much support available for families with aged members might precipitate an avalanche of families wanting to abdicate their responsibilities! Land points out that no statutory service in Britain has ever been called a family service. Even the supposed family-focused social service departments use the word 'personal' instead of 'family'.

Why is the State so backward on its view of the changes going on within families? We have suggested that there exists an important political lobby that has definite views on the family. This lobby may not be active in pioneering new views on family policy, but always rises to the defence of the family when it appears to be under attack. One has only to read Hansard during a debate on issues such as abortion, homosexuality, housing for single people, marital roles, youth movements, or the age of consent, to appreciate the significance of the 'moral majority'.

The State will inevitably discriminate against any woman who challenges the prevailing order by becoming financially independent of men. Since social policy is predicated on this assumption, any change might easily involve the State in paying housewives to stay at home, if they claimed they wanted to be independent of their husbands!

Land suggests two other reasons. The notion of the State and the family fulfilling a caring function in partnership, even though true, is unacceptable to many professional workers who feel that their claim to professional status is weakened in the process. She also suggests that resources devoted to social welfare have to be rationed in some way. It is merely convenient to rationalize planning to ignore the extent of family care (or at least to overestimate it).

There is, then, both a weak link between demography and social planning and an ideological block on the State's part in making a realistic assessment of the part families play in social provision, and the part that governments should play in partnership with families. Governments cannot afford to be too realistic: they still need the family to reproduce, nurture and socialize the labour force in the cheapest possible way.

Social policy is made in an ideological context. That context makes assumptions about the nature of man's and woman's relationship with each other. Just as we argued in Chapter 3 that men get a lot of support under this ideological framework for ducking out of domestic responsibilities, so the State supports the same ideological context. That context assumes that gender differences are fundamental in the way in which work and home relationships are structured. Whether or not this should be so is up to every reader to decide.

QUESTIONS

1. In planning social policies, it is necessary to know how the population has changed. Discuss.
2. The allocation of resources for social welfare depends more on power politics than it does on rational planning. Discuss.
3. It is easier to allocate resources for social welfare services according to individual need than it is to take account of the social and family context of need. Discuss.
4. Cuts in social provision are more difficult to make in services where client numbers are declining than those where client numbers are stable. Say why you think this is the case.
5. What factors are implied by the notion of family policy?
6. In what ways does the state continue to discriminate against women, in spite of its commitment to sex equality?
7. What are the basic contradictions between an equitable family policy and sex equality?

FURTHER READING

(There are very few books specifically on this topic.)

Hammerman S. B. and Kahn A. J., (eds), *Family Policy: Government and Families in Fourteen Countries*, Columbia, 1978.
Moss P. and Fonda N., (eds), *Work, the Family and Equal Opportunities*, Temple Smith, 1980.
Study Commission on the Family, *Happy Families?*, 1980.
Wynn, M., *Family Policy*, Penguin, 1970.

Six

An unequal society

The second half of this book will explore the extent to which inequalities of various kinds still exist in Britain. We shall discuss the significance of social class as an indicator of basic, underlying inequalities that determine what sort of opportunities people have during their life spans. We shall also consider whether the privileges that some people are born into are as important today as they used to be in determining the future course of people's lives.

What is social class? Can we categorize people according to their social-class positions to reveal basic differences in the amount of rewards and opportunities that people receive? Are the terms 'working class' and 'middle class' still meaningful categories, or is it true that everyone is middle class today? Do people get equal rewards for equal work, regardless of their backgrounds? Are people rewarded according to their abilities or according to their social positions?

A CLASSLESS SOCIETY?

When Harold Macmillan said, in the late 1950s, that the class struggle was now obsolete, he put in a nutshell what many people believed. His argument went like this.

Economic growth in post-war Britain had brought its fruits to both working- and middle-class people alike. The British had never had it so good. Between 1920 and 1960, real incomes had doubled. Economic growth in the 1960s was running at the rate of 3 per cent a year. The average conditions of working-class life had improved enormously over what they had been in the past. Technical changes were offering a wide range of opportunities to anyone with ability, regardless of social background, as long as they were prepared to work. Everyone who wanted to could reap the benefits of this economic prosperity.

Mass unemployment, it appeared, had been abolished for ever. The symbols of middle-class existence, consumer durables in abundance, were available to all, thanks to hire purchase arrangements and full employment. Educational opportunities were expanding. Social barriers appeared to be breaking down. The remnants of class distinctions that remained were only in people's minds. They were the cultural residues of an earlier class-bound society. Even working-class accents had become fashionable!

It also appeared that the old establishment – the church, the landed gentry, the older professions, the public schools and those in charge of the armed forces – was finally breaking up. The old inequities, the high positions accorded to a few, the enormous privileges handed out to a minority at birth: all these seemed to be fast disappearing. Money and power could no longer perpetuate itself. Poverty had finally been abolished, thanks to the redistribution brought about by the Welfare State, and a progressive tax system. The country now offered equality and opportunity to all.

But was this really so? While class conflicts were less apparent during the economic boom period, the optimism that Macmillan generated was not to last. Britain began to stagnate during the 1970s. As the recession deepened, so the old class conflicts once again appeared as people fought to hold on to the gains they had made earlier. These conflicts revealed a bitter struggle between the two sides of industry – workers and management – both of them intent on getting as much as they could out of the enterprises that employed them. As world trade declined, so the struggle intensified. The owners of factories tried to keep wage levels down and productivity up in order to maximize profit margins and maintain a return on their investments. The workers tried to resist any attempt to cut their living standards with wage rises below the rate of inflation. Class relationships, their impact blunted in periods of economic growth, appeared to be just as significant as ever.

SOCIAL CLASS

Social class is about the system of rewards in society. The range of these rewards is still enormous. In 1983, the chief executive of British Airways was paid a salary of £85,000 whereas the legal minimum wage for a hairdresser was only £2,000 a year. These vast differences in incomes are still so integral a part of society that we hardly pay any attention to them. While few could deny that such inequalities still exist, our concern is to assess their importance in determining other opportunities afforded to people and to determine how much they have changed, if at all.

A social-class system of inequalities is more fluid than the caste system that Britain had when it was an agrarian society. Under feudalism, there were landowners, yeoman farmers, peasants and landless serfs. Each person's position, fixed at birth, was almost impossible to change. The relationship of each group to the others was fixed and legally binding.

In a social-class system, the separate strata in society are not as rigidly defined. It is possible for people to move from one stratum to another, up or down the scale. Social class has no formal legality: nor does it depend solely on position at birth. As we shall see later, the opportunities for people to move are much greater than is popularly supposed. Nevertheless the inequalities of a social-class system are systematic and the positions in the structure are stable, so much so that we can talk about a structure of social class. Schumpeter (1943) described the class structure as something like a hotel or a bus: the positions inside are always full but not necessarily with the same people. There are always people at the bottom of the class structure, people in the middle and people at the top, even if some of them are free to move around. It is not the people that make a class structure, but the positions they fill within the structure.

The structure persists in spite of social changes that happen. Its shape may change from decade to decade depending on technical developments. Each industrial change throws up new opportunities for capital investment and labour, the two most important inputs in any productive system. Both inputs are well rewarded in any growth industries when a particular factor of production is in short supply. The opening up of the mass air travel market, the discovery of North

Sea oil, the development of space research, and the invention of the micro-chip all produced enormous opportunities for capital, expertise and workers who had the necessary experience to do the jobs required to be done. Because they were in short supply, they were paid well and this may have given some people the opportunities to use those rewards to enhance their positions in society. For example, pilots from a working-class background demobbed after the war, may have decided to remain in aviation where there were good opportunities. Their salaries were exceptionally good: they were able to send their children to public schools if they wanted, and thus they gave their children opportunities to enter top professional jobs that they themselves could never have attained.

Nevertheless, in spite of such opportunities, the inequalities of the class structure remained the same. Those who had substantial wealth could continue to invest it in lucrative ventures when they found them; those without such capital were still obliged to work for others. The most straightforward analysis of the class divisions in society is that provided by Marx. We shall use this in the rest of the book in preference to other approaches because it highlights the divisions between social class groups and this makes the basic divisions easier to grasp.

At its simplest, social class is about the unequal distribution of four basic resources in society – income and wealth, power, security, and the opportunities to change one's position in society – four resources needed by all, each of them important (Westergaard and Resler, 1976). (Various writers categorize these resources differently but we shall follow this approach in the next five chapters in order to provide some coherence to the analysis.) These four resources are fundamental to most of the opportunities and experiences people get throughout their lives. They determine the sort of existence people have and the kind of life style they can lead. In fact one's position in the class structure at the time of birth is still an important determinant of future life chances (Taylor and Ayres, 1969).

People can still be grouped into distinct levels or strata according to the amount of these resources they have (there may be gaps between the strata or overlaps: it does not matter which). What is important is that there are certain barriers between each stratum, making it difficult for people to move from one stratum to another.

A popular misconception about social class is that its most

important determinant is occupation. It is a view frequently put forward by the media in discussing which groups get what of the 'national cake'. These discussions grossly distort reality by missing out a group of wealth holders who do not directly benefit from occupational incomes but nevertheless derive a large share of the national cake from their ownership of property, much of it lucrative industrial property, or capital, as it is usually called.

The key to class division in Britain, as in other industrialized countries, is the ownership of capital. The possession of private property (owning parts of the productive system), remains the crucial source of wealth and the most important source of income inequalities. Most of us know this fact so well that we tend to forget it in our calculations. When we talk about property, we immediately think about the ownership of housing since that is the most achievable source of property ownership for the bulk of the population. We completely ignore the ownership of stocks and shares, of government bonds, and the ownership of houses for rent, as well as the ownership of office blocks and factories.

Oliver Marriott (1967) records the fortunes of developers and speculators, with the change of town planning law in Britain in the 1940s and 50s. Overnight, many developers became millionaires as the law was changed. He documents the fortunes of a hundred men who made their money through dealing in land speculation. We all know of examples of this through our reading the press but tend to forget about them since such experiences are usually foreign to us. Wealth to us is something much more humdrum. It is often about hundreds of pounds in the bank. Or it is about having a house of our own with the help of a mortgage.

This is not surprising. In 1970, 93 per cent of the adult population did not own a single share or government bond. The conception of Britain as a property-owning democracy does not refer to property in general. It refers only to the houses that people live in. The ownership of the property of Britain – the real property of the country's economy – is in the hands of a very small minority.

THE PRODUCTIVE SYSTEM

A person's position in the class structure is determined by her or his relationship to the productive system. In feudalism, social position was determined by one's relationship to land. Some owned it, others rented it, and others had none and worked for those who owned some. Similarly, in industrial societies, there are those who own productive resources, and those who work those resources (the factory hands, the clerks, and the maintenance workers).

Basically, if we ask the question: what is a person's relationship with the productive system, we get an indication of any person's social class. Does the person own, manage, or work for the productive system? The owners of the productive resources are the propertied or ruling classes, the managers are the middle class, and the factory hands, the clerks and maintenance workers are the working class. Of course, the classification of occupations into social classes is far more complicated than that, given the variety of occupations that exist in any complex industrial society. Nevertheless, this is a good rule-of-thumb account of the class structure.

Each of these groups has a particular amount of the four basic resources already mentioned. As we shall see in the next two chapters, the distribution of income and wealth is clustered into bands that are broadly distinct for each of these social classes. So is the distribution of power, as well as the amount of economic security a person has. Similarly, opportunities for advancement can also be grouped by social class. This is not to suggest that these groupings are rigidly defined or that opportunities to move between social classes are severely limited. Some people now at the top end of the social structure began life from humble origins but they are the exceptions that prove the rule.

Let us take the distribution of power as an example of the constraints within the social structure. Each social class has a varying amount of individual and corporate power to change things within the economic system. The owners of the productive resources are free to make decisions about where to place those resources. They can move a factory from an inner city area to a new town, if they think it will bring about some advantage. They can sell a factory in one country and re-establish it in another where perhaps the cost of labour is lower. They can merge companies and close down factories. They can convert their wealth holdings from one form to another merely by instructing their executives to make the necessary alterations. They can sell their factories and move their wealth into other property holdings or buy art treasures instead, or even hold their wealth in gold and foreign currencies until they find a potentially lucrative opportunity for investing their money.

Managers are rather more constrained in what they can do. They are answerable to the owners of the resources they manage. They can develop new products, open new sections of the factory, and hire new workers. In fact they may be called on to make complicated decisions involving the future of the plant and machinery as well as the labour they control. In consultation with the trade unions, they can set new wage rates and fix the demand for labour. But they are constrained in the final analysis by their performance as measured in terms of output and profits. They are expected to manipulate those resources (the factories, plant and machinery and the labour) in such a way that profits are better than what other managers might have achieved if they had the jobs. If they are not doing well, they are likely to be dismissed or down-graded in favour of someone more promising (Glyn and Sutcliffe, 1972). If they do well, they may be promoted, with perhaps the opportunity to own shares or to have a seat on the board of the company. Top management may be a precarious existence for those in the jobs: it can also be highly lucrative and a potential avenue to property ownership in one's own right.

Factory hands are the most constrained of all. They have very little control over the productive resources. They have muscle power to sell and, in times of shortages, they can probably bid up the value of that power so that their wages improve. But their muscle power can be substituted for machines if their wages get too high. They also have the power to withdraw their labour from the factory owners by industrial action, if they can unite sufficiently among themselves. In times of labour shortages, this is an effective bargaining counter. It might help to raise the price of their labour at the cost of the level of profits. But they are not free to give up their work and refuse to be controlled by the managers. They have to eat and the only way to do so is by the sale of their labour. To some extent, they can give up work and get the support of the state but the welfare benefits paid will be so low that working for a low wage under poor conditions is usually a better alternative. For factory hands, then, work is a means to an end – the supply of a cash wage that will enable them to live.

This description highlights the essential characteristics of social classes. Capitalism is based on competition. Some will succeed and others will fail. Competition supposedly offers opportunities to all. In good times, those opportunities are more widely available for people to succeed if they have the will to do so. At times the opportunities have been enormous. People have been known to work their way up from factory hand to supervisor and on to manager and even to factory owner. But competition also implies that, while some succeed, others will fail. Any competitive society is structured on unequal lines. This inequality is institutionalized: it is built into the system of social relationships.

One of the characteristics of this type of competition is the value it puts on the acquisition of wealth. There are opportunities for those who are successful to reap the benefits of success and obtain a bigger stake in society. Those who have a bigger stake can use that stake to consolidate their position, thereby making it more difficult for others to succeed.

Wealth holders are also permitted to pass on their privileges to their offspring, ensuring that they can set out on their own careers with all the advantages that their parents can afford to pass on to them; an elite education that puts them in touch with potentially fruitful contacts ensuring them opportunities later in life; a social grooming that will instill confidence in them and convince others that they have good potential for leadership jobs; and access to job opportunities that are still reserved for those with the 'right' amounts of wealth and the 'right' social background.

But one person's privileges are another person's constraints. At any stage of industrialization there are only a finite number of positions at the top of the class structure. If these positions are already reserved for the children of the rich, this means that other, talented people will find entry to those positions already barred. Privilege is thus institutionalized, making social circulation limited. Think of the front-seats-of-Schumpeter's-bus analogy as the top positions in the class structure. If those seats are already reserved for a small privileged minority, there is very little room for ma- noeuvre left to the other passengers who may also want to sit in the front!

The institutionalization of inequalities means that those from a managerial background can also use what money, social connec- tions and social grooming they have to ensure that their children gain access to professional or managerial jobs themselves. Those with property can pass on that property to their progeny; they can try to ensure that their children marry into other families with property. Those without this kind of property will find it difficult to acquire it themselves. The owners of substantial wealth have an array of professional services available to advise them how to ensure that their wealth is invested in the most rewarding ventures and how to ensure that it gets passed on intact to their children.

Factory hands still have only the sale of their labour to help themselves and their children. The Welfare State will help to protect them from destitution but it will not help them to rise out of their position in the class structure. Universal education can benefit their children but they still lack the social connections and capital to gain access to 'exclusive' institutions.

That some succeed in spite of these handicaps is undeniable: but this is more likely to happen in times of economic growth when there may be a shortage of talented people to fill the well-rewarded positions. Westergaard and Resler (1976) put it:

> property, profit and market – the key institutions of capitalist society – retain their central place in social arrangements, and remain the prime determinants of inequality.

This is so in spite of attempts on the part of the State to curb the power of privilege. Trade unions are an acceptable counter to the power of capital. Government policy attempts to curb the unacceptable face of capitalism. Educational opportunities have been widened in an attempt to ensure that individual talent is not thwarted. But the impact is limited. Privilege in a competitive society has never been fully outlawed. The impact of greater opportunities brought about through the Welfare State has been limited by the boundaries fixed by the maintenance of private property. For instance, although Denis Healey proposed a wealth tax in the 1970s when he was Chancellor of the Exchequer, he quietly changed his mind after representations from the propertied class showed how it could 'damage' the economy. Those with property had the power to move their own wealth holdings into other countries, thereby straining the country's balance of payments.

The inequalities we are discussing are the product of capital holdings (or the absence of capital). This is such an obvious point and one so outside the realm of many people's experiences, it tends to be forgotten. Inequalities are reinforced through privilege. Privilege ensures that the rewards in society are based, not on personal ability, skill or intelligence, although each of these may be important. The hierarchy of wealth does not reflect a hierarchy of natural endowment. It is not even the product of the workings of the labour market (although this too is part of it). It is the product of capital and property holdings. Those with property holdings can use them to buttress their positions against encroachment by those with less.

We shall now examine the distribution of each of these resources – income and wealth, security, power, and (in Chapter 7) opportunity. This is not as easy as it may sound: these inequalities are still often shrouded in mystery in some official statistics. Many tables on the distribution of income give figures for family units and even industries but are more reticent to give information by class groupings. Until the 1970s, unravelling the complex data on income distribution was left to a handful of academics. But in 1974, a Royal Commission on the Distribution of Income and Wealth (RCDIW) was appointed to bring together existing information as well as to commission new work on many aspects of income and wealth. Much of the analysis in this chapter draws on this data.

INCOME AND WEALTH INEQUALITIES

People receive their incomes from three sources – what they can get for themselves in the labour market if they have a job, the money they derive from any property or investments they hold, and any benefits they get from the state if they are unable to support themselves. In the 1976/7 tax year, the total amount of money earned in the UK came to £93 billion. This was paid to 28½ million income units, that is, single people or other units who receive incomes.

The money was divided among these units very unevenly. Figure 6.1 shows its distribution both before and after tax. It shows a striking range of incomes between the top and the bottom earners. It also shows that tax deductions had very little effect on reducing that range. After tax, the highest paid 10 per cent still received more than the lowest paid 40 per cent. And the top 20 per cent enjoyed almost 40 per cent of the entire personal income of the country. Put another way, the top 10 per cent of earners received almost eight times the share that the bottom 10 per cent of earners received. To anyone who thought that incomes were distributed equitably, these figures provide food for thought!

Figure 6.1. The spread of income

Population divided into tenths

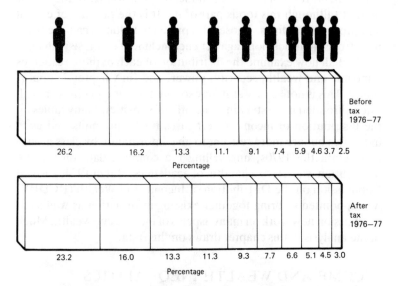

Before tax 1976–77

26.2   16.2   13.3   11.1   9.1   7.4   5.9 4.6 3.7 2.5

Percentage

After tax 1976–77

23.2   16.0   13.3   11.3   9.3   7.7   6.6 5.1 4.5 3.0

Percentage

Source: The Royal Commission on the Distribution of Income and Wealth, *An A to Z of Income and Wealth*

Furthermore, these disparities have persisted over time. Figures 6.2 and 6.3 show the changes in the distribution of incomes between 1949 and 1976. We can see that the share of the top 10 per cent fell steadily from the early 1960s onwards and the share of the bottom 50 per cent rose during the same period. But the overall change in distribution has been quite slight. The figures are given in Table 6.1 and show that the only marked change has been the fall in the share of the top one per cent of income earners, from 6½ per cent in 1949 to 3½ per cent in 1976. Otherwise, the share of each group of income earners has remained remarkably steady.

What is striking is the share enjoyed by the top one per cent of earners. They continue to get three-and-a-half times the share of what they would get if incomes were divided equally. In fact, this is roughly the same as the share that goes to the poorest ten per cent. The top 5 per cent continue to get two-and-a-half times their share and the top 10 per cent still get double their share.

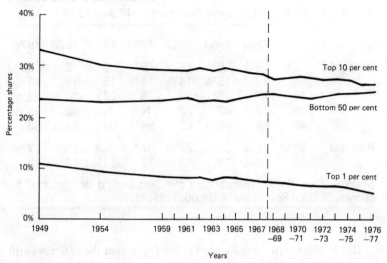

Figure 6.2. *Distribution of personal income – percentage shares before tax income*

Source: The Royal Commission on the Distribution of Income and Wealth, Report No. 8, 1979

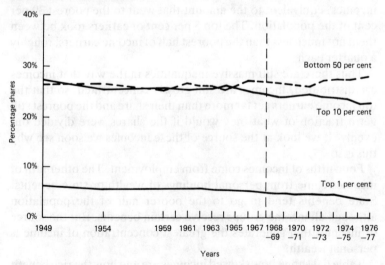

Figure 6.3. *Distribution of personal income – percentage shares after tax income*

Source: The Royal Commission on the Distribution of Income and Wealth, Report No. 8, 1979

Table 6.1. Shares of income between 1949 and 1976

		1949	1954	1957	1963	1967	1970	1976
Richest	1%	6½	5½	5	5	5	5	3½
	5	17	15½	14½	15½	15	15	13
	10	27	25	24	25	24½	24	22½
	20	42	42	38	NA	NA	40	38½
	40	64	65½	63	64½	64	64½	63
Poorest	50%	26½	25½	27½	NA	NA	26	27½
	30	14½	11	13	12	11½	12	13

Source: Blue Book Estimates on the Distribution of Personal Incomes, RCDIW, Report No. 7, Cmnd. 7595, 1979.

But Westergaard and Resler (1976) argue that these figures still grossly underestimate the extent of the disparities. The figures do not include undistributed profits or the many fringe benefits that top earners tend to receive. They also exclude evaded taxes. Various writers (Lydall, 1959 and Meade, 1964) have estimated the distribution after these items have been taken into account. They conclude that in 1959/60 the top 1 per cent in fact received 10 per cent of incomes, equivalent to the amount that went to the poorest 30 per cent of the population. The top 5 per cent of earners took between them not much less than the poorest half of income earners, roughly a quarter each.

Thus there are still massive inequalities in the way that incomes are distributed. Incomes are still grossly concentrated, so that the top income earners get far more than their share and the poorest still get a fraction of what they would if the shares were divided out evenly. If we look at the source of these incomes we soon see why this is so.

Four-fifths of incomes come from employment. The other fifth of incomes come from personal holdings of wealth or state benefits. State benefits tend to go to the poorer half of the population although all income groups receive certain benefits. But the source of incomes that generates the greatest concentration of income is personal wealth.

Table 6.2 shows how skewed incomes are and how the rich benefit from every source of income except state benefits. The top 10 per

Table 6.2. Distribution of income by source, 1976–7

	share of total income %	share of employ- ment income %	share of self employ- ment income %	share of invest- ment income %	share of transfer income %
Top 1%	5.5	3.6	23.6	23.4	0.7
Top 10%	26.2	25.5	47.8	51.6	5.6
11–20%	16.2	18.3	9.9	11.1	6.0
21–30%	13.3	15.1	7.7	8.2	6.1
31–40%	11.1	12.0	7.7	7.4	8.0
41–50%	9.1	9.3	7.9	6.5	9.6
51–60%	7.4	7.0	6.7	5.2	11.9
61–70%	5.9	4.9	5.0	4.3	14.6
71–80%	4.6	3.4	3.5	3.0	15.1
81–90%	3.7	2.6	2.5	2.0	14.3
91–100%	2.5	1.8	1.3	0.7	8.8
Total	100.0	100.0	100.0	100.0	100.0

Source: RCDIW, Report No. 7, Cmnd. 7595, 1979.

cent of earners receive a quarter of employment incomes, almost half of self-employed incomes, and over a half of investment incomes. If we look at the top one per cent, this concentration is even more striking. They receive a quarter of all investment incomes and a quarter of self-employed incomes. Even the top 20 per cent do well from these sources. The table shows that, while investment incomes are actually spread throughout the entire population, the share is so heavily concentrated at the top that the amount that the rest of the population get is almost insignificant.

So overall, in spite of some redistribution of incomes, there is still an intense concentration of incomes. This is true for all payments except state benefits. It is particularly so for investment incomes and incomes from self-employment.

Incomes from Occupations
The labour market is an important source of inequalities in rewards. The living standards of those without property are set primarily by the terms on which they can sell their labour. Some sell it for very

little: others sell it for enormous sums. Incomes in 1983 from the labour market range from around £2,000 (for a full-time job) at the bottom of the market to tens of thousands for top executives. Executives in the nationalized industries earn between £40,000 and £80,000; executives in private companies may earn more.

What is surprising is that these disparities persist in spite of the very substantial improvements in real wages. Between 1886 and 1970, real wages rose twenty times (George, 1968). Yet changes in the distribution of wages during this period have been only slight. The range has merely narrowed slightly.

In fact the broad pattern of inequalities in earnings between groups has remained remarkably stable over the last sixty-five years. Table 6.3 shows the earnings of six occupational groupings, calculated as a percentage of average male earnings between 1913 and 1978. Over this period the range of incomes fell considerably. The differential between what top professionals can earn, compared with what unskilled workers earn, has fallen from five-and-a-half times in 1913 to two-and-a-half times in 1978. We need to remember, again, that these figures are averages and that the extremes are many times broader in range.

If we look at the range in more detail, we can distinguish three broad bands of earnings. At the bottom of the scale is a broad mass of manual workers – skilled and unskilled, of service workers and shop assistants, as well as clerks below senior grades. The range of earnings in this group is limited. In 1968 it was about £5 a week. Large numbers of them earn very low pay. In 1971, 30 or 40 per cent

Table 6.3. Average male earnings

| | As a percentage of all male earnings | | | | | | |
	1913	1922	1935	1955	1960	1970	1978
Unskilled	67	71	69	69	63	68	71
Skilled	113	100	105	98	94	84	91
Foremen	131	149	147	124	120	98	98
Clerks	105	101	103	82	80	78	77
Managers	213	267	237	233	218	199	168
Higher							
professionals	349	323	341	243	240	172	173

Source: RCDIW Report No. 8.

of some occupations were earning less than £20 per week. An average for the group was around £35 a week while a few skilled and semi-skilled workers earned more than £40.

Next to this group is a band of workers – foremen, supervisors, technicians, senior clerks, and also school teachers and some social services workers. In 1968 two-fifths of them earned more than £35 a week, just over a quarter earned £40 or more and a small proportion of them earned as much as £50 a week. These are the two broad earnings bands of working- and lower-middle-class jobs.

Between these groups and the rest of occupational groupings there appears to be a major division. Above the line, managers, professionals and directors in 1971 were all earning substantially more than the other two groups. Between a third and two-thirds of them earned more than £50 a week. And there were wide variations in the earnings of this group. When the earnings range for manual workers was £5 a week in 1968, it was £20 a week for the professionals.

These disparities between earnings of the three occupational groupings gives us a simple picture of the earnings gaps in the class structure, determined by the labour market (remember, this is not the complete picture of the class structure). We can call the groups professionals, lower professionals and manual workers.

These differences are even clearer when we consider how they change over any person's working life cycle. The average earnings of any group tends to increase to a peak over their life cycle and then fall off before retirement. In fact, most men (we are not at present considering women's earnings) tend to start off their working lives earning much the same as each other, regardless of occupation. In 1970, all twenty-one to twenty-four year olds earned between £20 and £25 a week. But after that age, their earnings diverge sharply.

The earnings curve of all manual workers is nearly flat throughout the life cycle. It peaks slightly at about 15 per cent above their starting wages, when workers reach their physical peak at around age thirty. After that, earnings decline slowly and eventually end at retirement at less than comparable starting wages. Earnings for white-collar workers (sales assistants, office and communication workers) follow a similar curve. They start initially at a lower point than other manual workers but eventually finish up at about a fifth below their peak earnings, a little ahead of manual workers. The earnings of technicians, a group on their own in life cycle terms, rise to a peak in their forties at about 45 per cent above starting wages.

But the top group of earners – professionals, academics, and managers – have a radically different earnings profile over their life spans. Their salaries rise substantially during the course of their careers. They can expect to reach their peak earnings in their forties, at double their starting salaries. After their forties, their earnings curves flatten out and may even drop a little by the time they retire.

Of course, this data simplifies the picture considerably. It gives us no information about what happens to people's earnings as and when they change jobs throughout their working lives and we know that job changes occur frequently for many groups in the labour market. We would need much more information to know what happens, for instance, to a person who starts off working in a shop with few qualifications, and moves around from shop to shop as he or she gains experience. We shall be looking at these issues in more detail in Chapter 7. But the description so far makes one thing clear. People are paid for different qualities in the labour market. Manual workers are paid for their output measured in terms of what the organization produces. The ability to produce high output depends partly on physical abilities, partly on dexterity and, to a smaller extent, on organizational skills. Physical strength and dexterity decrease with age. After reaching, say, thirty-five, it is not so easy to make extra money by working long overtime; younger workers are more valuable to the organization.

That is not so true of professionals or managers whose manipulative skills can increase with age and experience. But it is likely that their energy and assertiveness may decrease after forty and they then may become less valuable. It may be that the ones that are good get promoted to higher grade jobs and the ones who are not promoted are less valuable. It is easy to see that class is determined by one's relationship to the means of production in the case of earnings. There is a direct relationship.

But there are other differences between these groups in fringe benefits. We shall look at these later on in the chapter.

Incomes from Wealth Holdings

Personal wealth in Britain is still heavily concentrated at the top, in spite of quite substantial changes in its distribution over the last

Figure 6.4. **The distribution of wealth, 1976**

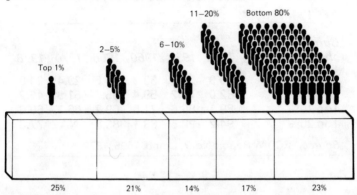

Source: The Royal Commission on the Distribution of Income and Wealth, *An A–Z of Income and Wealth*

sixty-five years. Figure 6.4 shows the distribution of wealth in the population in 1976. It indicates the scale of concentration at the top. The wealthiest 1 per cent own a quarter of all personal wealth, the top 5 per cent own 46 per cent of all personal wealth.

In fact, wealth is far more heavily concentrated than incomes. In 1976 the top 1 per cent of income holders earned only 3½ per cent of incomes but their equivalent wealth holders held a quarter of personal wealth. The top 1 per cent of wealth holders own more than the poorest 80 per cent of the population. These figures do not include pensions (since they are not disposable). However, even if we include pensions, the bottom 80 per cent increase their holdings of wealth only up to 45 per cent.

The concentration of personal wealth has fallen quite dramatically this century. Table 6.4 shows the amount of wealth owned by the top 20 per cent between 1923 and 1976. In that fifty years the share of wealth owned by the top 1 per cent has fallen from 60 per cent to almost a quarter. The share owned by the top 20 per cent similarly fell from 94 per cent to 78 per cent. This latter fall is far less dramatic and confirms what Westergaard and Resler point out, that the ownership of capital in private enterprise is still intensely concentrated in the hands of a tiny minority of the population.

The most recent figures, however, show that the concentration of

Table 6.4.   Trends in the distribution of personal
wealth

Cumulative share	1923	1930	1960	1966	1970	1976
Top 1%	60.9	57.9	33.9	30.6	29.4	24.9
Top 5%	82.0	79.2	59.4	55.5	51.9	46.2
Top 10%	89.1	86.6	71.5	69.2	66.1	60.6
Top 20%	94.2	92.6	83.1	83.8	NA	77.6

Source: RCDIW Report No. 7, Cmnd. 7595, 1979.

wealth is beginning to narrow again. While the top 1 per cent now hold only 23 per cent of all wealth, the richest 5 per cent have increased their holding from 43 per cent in 1980 to 45 per cent in 1981. The richest 25 per cent have also increased their share from 81 per cent in 1980 to 84 per cent in 1981.

There are three assets that are particularly important in shaping the distribution of personal wealth – dwellings, company securities, and land. We shall consider each. The ownership of dwellings has increased substantially since the sixties when both political parties began to support owner-occupation. Ownership increased from 13.9 million homes in 1951 to 20.4 million in 1977. Also, since the value of dwellings has increased relative to other goods, this source of wealth has assumed more importance. Between 1960 and 1976 the price of dwellings increased sixfold. This means that dwellings, as a proportion of net wealth, have increased from 17.7 per cent in 1960 to 35.5 per cent in 1977. The ownership of dwellings is the least heavily concentrated form of personal wealth (although we must remember that there are still some very large landlords owning numbers of rented properties). Their ownership is concentrated in the middle range of wealth holders.

The ownership of company securities reflects the ownership of capital by a tiny minority. 60 per cent of listed ordinary shares and 24 per cent of unlisted ordinary (that is, private companies) are owned personally. They are heavily concentrated in the hands of the top wealth holders especially among older people. According to the RCDIW, while the top 1 per cent held 17 per cent of total net wealth (unadjusted), they owned 54 per cent of all listed UK

Table 6.5.   Distribution of total net wealth, 1978

	Total net wealth %	All company securities %	Land %	Dwellings %
Top 1%	17.0	54.2	52.0	8.6
Top 5%	34.0	80.7	73.7	24.4
Top 10%	46.5	89.6	84.1	37.5
Top 20%	62.3	95.1	92.2	57.5

Source: RCDIW Report No. 7, 1979.

ordinary shares and the pattern of company securities was similar. Hence the pattern of ownership of shares was a major determinant of the shape of wealth distribution.

The ownership of land is similarly highly concentrated. It accounted for only a small proportion of wealth (about 5 per cent in 1978). The top 1 per cent of wealth holders owned 52 per cent of all land, the top 5 per cent owned 73.7 per cent, and the top 10 per cent owned 84.1 per cent of all land.

Table 6.5 shows the distribution of all forms of personal wealth among the top 20 per cent of wealth holders. It shows a very high concentration of both company securities and land. We said earlier that the ownership of dwellings is shared among the middle-range wealth holders. It is notable from the table that the top 20 per cent of wealth holders still own two-and-a-half times their share of dwellings (if the ownership of dwellings were evenly distributed throughout the population).

In conclusion, therefore, we can still say that wealth in Britain is still highly concentrated at the top. There is still undoubtedly a propertied class in Britain and it is a very small minority of the population.

INEQUALITIES IN SECURITY

Not only are incomes and wealth distributed unequally; some people's holdings of them are less secure than others. There are three ways of deriving an income in industrial societies. As we have seen, the wealthiest group derive their main incomes from their holdings of wealth. The bulk of the population derive their incomes from their earnings in the labour market, and those who have no means of support depend on state benefits. There is thus a hierarchy of security. Those with most wealth are the most secure. They can switch their wealth holdings to give them the highest return. Those who derive their incomes through their jobs have a varying amount of security, depending on the demand for their skills. Some have a very insecure foothold on the labour market. Some are employed part-time, some work on a casual basis, some are often unemployed depending on the vagaries of the demand for their skills.

Those who are dependent on the state for support will be discussed in Chapter 8 when we discuss poverty. Those in the labour market sell their labour on differing terms. This applies not only to the price at which they sell their labour: it applies to the terms and conditions on which they are employed.

First, the amount of money out of a pay packet that is secure and predictable varies. Over 90 per cent of non-manual workers' earnings is derived from their basic pay. The bulk of the income is known and predictable. But only about two-thirds of manual workers' earnings is derived from basic pay. The rest comes from overtime and bonuses. When there is a strong demand for their labour, they may be able to make considerable amounts from overtime, but they cannot rely on this. For many manual workers, basic wage rates may be low and they are likely to find it difficult to exist only on their basic wages. Also, while only 2 per cent of non-manual workers lost any pay through sickness, lateness or other forms of discipline, this applied to 15 per cent of manual workers. It is still possible in some trades for workers to lose money because of losses from cash tills or because customers have left without paying their bills.

Second, hours of work vary. Non-manual workers work shorter hours than manual workers. In 1971, the average working week for manual workers ran to about 45 hours, and one in five manual workers worked more than 50 hours, compared with only three in a hundred non-manual workers. Long working hours is the only way for manual workers (if they are lucky) to reach earnings comparable to the lower paid office manager. To get to these levels, seven in every ten had to work more than 45 hours and five in ten for more than 50 hours. For non-manual workers, earnings rarely vary with hours.

Third, pensions, sickpay, and holidays for manual workers are in general far less generous. There has been a considerable growth of employers' pension and sickness schemes for manual workers. But the schemes conceal wide variations in the types and quality of benefits. In general, half the pension schemes for manual workers provide a pension based on a fixed sum each year, compared with schemes for non-manual workers based on earnings levels (usually three-eightieths) of the final years of service. Some non-manual pensions are also indexed-linked to take account of inflation. In 1970, 90 per cent of non-manual compared with only 65 per cent of manual workers were covered by sick pay schemes.

Fourth, general working conditions varied. The TUC recently reported: 'every worker can expect on average to be the victim of at least two disabling accidents during his or her lifetime'. By worker, they meant, manual worker! Because of the dangers inherent in much manual work still, certain workers are liable to be disabled at work through industrial accidents or having to work in dangerous conditions. Those who are will be destined to a future of unremitting poverty. Even worse is the plight of the household head who contracts illnesses such as bronchitis and is only able to work in the summers.

Fifth, workplace relationships vary. Various studies have shown the marked variation in the way manual and non-manual workers are treated at work. Manual workers are subject to rules while non-manual workers are treated with discretion on the assumption that they will 'behave responsibly' or 'not abuse privileges'.

Much of this inequality is inevitable in a system based on the need for profit. Every entrepreneur can afford only to take on labour up to a point where the worker is contributing more than what it costs the employer to employ the person. The entrepreneur is buying a person's labour power and the worker is giving the employer the right to organize the working hours as the employer decides. Employees can be dismissed if the employer decides that the enterprise is no longer viable. There have of course been many improvements to employment law that mitigate against some of the insecurities. But jobs are still not protected. Any employer is free to sack a worker and risk having to pay out compensation for unfair dismissal. Having sold one's labour power, the worker is no longer in control of it. Management has the initiative in utilizing it in whatever way will maximize profits. One example of the inequalities in employment is shown in death rates for different occupation groups. Holding age constant, death rates for adult men in 1930–2 ranged from 10 per cent below the average for professionals and administrators to 11 per cent above the average for unskilled workers. By 1959–63 this gradient had increased to 25 per cent below for professionals and 40 per cent above for unskilled workers.

The most important source of insecurity rests in the labour market and applies to manual workers. Rank-and-file wage earners live with the risk of poverty over their heads throughout their lives. They face the likely prospect of poverty on retirement but they also face the prospect of poverty before that – on redundancy or if they are obliged to work short-time, or by being transferred to low paid work as they get older, or through sickness. Poverty towards the end of the work cycle is a real fear for many manual workers.

For non-manual workers, the risk of poverty is remote. High earnings, fringe benefits and greater job security as well as the incremental rise throughout their work cycles all reduce the risk of poverty considerably. And those who own the means of production get total immunity from poverty.

The inequalities of security are another dimension that go along with earnings and wealth. In general, the higher the incomes earned, the greater the security that goes with them.

POWER INEQUALITIES

It is not possible to map out the distribution of power in the way we have mapped out the distribution of income and wealth. Power cannot be seen or measured so easily. It is only visible in its consequences. We can deduce something of the power held by certain people by the changes they can effect on organizations and groups of people. Power is usually not related simply to individual people but, rather, to their connections with certain organizations. The source of personal power, in these situations, is that certain individuals have the power and authority to make sweeping changes to the policies of these organizations. But the mechanisms through which such activities happen are highly complex and make it difficult to describe in any simple terms.

In any case, few people have absolute power to do exactly what they want. Usually there are a number of complex struggles that go on between different groups each with their own sets of interest in the outcomes. Nevertheless, the balance of power in organizations is usually heavily weighted in favour of those with capital. For example, few boards of directors are able to determine what productivity levels they want their workforces to achieve. They may know what they would like, but they then have to negotiate any changes they want to produce with the organizations that represent the labour force. But each side to these negotiations (or struggles) know that, in the last analysis, the power of the workforce to hold out for productivity levels that they think are reasonable, is limited by both their collective strength as workers (standing together in opposition to the management), their trade union bank balances (for paying out any strike money), and their need for wages each week to meet their family commitments. Many corporations can afford to close down factories, even if they lose millions of pounds through doing so, knowing that these losses can be recouped over the long-run from increased productivity if they get the sort of agreements they want from the workforce. Given that sort of example, it is very difficult to disentangle who has what amount of power on an individual level.

It is also rather difficult to decide which of the many complex decisions made each day in organizations are the crucial ones that will illustrate the distribution of power in the organization. Studies of power have tried this in the past and come up with very confusing results. Westergaard and Resler (1975) do not discuss power in this way, but they highlight other aspects of power that are important to the discussion in these chapters. They highlight the power of capital, and the system of profit on which it is based, to perpetuate itself. It does this through a range of institutions (including the government of the day) that take the gross inequalities in rewards for granted and make it inevitable that such a state of affairs will continue.

Ideological Consensus
It is not easy to appreciate the significance of this. Our society operates within an ideological consensus that is determined by this

powerful minority. The interests of capital are largely presented as a dominant and acceptable view in most forms of the media. This is not because those who control the most powerful corporations in this country also control the means of press and television communication, although that is sometimes the case. More often than not, it is because those who determine what goes out in the media come from similar backgrounds and share broadly similar ideological positions as those who control capital. Both groups believe basically that there is no alternative to the current way of organizing society. Thus any critical analysis of what goes on is made within very narrow confines of what is appropriate to criticize. The broad parameters of this society, the facts of inequalities, and whether or not they could be changed are not usually serious issues of debate.

In other words, the major institutions that control British society all agree that the prevailing level of competition and inequality (give or take a little in either direction) is as it should be. This is not surprising, since any serious redistribution would be at the cost of every major power institution. It would affect all those in whose hands wealth, income, and power are pesently concentrated.

Thus any discussion of an alternative arrangement, based on an equable distribution of resources, is relegated to fringe groupings, whose existence and authenticity can be questioned because they are not in the mainstream of nationally-recognized opinion makers. The power that can produce this kind of consensus does not need to censor such alternatives: it can ridicule them precisely through marginalizing them. We need only consider an alternative scenario to appreciate the force of this ideological power.

Let us assume that the government has decided to introduce complete equality in the distribution of our basic four resources within the next five years, and has decided that it is essential that the public fully understand the implications of these changes. So it insists that a debate is developed about inequalities, their current dispersion, the damage they do to individuals, the amount of talent lost in the country because able people are not permitted to develop their abilities fully, the cost of production lost through much of the workforce being somewhat alienated from their jobs and feeling powerless to suggest changes to industrial processes, etc. We can all imagine many different aspects to the debate that would be necessary.

The quality of the debate would be good: it would be presented simply and graphically so that everyone understood the issues as clearly as they understand any complex advertising material. Television programmes would present dramatic accounts of this new kind of society about to be introduced: a new film genre would develop a new awareness of this new society and would challenge much of the sexism, racism and classism inherent in current films. People themselves would be educated into this new participative society through being encouraged to take part in debates. The layperson would no longer be treated as lacking in intelligence on live television debates. Lay people would be given more support to acquire the necessary information so that they could take part in an intelligent way. Experts would no longer be treated as if they alone knew the answers. The possibilities are mind-boggling! Thinking up such alternatives shows the extent to which the current power holders can stifle alternative debates and engineer a consensus to hold on to the existing concentration of power, merely by not actively encouraging such different viewpoints and ensuring that, although such viewpoints are put forward from time to time, they are always marginalized.

Power is the capacity to determine events despite resistance. It is the capacity to determine the extent to which any resistance is given space in the public communications machinery.

The Concentration of Enterprises

The power of capital has been considerably strengthened through the concentration of business resources into a few hands. A small number of giant organizations now holds the keys of the economy. Fifty such corporations accounted for a seventh of the total manufacturing labour force in the UK in the mid-1930s, a fifth by 1958, and a quarter by 1963. Although there are many small businesses as well as these giant corporations, the number of them alone gives no indication of their power. The industrial labour force is employed predominantly by big businesses. Over 70 per cent of employees in manufacturing in 1963 worked in firms employing more than 500 people. We can see the impact of this concentration by looking at sales figures. In 1963 the five biggest firms in each manufacturing trade accounted for an average of 60 per cent of sales. Outright monopoly is rare: monopolistic competition is the usual state of affairs.

This concentration of power in companies is also transnational. The biggest of these multinational companies now control assets that are greater than the productive resources of some European countries. For example, the sales turnover of General Motors in 1967 was greater than the GNP of Belgium; Standard Oil's turnover was about the size of Switzerland's or Denmark's GNP, and Ford had a turnover greater than Norway's GNP (Westergaard and Resler, 1975). But it is not in the size of the organizations that this concentration of power shows its effects. It is in the way that such mammoth corporations act. After all, most of these corporations have an enormous number of shareholders and most of them are small. Crucially, the power of these corporations is seen in the way that a very small minority of shareholders control a majority of the share capital. For example, in 1970 people owning shares worth at least £20,000 were a small minority among a tiny minority – 8 per cent of all shareholders (about 0.5 per cent of the entire population). But they disposed of nearly 70 per cent of all corporate capital in private hands.

That is not all. Big corporations are in fact closely connected with other big corporations and financial institutions, through overlapping board memberships and interpenetrating stockholding. Although the ownership of shares is in general fragmented, it is also and at the same time highly concentrated. The irony of the fragmentation of shares is that it lowers the amount of concentration in stock ownership necessary to have a controlling interest.

Power in Britain rests in the hands of a small group of people. We have looked only briefly at certain aspects of this. The assumptions on which British society runs are firmly in line with the interests of one small group. This group consists of the top business and large property owners. The power is concentrated through very large organizations, often transnational in scope, and the interests of the large organizations have to be carefully considered by any government since they in large part control the economy.

Within these organizations there are a number of persons who are immensely powerful, since they have controlling interests in some of these conglomerates. But they are not the only ones who make up the power elite. There are others who derive substantial privilege

from their association with this group of powerful people – those in
the senior ranks of the public services as well as those in the older
professions.

Of course there are other societies where power is even more
concentrated. British society permits a certain amount of dissent
and even works with it. The labour movement is the main source of
opposing power, but its strength is limited by the need of the
workforce to participate in the productive process that is largely
shaped by the owners of production. It is in this sense that we can
talk about a ruling class in Britain.

THE STRUCTURE OF SOCIAL CLASS

To sum up, we can discern three groups of people in the labour
market who sell their labour on distinctive terms and conditions. At
the top, the most privileged is a small group of directors, managers,
established professionals and senior public service officials, consisting of about 5 to 10 per cent of the working population. They are
often able to set their own salaries and have a say in shaping the
conditions of the labour market. They usually belong to powerful
societies that control entry to their professions, and they can
determine the nature of their work as well as the demand for their
services. They are usually very close to those who administer state
power and are likely to be made special cases in times of wage
restraint. They also have the contacts to get sufficient advice to
evade many taxes. And many of them hold property in their own
right. The barrier between this group and the next is distinct,
although there are channels of mobility between these groups.
Nevertheless, upward mobility to this group is limited, as we shall
see in Chapter 7.

At the other end of the structure is the broad mass of ordinary
wage earners, those entirely dependent on the sale of their labour in
which the only power they can exercise, to set their terms and
conditions, is essentially defensive. They comprise about three-
quarters of the working population. Although their terms and
conditions vary from group to group, they have four things in
common. All earn relatively low wages; their earnings are insecure
and unpredictable (unemployment among this group is still far
higher than for any other group); they depend on overtime to
supplement their earnings and are likely to lose pay for any time

they have off work; and they are in general excluded from em-
ployer-run security schemes. The status distinctions between unskilled, semi-skilled, skilled and junior non-manual may appear
significant to those who experience the distinctions. But they do not
amount to much when measured in material rewards. According to
the Royal Commission, the variation in earnings between any
working-class job is about 15 per cent (excluding junior non-manual
jobs). All of this group faces the risk of poverty both during and at
the end of their working lives.

Between these two groups is an intermediate cluster of workers.
Their jobs are usually more secure, they are paid annual salaries
with increments each year and they benefit from employer-based
security schemes. They also enjoy some of the fringe benefits paid to
the top group.

But this group depends no less than rank-and-file workers on the
sale of their labour, although they can sell it at a premium compared
with ordinary workers. Their life cycles follow, at least in part,
an upwards, incremental rather than the long low hump and downward slope of most manual and routine workers. But they are to
some extent protected against poverty. They run very low risks
of accidents during their working lives; they usually are eligible
for employer-based pension schemes to cover their retirement,
and they are likely to have been paid sufficiently highly during
a part of their careers to have amassed some savings of their
own.

Outside the labour market are two other groups who are part of
the class structure. At the bottom are those without other means of
support. Some of them will have retired from work; others will be
sick or disabled and others will live outside of households with
incomes from the labour market. Many of this group are not distinct
from those at the bottom of the labour market. Some of them are in
and out of work throughout their lives. There is thus no distinct line
to be drawn between those in the labour market and those dependent on state benefits.

At the other end are those who do not work but rely on the
earnings of their wealth holdings. They are often forgotten in any
discussion of social class. This is the group that has massive amounts
of wealth compared with the rest of the population: wealth that is
theirs to dispose of as they wish.

There are still widespread disparities in the distribution of wealth, income, security and risk, and power that people experience. The evidence available suggests that these disparities have changed very little since the last war.

Capital is still concentrated and carries with it considerable power. The labour market still dictates the conditions of workers without property. These conditions of inequality are what Westergaard and Resler call the brute fact of the existence of class.

We shall examine in the next chapter how much inequality of opportunity there is. This is a different aspect of social class – the movement of people within positions in the class structure. This tells us nothing about the existence of social class. Only if there were no inequality of wealth, income, power and security, with no privilege and no contrasting dependence, would there be a classless society.

QUESTIONS

1. The dimensions of social inequality are only considered relevant by sociologists who cling to Marxist doctrines which the facts contradict. Discuss.
2. Private ownership of capital is the key to class divisions in Britain. In what ways has that ownership changed since the last war?
3. The backbone of the class structure, and indeed of the entire reward system of modern western society, is the occupation order. How useful is it to regard occupation as the basic economic inequality?
4. The correlation between social class and income is . . . one which only holds up in very general terms. If this is so, is it possible to see British society as stratified into social classes?
5. How useful is it to regard the dichotomy between manual and non-manual workers as the principal line of demarcation in the class structure?
6. Britain has not become a more egalitarian society in the last twenty-five years. Discuss.
7. The power elite . . . are in command of the major hierarchies and organizations of modern society. They rule the big corporations. They run the machinery of the state and claim its prerogatives. They direct that military establishment. They occupy the strategic command posts of the social structure, in which are now centred the effective means of power and the wealth . . . which they enjoy. Do you agree with this description of modern industrial societies?
8. We are all middle class now. Discuss.

FURTHER READING

This chapter draws heavily on the approach of Westergaard and Resler's book *Class in a Capitalist Society*. Any reader who wants to explore these issues more fully could find their book very rewarding.

Seven

Inequalities of opportunities

We have discussed so far the distribution of rewards that people are given at different points in the class structure and concluded that the inequalities are still as great as ever. The British class structure remains intact; people are still rewarded according to their position in the productive system – owner, manager, worker or dependant.

In this chapter we shall consider how these inequalities affect people's opportunities to move up or down the class structure. Is it the case that people from a working-class background can, by their own effort, move into middle-class positions and vice versa? Are there particular barriers in the class structure that it is difficult to break through? For instance, how significant is a public school education in bestowing on a person privileges that help him or her to move into well paid, powerful jobs? Similarly, does a life of poverty or social deprivation predispose those so born to remain there? These are common questions asked about the amount of social mobility in British society.

WHAT IS SOCIAL MOBILITY?

Social mobility is a complex question: there is no one single measure that will indicate how mobile the society is. So we shall begin the chapter by posing some of the questions usually asked about the subject. For the purposes of this book, it is not necessary to answer all the questions. They will help us to understand the ramifications of social mobility and will dispel some of the common misunderstandings that many people have on the topic.

How many people in the population get the opportunity to move away from the position they were born to, in the class structure: a few, some, many, or most of the population? Would we describe the British class structure as rigid or fluid? It is popularly believed that the class structure here is more rigid than the American class structure. Is that the case? If a third of the population have the opportunity to move from their social origins over their life span, would we regard that as an indication of a fluid or rigid structure?

The way we formulate the questions will determine the answers we arrive at. Some people interpret equality of opportunity to mean that children of working-class parents have an equal chance with middle-class children of obtaining middle-class jobs. That is one measure of equality of opportunity, but not the whole story. Others regard equality as the freedom for all people with talent to move into jobs at the top of the social structure.

How far do people need to move away from their origins for us to regard the move as a part of social mobility? How do we compare one step up or down the ladder on the part of a majority of the population with a lot of steps for a few people, since there is likely to be a good deal more short-term mobility than long-term?

If people do move, then is education the key to this movement, as is commonly supposed? Many more people had the opportunity to go to university after the post-Robbins expansion. What effect has that had on social mobility? Most readers will have answers to these questions based on their own understanding of the fluidity of the British class structure.

Many people tend to ignore completely the existing distribution of rewards (security, wealth, income and power) in favour of using the rate of social mobility as the best indication of the class structure. Low mobility is then regarded as the identifying mark of a class-divided society: high mobility as the hallmark of a classless society. Existing disparities of wealth are taken for granted. Rather than assess how much wealth can be acquired and retained by birth or accident, popular attention focuses on how much some people can achieve by personal merit and drive.

Westergaard and Resler complain that this is a particularly American way of looking at things. 'Equality' in the United States has come to mean equality of opportunity, with the ideal being a state of affairs where each individual can find a level in the hierarchy of inequality, according to their own abilities and drive, regardless of parentage or the circumstances of their early life. But equality of opportunity is always limited by the extent to which wealth and property can still confer on some privileges that can be passed on from one generation to the next. Social mobility is about social circulation. Just as the arteries can clog up and slow down blood circulation, so can privilege clog up the opportunities for social mobility. In any case, it is easy to underplay the significance of social background in conferring advantages and to assume that a person's limited progress is due to limited, innate abilities. Clearly we need to investigate such an assertion more closely.

The reader who has followed the arguments of previous chapters will soon realize that a truly mobile society, in which individuals of talent and character can freely transcend their parentage and poverty, rising to wealth and power, is not possible within a profoundly unequal class society.

> Only the presence of a high degree of practical equality . . . can diffuse the general opportunity to rise. The existence of such opportunities, in fact not merely in form, depends not only upon an open road but upon an equal start (Tawney, 1964).

In Britain, the left has always stressed the importance of equality of condition in its definition of social equality. The labour movement has a vision of a society in the future founded not on merit established by competition or the possession of property but on the distribution of resources according to some notion of a person's needs. The right, on the other hand, tend to stress the significance of equality of opportunity (while ignoring the social advantage of personal backgrounds) in its definition of equality.

Clearly, social mobility is closely related to the issues raised in the earlier chapters, where we concentrated our discussion of the class structure on its cleavages, and defined class primarily in economic terms. We have ignored such considerations as prestige or social status. In this chapter we shall be interested in finding what barriers there are that inhibit the movement of people from one social class to another. We are not interested in the barriers of social acceptance: they are merely the small change of social inequalities.

We can define social mobility, for the purposes of this book, as the measure of changes in a person's access to different positions in the class structure. In crude terms we want to know how easy it is for the managers, owners, and workers of the country's productive resources to move to other positions in the class structure, over their life spans. How likely is it that workers will be obliged to remain as workers throughout their lives? Is it possible for people without capital to acquire some of the means of production over their life times? We are not including the possibility of merely buying a few shares on the stock market. We mean the chance to buy a factory and make important decisions about its output. And what of the social dependents we referred to in Chapter 6? Does poverty breed poverty? Is the so-called cycle of deprivation so severe that few stand any chance of breaking out of it?

MEASURING SOCIAL MOBILITY

Social mobility is about measuring change of position over time. To do this we must both simplify people's individual mobility experiences so that we can aggregate them and we must apply certain basic concepts to any available data in order to measure the main outlines of social mobility.

First, we need to apply the concepts we have used elsewhere in this book to measure the movement of people over time: stocks and flows. People flow from position to position within the class structure, and the structure itself (the stock of positions) changes over time. At times there has been an expansion in the number of jobs at particular points in the class structure: at other times there has been a contraction. We must not confuse these two processes – flows of people and changes of stock – when we consider social mobility.

Social mobility data can be presented in three ways. We can measure *outflows*. For example, we can calculate the chances of working-class children moving out of working-class jobs, expressed as the number of children who left their working-class backgrounds as a proportion of all working-class children. Alternatively, we can use *inflow* data to measure the number of new entrants to middle-class occupations from elsewhere, expressed as a proportion of all current middle-class job holders. These two measures will give very different rates (they have different numerical bases) yet they both measure the same movement but from different points in the class structure. A third way of presenting the data is to measure the proportion of people who maintain their social class position over their life spans. For example, a study of social mobility in 1949 showed that 40 per cent of the sons of men with the top 3 per cent of the jobs themselves had similar jobs. In other words, children with fathers in top jobs had a very high probability of holding on to those privileged positions.

Flow data is easy to understand once we know exactly what we are talking about. Similarly with stock data. A lot of the increase in middle-class job opportunities since the war has been due to a massive expansion in the jobs available. Thus social mobility between working- and middle-class jobs can increase merely because the stock of middle-class jobs has increased relative to the stock of working-class jobs. If we wish to measure the fluidity of the class structure only with reference to the rates of flow of people between positions, we need to standardize the figures to eliminate these stock changes over time.

Second, we need to decide how to measure change of social position. We can ignore many changes that people go through that affect their life chances. For example, changing from the night to the day shift at work is irrelevant. So too is the arbitrary acquisition of capital through unforeseen circumstances. Social mobility is not primarily about pop stars or pools winners. It is more about the move from semi-skilled to skilled or non-manual jobs. But some people make many, complex moves in their journeys through the labour market. Much of this complexity will have to be ignored if we are to make sense of the major trends in social mobility.

The most usual way to consider social mobility is to measure two points in time. We can note the point at which people join the labour market and measure the point they reach when they retire, or we can note their position at a particular age and compare it with the position reached by a parent (usually the father) at a similar age. The first, measuring mobility over a person's own life span, we call intra-generational mobility. The second, measuring a person's position compared with a parent, we call inter-generational mobility.

They are two measures of the social origins and destinations of people. Using both measures has the advantage of being able to include more people in any study. If we used only intra-generational mobility, we would exclude all those people living who had not completed their working lives. This would cut out a lot of

information about recent mobility experiences. Also, both measures are important since they emphasize different aspects of social
mobility. Intra-generational mobility looks at what happens once a
person has completed education and acquired qualifications, to see
how well a person does over a career span. Inter-generational
mobility includes the effects of family life and cultural background
in opening access to educational institutions and initial career
opportunities, derived from possible family connections.

Third, we need to devise a classification of positions. This will
include not only people in the labour market but also the owners of
production as well as the social dependants. Taking the labour
market first, its broad structure is easy to define. We could simply
take the Registrar General's classification of occupations. But
problems arise as soon as we look at this in any detail. The
occupational structure changes over time not only in the stock of
different jobs, but also in the position of those jobs. A clerk's job at
the turn of the century was different (measured by its security,
wealth, income, and power) from clerical work in the 1980s.
Technological changes in the means of production (the introduction
of word processors and computers, for instance) have downgraded
the position of clerking. This makes it difficult to use a broad
classification to measure mobility over generations. Also, we know
from earlier discussions that some similar jobs also have important
differences. For example, technicians' jobs have a similar reward
structure to nurses' jobs, but the possibilities that both offer for
advancement are different.

Most researchers have treated these problems by reclassifying
occupations. This makes it difficult to compare the different studies
to draw a picture of social mobility over time. Because of this, we
shall marry up the studies by simplifying the data. We shall concentrate on the broad barriers to social mobility that exist over time. A
particular problem is how to classify low-skilled white-collar work.
It hangs ambiguously between working-class work and middle-class
work. We shall not be consistent here, since for some purpose it will
be convenient to regard it as middle-class and for other purposes as
working-class work! Similarly, there is no clear-cut distinction
between top professionals and managers, and the owners of capital
who are working directors. They often merge together.

The greatest difficulty lies in marrying the studies of social
mobility with the analysis of social class outlined previously. Most

mobility studies concentrate on occupational groups. We are interested in groups of people whose activities lie outside the labour force. Those who have substantial holdings of wealth, without themselves being economically active, may have a controlling interest in the means of production. Also, at the other end of the scale, we are interested in those who are dependant on others for their livelihood, either on the state because they are unable to work themselves, or on those who are economically active.

Most studies of social mobility tell us little about the opportunities to move out of poverty. Poverty affects two particular groups usually omitted from mobility studies – the old and women. While we may reasonably ignore the first group since they have already passed through the labour market, we can by no means ignore the second group.

This exclusion of women from studies of mobility in any case presents a biased picture of the labour force. As we know, women occupy different positions to men in the labour market. By and large, there are many more semi-skilled female occupations compared with more skilled male ones. Also, there are more junior non-manual positions available to women, compared with more senior middle-class jobs available to men. Thus social mobility for women is severely constrained by segregation of women in the labour market. To exclude women gives a distorted and male-centred picture of social mobility.

This is true also of studies of the transmission of poverty between generations. Low-income families include a preponderance of single female parents. A major defect of many mobility studies is their continued insistence of defining a family's social class by the occupation of the father (and ascribing the occupation in those families without fathers!).

BRITISH MOBILITY STUDIES

There have been two major studies of social mobility in Britain, one carried out in 1949 and the other in 1972. We shall draw on both of them to look at the main structure of opportunities and the changes in mobility between the two dates. The first, carried out by a team of researchers headed by David Glass at the London School of Economics (Glass, 1954) produced findings that have become so well known that many of the results may now seem commonplace. The second, carried out by a team under John Goldthorpe (Goldthorpe, 1980) set out to replicate much of the earlier work in order to make comparisons. Both researchers chose a sample of 10,000 men and measured their present position in the occupational structure, how far they had moved since they first entered the labour force, and their progress in the class structure compared with their fathers' positions. The second study has been widely criticized for omitting women but one of the reasons for this was that it was an omission necessary if the study was to follow the procedures of the 1949 study.

Both studies used a seven-fold classification of occupations. Glass looked at seven 'status' categories defined by the amount of social prestige attached to them. Goldthorpe defined the seven groups more in terms of income, security, opportunity for mobility and social relationships at work (that is, characteristics more in keeping with our definition of social class). Their classification scheme differs also because of changes in the position of some jobs in the labour force as well as the stock of jobs in the overall structure. These changes have been substantial over the last fifty years. For instance, of the men born between 1908 and 1917, only about 22 per cent came within Goldthorpe's top two classes whereas the size of these classes had increased to nearly 30 per cent for the men born between 1938 and 1947. Other groups declined. Goldthorpe's classes III to V (white-collar workers, small shopkeepers and the supervisors of manual workers) declined from 32 per cent to 27 per cent for the respective birth groups.

Both studies indicate a fair amount of social mobility. Fewer than a third of men in the 1949 study proved to be in a job of the same level as their fathers. Even when those who had moved only a step away from their fathers' positions are excluded, forty per cent had either improved upon or slid down from the circumstances of their birth. Men in the 1972 study showed a similar pattern: the precise comparison is difficult to make.

Westergaard and Resler comment that this fact is sufficient to dispel any notion that Britain is a society in which individual position in the class structure is fixed at birth. Capitalism here, as elsewhere, allows a fair degree of social circulation. But this may not be very significant. A fluid circulation is not the same as free circulation, as any heart specialist knows!

We can formulate this result more clearly by reference to the notion of 'perfect' mobility. If mobility were perfectly fluid, then we would expect the sons of fathers in any particular social class to be distributed throughout the class structure in a pattern that reflects the current dispersion of occupations. In other words, some class positions would be independent of social origins. But if we look at the sons of fathers in the top social class we find that, while they are dispersed throughout the class structure, they are still overhwelmingly bunched in the same class as their fathers. That goes for most of the groups. Any society that had perfect mobility would permit much greater freedom of movement so that social origins would truly be insignificant.

Both studies agree, too, that there is a lot more short-range than long-range mobility. In the 1949 study, three-quarters of the sons of unskilled fathers managed to move at least into semi-skilled work. But only about 1 per cent of the men from semi-skilled or unskilled backgrounds managed to achieve middle-class jobs. And only 6 to 7 per cent of the sons of professionals and managers landed up in semi-skilled or unskilled work, at a time when these two categories contained a third of the workforce.

The dominance of short-range over long-range mobility is confirmed in Goldthorpe's study. Although two-thirds of the population were inter-generationally mobile, less than 10 per cent of men from Class 1 origins had dropped to semi-skilled or unskilled manual work, while over a quarter had dropped the shorter distances to Classes III–VI. Similarly, 15 per cent of men from the bottom class achieved long-range upward mobility while 50 per cent achieved some short-range movement. (Any precise comparision in figures between the two studies is meaningless because of the difference in the categories.)

Goldthorpe found that 18 out of every 100 boys from manual homes went on to become profesional or managerial workers: while 30 out of every 100 boys in intermediate homes reached professional jobs. But 62 out of every 100 boys in professional or managerial homes remained in that class. In other words, the opportunities for mobility into the professional classes are distributed in the ratio 1:2:4 (one manual boy to every two intermediate boys to four professional boys).

This raises the question of the extent to which there is a barrier in British society between working-class and middle-class jobs. Glass pointed out that descent from professional and executive backgrounds usually stopped short of the line dividing white-collar from blue-collar work, and that the groups just above and below this barrier had distinctly different chances of movement across it. Thus, while only 6 per cent of the sons from routine white collar homes moved into at least executive positions, this was three times the figure for those from skilled manual homes. All told, 29 per cent of routine white-collar sons but only 22 per cent of skilled blue-collar sons managed to rise as far as supervisory jobs. But both Glass and Goldthorpe found that about a third of the workforce did move across the barrier. And Heath (1981) points out that the men who did cross from working-class origins did not then collapse from exhaustion, but were just as likely to carry on into the higher grade professional or managerial posts as they were to end up in routine clerical work.

Goldthorpe found that while about a quarter of the sons of working-class backgrounds breached the barrier, rather fewer moved in the opposite direction. This assymetry, found in other countries too, has led some writers to describe the barrier as a one-way screen which is easier to pass through in one direction than it is in the other. This suggests what many people believe: the barrier between white- and blue-collar work creates relative protection for the sons of white-collar parents who do not gain the necessary qualifications for most middle-class job opportunities but have the option of remaining in the unskilled white-collar jobs like retail sales and routine clerical work. In fact, this is not the case. The great majority of educationally unsuccessful white-collar sons with 'inferior abilities' seem to end up in some kind of blue-collar work.

What does happen is that educationally unsuccessful sons from middle-class homes do distinctly better than their counterparts from working-class homes. They are more likely to get apprenticeships leading to skilled manual work. White-collar families know that qualifications improve the chances of getting better-paid work and that vocational qualifications are a good second best to academic ones. They are also good at securing such advantages as school credentials and contacts in ensuring that their sons find apprenticeships.

There is one clear difference in the findings between the two studies. This concerns the amount of absolute mobility which measures the increase in opportunities caused by an increase in middle-class jobs compared with working-class jobs. We have already pointed out the increase in the size of the middle-class sector over the last fifty years. Glass found little overall change in the social structure: the number who rose was roughly equal to the number of those downwardly mobile. Goldthorpe concludes therefore that the marked expansion of white-collar work happened after 1949 and that it is this growth that accounts for most of the increased mobility this century. But if absolute mobility has increased, relative mobility (the prospects for working-class compared with middle-class sons) may have worsened. This seems to reflect the tightening of opportunities for younger working-class sons.

The other important finding confirmed in both studies concerns the amount of self-recruitment at both extremes of the social structure. A third of the sons in the 1949 study who had unskilled manual jobs came from homes where fathers had similar jobs. A half of the sons in top professional jobs came from backgrounds where fathers had similar jobs. To some extent, we can say that the unskilled are born to fail and the privileged are born to succeed. As Westergaard and Resler point out:

> If parental origin played no part in determining life chances, whether directly or indirectly, only 3 per cent of the sons of the 1949 sample (the sons of the professional and administrative classes) . . . would have found jobs of a kind to secure them a place in this privileged minority (of established professional and high administrative jobs). In fact nearly 40 per cent did so.

This is roughly thirteen times as many as one would expect if there had been perfect mobility. Sons of fathers at the top have a thirteen-to-one head start on other sons. The 1972 study shows a similar head start (the ratios are not the same due to the massive expansion of top jobs recently).

We need to distinguish, however, between the ability of men at the top to maintain those privileges for their sons and the opportunities for others to move into top jobs. The two are not incompatible (at least in the period in question). While nearly half the sons of fathers in Class 1 remained there, three-quarters of the men in Class 1 in 1972 had come from lower social origins. The distinction makes sense when we remember that social mobility can be conceived either as social origins or destinations. Heath remarks: 'even if every single person from Class 1 origin had managed to stay there, expansion would have meant that a large number would still need to have been recruited from elsewhere to fill all the new vacancies'. Self-recruitment is not the same thing as closure.

At the bottom we find the reverse picture. While three-quarters of Class 1 are upwardly mobile 'new men', 40 per cent having come from blue-collar backgrounds; nearly three-quarters of Class VII members are 'second generation' working class and less than 10 per cent are from white-collar backgrounds. Again this can be accounted for by the expansion at the top of the class structure.

ELITE SELF-RECRUITMENT

Although both studies found that the highest levels of self-recruitment were at the two extremes of the class structure, this was particularly so at the top where the rich clearly remain 'born to succeed'. But the patterns of self-recruitment at the top vary among the social groups that make up Class 1. The new men that have arrived at the top to fill the increased number of positions are not necessarily spread throughout the top class. Middle-class jobs consist of many different types. They range from the self-employed professional like a doctor or lawyer to the salaried professional like a university teacher or scientist, to the senior administrators of large public or commercial bureaucracies, to industrial managers in the large conglomerates and to the large proprietors, the working owners of large shops and enterprises. We need to consider each of these: in doing so we shall get some appreciation of the connections between the managers and the owners of capital.

Room at the top for those from elsewhere is available in certain places. The majority of industrial managers had come from blue-collar backgrounds. But few of the new men landed up as pro-prietors or self-employed professionals (in fact only a quarter of these had blue-collar backgrounds). The middle-class jobs which are the most autonomous – the self-employed – are the most exclusive in their recruitment patterns. The archetypical profess-ional still comes from a privileged social background and receives an élite education, going straight into a good job with a secure future, probably beginning in a partnership of self-employed pro-fessionals and ending up as one of the senior partners.

The extreme position is that of large proprietors. Over 44 per cent came from a Class 1 background. For them the direct inheritance of property is likely to be very significant in spite of the impact of inheritance taxes. No less than 47 per cent of the large proprietors were themselves the sons of proprietors. There seem to be two distinct types: the self-made men and the inheritors. A typical inheritor goes to a private school, starts working life in a subordinate position in his father's firm, and eventually takes over the business. A self-made man is more likely to receive minimal education and start out in a routine white-collar or blue-collar job.

The occupations offering the best channels for upward mobility are the salaried professional ones in industrial or government bureaucracies. Nearly 54 per cent of industrial managers and 43 per cent of senior administrators came from blue-collar origins, compared with only 24 per cent of self-employed professionals and 26 per cent of the large proprietors. Industrial management thus recruits more than the other channels from blue-collar homes; its recruits have somewhat lower educational levels and more of them have spent some time on the shop floor. Well over half of them began their careers as manual workers or technicians. In contrast, nearly two-thirds of the administrators began in white-collar jobs especially routine clerical ones. The members of social class I have an extremely varied social experience between them. There are three routes to the top – the inheritance of privilege, the scholarship ladder into white-collar work, and promotion from the shop floor. The largest group at the top are the scholarship boys, followed by those promoted from the shop floor. The privileged route accounts for only a tiny minority (less than 10 per cent).

Finally, what about the connections between Class I job holders and the very highest echelons of society, the posts of cabinet ministers, senior civil servants from under-secretaries upwards, directors of major financial institutions and the 'command posts' of industry, that all go to make up the group of 'top decision-makers' as Lupton and Wilson (1959) call them? After all, in the early 1970s there were well over a million men in Class I occupations but only a few of those reach the very top.

Good data is difficult to find. Boyd (1973) used membership of *Who's Who* to investigate the backgrounds of all people who were top civil servants, ambassadors, High Court judges, bishops, and bank directors. Heath calculated the chances, for each group, of the sons remaining at the same position as their fathers, compared with completely free mobility. The results are illuminating. Thus if élite membership were entirely independent of social origin, only 0.15 per cent of the people in *Who's Who* were to be expected to have had fathers who were also in. In fact, 11 per cent of the top civil servants had such fathers: this gives us a self-recruitment ratio of 75:1. For bank directors it is as high as 300:1. The civil service was more open than the judiciary, the Church, or the City. The same can be done with wealth holders. In 1973, 36 per cent of top wealth holders (with over £100,000) came from similar backgrounds, giving a ratio of 257:1. These data reveal that the great inequalities of opportunity are not those between children from white- and blue-collar homes, but between the élite and non-élite. Heath gives the rough figures as follows. A man from a working-class home has about 1 chance in 1500 of getting into *Who's Who*; the man from a white-collar background has about 1 chance in 500; the man from the higher professional or managerial background about 1 chance in 200; but the man from the élite home has a 1 in 5 chance of remaining there. As he points out, 'silver spoons continued to be distributed'.

MOBILITY OF WOMEN

None of the major mobility studies have included women in their analysis. This may have been understandable in the past when women made up a smaller portion of the employed workforce. Since 1970 women have made up more than 40 per cent of the labour force. Even when we exclude those who work part-time, women still make up a quarter of the workforce.

Fortunately, Heath has brought together what data does exist to provide useful information. He compares women's marital and occupational mobility chances with the social mobility of men. He also considers the extent of inequalities of opportunity dividing women themselves.

There is, of course, some relationship between a woman's class position and her husband's occupation. It is not necessarily an obvious one. In fact Heath's findings dispel certain myths. It is not the case, for instance, that women in general achieve social mobility through marriage. There is no large-scale tendency for women to marry up. Nevertheless, there is a great deal of marrying up which is balanced by other women marrying down. In fact the interchange is more extensive than the interchange between fathers and sons.

Hence, the class structure is rather more fluid than an analysis of father-son mobility suggests. The typical father from Class 1 is more likely to see his daughter downwardly mobile than his son. And women from an unskilled or semi-skilled home are more likely to be upwardly mobile than their brothers. Because of the possibility of marital mobility a woman's class fate is more loosely linked to her social origins than is a man's. But this presupposes the usual sexist assumptions that it is the man's occupation that determines a family's class position.

When we consider the differences between male and female inequalities of opportunity we need to bear in mind the distinctive distribution of occupations for women. It is bimodal: women's work is heavily concentrated in lower white-collar work and semi-skilled or unskilled manual work. It is grossly underrepresented both in skilled manual and higher grade professional and managerial work. This means that women find it easier to move into certain parts of the class structure than men and in other parts they have much greater difficulty. Women from Class I and II origins tend to be downwardly mobile in large numbers: a gross inequality between men and women. Although there is a surplus of upward over downward mobility, this surplus is smaller for women. This is not surprising in the light of the enormous concentration of 'women's work' in routine non-manual jobs. Of course, considerable numbers of women from working-class backgrounds cross the barrier into routine clerical jobs but we need to remember that these jobs are usually badly paid.

Opportunities for single women differ. They do much better than men in gaining access to Class II jobs and avoiding Class VII jobs. The helping professions provide a definite channel of upward mobility for career-orientated women. But these results need to be treated with caution. Women have these opportunities only because so few pay the price of choosing between family life and a career, an option that is not necessary for men. If more women were to seek full-time, continuous work it is likely that the underlying sexual discrimination in the labour market would reveal itself more readily.

The significance of social background is less marked for women than it is for men. Men from a Class I background have a seven-fold advantage over those from Class VII in the competition to stay in Class I. For women this advantage is only five-fold. And while a man from Class VII is six times more likely to remain there than his Class I competitor is, a woman from Class VII is four times as likely to end up with a husband there than is her Class I rival.

While there may be greater equality among women than there is among men in the competition for routine white-collar jobs, this equality may simply be a consequence of the inequalities between men and women. Class discrimination divides men, but sexual discrimination brings women together. If women were given the same opportunities as men to enter jobs in management or skilled manual work, then the class differences that divide men would probably reappear for women.

ARE PEOPLE BORN TO FAIL?

Finally, we need to consider the social dependants in the class structure, those not found within the labour force. Does a life of poverty or social deprivation predispose those so born to remain there? This is difficult to answer, particularly in the way in which we have discussed poverty in Chapter 7. Poverty affects two groups in particular: the old and women, especially divorced or separated women with young children. Both are excluded from the available data which covers only those within the labour force. Heath discussed the issue and concludes that we cannot be sure exactly what we are measuring when we take various indices of deprivation since they often cover similar factors. He does point out, however, that our educational system destines a very large proportion of boys to fail. The British educational system is geared to the needs of the academic and social élite.

The majority of working-class boys leave school without educational credentials. He concludes what many other commentators have concluded that deprivation is a common mischance that many, almost at random, within the working class may experience. Job security, as we pointed out in Chapter 6, is unequally distributed. Many working-class families lose what foothold they have in the job market, faced with a personal crisis or an unforeseen circumstance. Also, we must bear in mind the physical handicaps that some working-class men acquire through their work, which may result in permanent disability and loss of job.

Nevertheless, there is little evidence of a cycle of deprivation. Some people (at least those that can be measured through workforce data) are not born to fail. This is in marked contrast with those born to succeed at the top of the structure.

Half the children born into a disadvantaged home do not repeat the pattern of disadvantage in the next generation. Over half of all forms of disadvantage arise anew each generation. . . . In short, family cycles are a most important element in the perpetuation of disadvantage but they account for only a part of the overall picture. (Rutter and Madge, 1976)

CONCLUSIONS

We began the chapter by supposing that a key question on social mobility is the extent to which children of working-class origins have the opportunity to enjoy the advantages of middle-class jobs and the security they offer. Any reader who has followed the discussion of this chapter may by now have come to a different conclusion.

Britain is not a society in which individual position in the class structure is fixed at birth. The sons of foremen and technicians, for example, are spread out across the class structure in an apparently random manner. Fluidity rather than occupational inheritance seems a better character-isation of the intermediate area of the British class structure. Occupation inheritance, however, is more in evidence when we look at the extremes. Almost half the sons from Class I homes followed in their fathers' footsteps into Class I jobs; well over half the sons from working-class homes likewise followed in their fathers' footsteps. But this still means that there were many men from these classes who experienced upward or downward inter-generational mobility. One in seven men from Class I homes were downwardly mobile into blue-collar jobs; one in five men whose fathers held semi-skilled or unskilled manual jobs were upwardly mobile into white-collar work. (Heath)

In spite of this fluidity, Britain is still a society where there are the most grotesque inequalities of privilege in the competition for élite positions among the ruling class. We must conclude that the divide between those who work for capital and those who manage it on the one hand, and those who own and control it on the other, is the greatest cleavage within the class structure. Some breach the gap; most remain on the side at which they were born.

QUESTIONS

1. How would you define social mobility: and how would you set about measuring mobility?
2. Equality of opportunity is limited by the extent to which wealth and property can still confer on some privileges that can be passed on to their offspring.
   Explain.
3. Goldthorpe, in his study of social mobility, found more upward mobility than Glass found in his earlier study. How would you account for this?
4. Is it true that the unskilled are bound to fail, and the privileged to succeed in the British class structure today?
5. Describe the pattern of élite self-recruitment in modern Britain.
6. Is there a barrier in British society between working and middle-class jobs that prevents working-class people from acquiring middle-class jobs?
7. What are the most important barriers to social mobility for women?
8. Goldthorpe concludes in his study that opportunities for mobility into the professional classes are distributed in the ratio 1:2:4 one boy from a manual home to two boys from intermediate homes to four boys from professional homes. Explain.

FURTHER READING

The most readable account of social mobility, written by a member of the Goldthorpe team, is undoubtedly the book by Anthony Heath, *Social Mobility*, Fontana, 1981.

Eight

Poverty

People in Britain today live in an affluent society. In spite of periodic recessions, the post-war economy has grown and wage rates have risen to levels hitherto unimaginable. Net national income per head more than doubled in real terms between the early 1920s and the middle 1960s. As a result of the prosperity of the 1950s and 1960s, people now take for granted a standard of material consumption that is unprecedented. We now live in a mass consumption society where many items, previously regarded as luxury goods for the wealthy, are now commonplace. High proportions of the population have such things as washing machines, television sets, fridges and 'luxury' kitchens. Car ownership and home ownership are now available to a majority of the population.

It seems something of a paradox, then, to discuss poverty in this context. Compared with anyone living in a Third World country, people living in Britain cannot possibly be regarded as poor. Economic life in the 1980s in Britain may not be as rosy as economic life in the 1960s. But most commentators expect Britain to revert to high growth rates eventually. In a society such as Britain that has experienced a long period of growth, where living standards have always been comparatively high, and where the benefits of the Welfare State are available to all in need, it is easy to conclude that something must be at fault with those who are poor. When work and money is available to all, surely only those who are feckless or inadequate will be poor.

Frank Field (1981) pointed out that many people believe that poverty is a self-inflicted wound. A recent EEC survey, which he quoted, showed that in Britain people were far more likely than elsewhere in Europe to take a personalized view of poverty. In Italy and France people generally blamed society for any poverty in the country. In Britain people were more likely to attribute poverty to the victims of it. They regarded such things as laziness, chronic unemployment, drink, and ill health, as causes of poverty.

This line of thinking has a certain logic. Compared with living standards in the 1930s, few can now be regarded as poor. And in an era where certain consumer durables are owned universally, it is difficult to imagine that some families may be unable to afford the necessities of life. How do we relate these issues to the possibility of poverty existing in Britain in the 1980s? The confusion arises because of differing notions of how to define poverty.

WHAT IS POVERTY?

To understand what anyone means by poverty today, we shall first summarize how poverty was defined in the past. The pioneers of poverty research in Britain were Charles Booth and Seebohm Rowntree. They began to investigate the conditions in which the poor lived towards the end of the last century. Their ideas have influenced this field of investigation ever since.

1. Poverty as Subsistence
It was Booth who created the notion of 'the poverty line', an idea that has been incorporated into the English language. We think of the poverty line as a standard below which people cannot afford the necessities of life. Of course it is difficult to decide exactly what we mean by this. People's view of what is a necessity will vary. Booth intended his notion to be a relative one. He defined families as poor when their incomes were insufficient 'according to the normal standard of life in this country' – that is, a relative notion of poverty.

Rowntree had a notion of the poverty line that was independent of the society he was investigating. It was a minimum subsistence level; a level of income just sufficient to provide enough clothing, food, and shelter necessary for the maintenance of merely physical health. If people's income fell below this poverty line, their standard of health would be likely to deteriorate, and their rates of death rise. In other words, this was an absolute notion of poverty.

The notion of a minimum subsistence level is still used in social policies in Britain. Beveridge relied heavily on Rowntree's calculations of subsistence levels in his blueprint for the Welfare State in 1942. And the recommendations of the Beveridge Report about benefit levels have had an enormous influence on the subsequent history of social security. Anyone not working who is living on an income below the State's definition of the subsistence level, is entitled to financial help from the state. The number of people entitled to, or claiming, benefits is thus a measure of the numbers of people in poverty.

The precise definition of this subsistence level has always been open to dispute. From time to time, nutritional and social policy experts have argued that the State's definition of poverty is too low for people to live on for any length of time. A study in 1975 argued that the State underestimated the food needs of children. Field (1981) argued that recent estimates of the cost of raising a child show that a fourteen-year-old child costs as much as an adult to feed. Studies in the USA have shown that the cost of feeding a sixteen- to nineteen-year-old male is one-and-a-quarter times the cost of feeding an adult. Yet the State continues to pay out less to keep a teenager than it does to an adult.

Also, there is evidence from official surveys (quoted in Field, 1981) that the State's definition of minimum income levels is insufficient to provide claimants with enough clothing stocks to meet the State's own definition of minimum requirements. 43 per cent of single sick or disabled claimants have stocks of clothing less than the State's recommended levels. The surveys also showed that a number of claimants had fallen into debt since being on state benefits. The State partly recognizes the inadequacy of its definition of subsistence. It has the power to make certain discretionary payments to claimants in need.

Whether or not the State definition of poverty is adequate is a matter of personal judgment. It is impossible to find any objective measure of assessing minimal subsistence. Booth and Rowntree have always been subject to the criticism that they took an idealized notion of behaviour to assess a person's minimal needs. Some people argue that a notion of subsistence, based on a measure of the basic necessities of life, can never be appropriate for dealing with the issue of poverty.

After all, society has changed drastically. Most families in Britain expect a standard of living where they have the money and freedom to make a series of choices about how to live. They would place a high emphasis on their right to choose their diet, how to spend their leisure time and what goals in life matter to them as we argued in our discussion of modern family life.

President Johnson, in his message to Congress on poverty in 1964, said that for the poor, poverty 'means a daily struggle to secure the necessities for even a meagre existence. It means that the abundance, the comforts, the opportunities they see all around them are beyond their grasp'. Thus we can talk of poverty in a relative sense as something more than just a minimum to keep people alive.

We can make three criticisms of the subsistence notion of poverty. First, as incomes improve, so living standards rise. People would not dream of doing certain things they used to. For example, few people would be prepared to walk long distances to work or school, as they used to in the past. The cost of public transport is no longer regarded as a luxury. Also, people rarely wash clothes by hand: it is too time-consuming. The use of a washing machine or a launderette is now regarded as a necessity. Houses no longer have built-in larders for storing perishable food: fridges are a necessity. Expectations of minimal comforts have widened too. The telephone and television set are part of our complex methods of communicating. Few people now expect to live near relatives or close friends. They need money to travel to see them, in order to maintain important social relationships. Processed foods, holidays, home improvements are all aspects of changed styles of living that most people take for granted.

Second, nutritional needs, used to determine subsistence levels, do not take account of social customs. Most people's eating habits are based on their cultural milieu, not on their nutritional values. Tea is an important drink to British people; yet its nutritional value is low, and would not be part of any subsistence diet. Food serving is an important part of social relationships. To be unable to afford to do this would cut one off from some important relationships.

Third, with improved living standards, people's expectations have improved. Few people now expect merely to survive. Educational achievements, individual hobbies, leisure activities enjoyed together, and the personal fulfilment of each member of any family, are all goals that are important to people. The needs of the present generation cannot be defined by the living standards of an earlier generation. Any satisfactory notion of poverty must take account of current living standards.

2. Poverty as Deprivation

Townsend (1979) attempted to relate poverty to living standards. He defined poverty as the inability of people to participate acceptably and then set out to ascertain what people thought we mean by that. He compiled a list of sixty measures of goods and activities that people could regard as basic requirements, the lack of which constituted a deprivation.

They range from not having a holiday away from home in any twelve months, to not going out for entertainment in the last two weeks, down to not usually having a Sunday joint three out of every four Sundays. Not everyone would expect to score positively throughout his whole list. Individual tastes depart from cultural prescriptions at times. But overall, a pattern emerges. He argues that there is a threshold below which the deprivation as measured by these notions of participation increases dramatically. He has, in fact, switched from a subsistence notion of poverty that measures basic physical survival needs to a measure of subsistence defined by cultural and social needs, since these are more important and reflect the dominant values of our society.

As living standards improve, so his list would need to become more inclusive. While we might disagree about individual items, a consensus exists about the broad measure of deprivation which his list contains.

3. Poverty as a Percentage

A third approach is to analyse the range of incomes distributed in our society and to fix a percentage about the mean (or median) below which incomes should not fall. George and Wilding (1976) argues that earnings range from about 140 to 157 per cent of the median earnings at the top, to about 66 to 70 per cent at the bottom decile. This spread of earnings has remained stable for many years. The Low Pay Unit argued that in 1970, although the lowest decile earned an average of 70.2 per cent of the median, some workers were earning rates as low as 50 per cent of the median. The Unit, in its report to the Royal Commission on the Distribution of Income and Wealth, suggested that low pay could be defined as anything below 80 per cent of the median.

When we look at State benefit levels as a percentage of average weekly earnings, we find that insurance benefits for a married couple are roughly a third of average weekly male earnings. Lansley (1980) pointed out that supplementary benefit in 1970 (i.e. the long-term benefit for a couple plus 30 per cent for rent and discretionary allowances) worked out at roughly 50 per cent of the median net income.

It is not easy to put these figures together. But the argument implicit in these points is that it is possible to find a consensus about the percentage levels that poverty is defined at, relative to average male earnings. If people earn less than this percentage, they could be defined as being in poverty. The advantage of this way of viewing poverty is that, although it is a relative measure, it is possible to abolish poverty by ensuring that no one earns less than this percentage of average earnings.

Another relative measure used to define poverty is to take a fixed percentage of the lowest incomes. This has the disadvantage that it does not define poverty relative to the standards of living of the country. Poverty, by this definition, is ever present.

Anyone who has gone along with the argument so far is likely to conclude that poverty can only be defined relative to average living standards. The problem then becomes a question of deciding at what level to put the poverty line in relation to living standards.

By convention, many policy analysts use a measure of poverty that is related to state benefit levels. Poverty is then defined as a certain percentage above Supplementary Benefit (SB) levels. It needs to be at least a certain level above SB rates since the rates do not include an allowance for housing costs. Even then, some allowance has to be made for the fact that a substantial number of claimants receive more than the SB rates. They may be given the short-term or the (higher) long-term SB rates; they may be awarded extra additions (to supplement their heating or food costs) or they may be awarded discretionary payments for exceptional purposes such as clothing and furniture.

This is not surprising. The State is in a dilemma. On the one hand, it has to ensure that the definition of subsistence is high enough to allow people to survive, but low enough to exclude those who work and are badly paid. We should not expect the State definition of poverty to be an objective definition of what people need to be able to live adequately!

Townsend argued that a realistic measure of poverty that takes into account the sort of payments the State provides to many claimants needs to be about 140 per cent of the ordinary SB scale rates, after allowing for housing costs. Few claimants get more than this level of benefits. A substantial number get somewhat near the level. According to an analysis of the Family Expenditure Survey data for 1953–4 (Field, 1981), single people receiving assistance were, on average, receiving about 26 per cent above the basic rates (plus rent) and, for nearly two-thirds of all claimants, benefits work out at approximately 110 per cent of the basic scale rates (plus rent) while a quarter of claimants receive about 120 per cent. Only a minority get about 140 per cent.

This explains how Townsend arrived at his definition of poverty. He concluded in his study that very roughly a quarter of the population fall below the poverty line, so defined. This is roughly similar to the portion of the population falling below his deprivation measure of poverty. It corresponds to similar conclusions arrived at by Layard (1978).

TRENDS IN POVERTY

While it is difficult to compare the different notions of poverty because of the definitions used, we can conclude that poverty affects roughly the poorest quarter of the population today (about 12 million people). That quarter has a standard of living that most people would deem as inadequate, judged by the standard enjoyed by the rest of the population. Poverty is, then, quite widespread in Britain.

Part of the reason for this scale of poverty lies in the distribution of incomes. The spread of incomes is so wide that the poorest quarter are too far below the average income to be able to manage on what they get. We have seen that the poorest 30 per cent in the population still receive only 10 per cent of the share of post-tax incomes. That share has been remarkably stable, in post-war Britain.

What does this imply about trends in poverty? How has the plight of the poor changed over time? It is difficult to obtain long-term data that enables us to make such comparisons. We can look at the number of claimants eligible for state benefits to see if they have increased over time. Or we can compare the value of state benefits with average wage rates over time.

If we take the supplementary benefit scale rates as our definition of poverty, there was a rise in the number of people living in poverty between 1948 and 1979. During that period, the number of households dependant on SB rose from just over a million to around three million. If we include the dependants of those households, the total number in poverty rises to around five million in 1979. Thus, depending on our definition of poverty, we can say that poverty affects between 5 and 12 million people in Britain.

The difficulty of using the SB scale rates as a measure is that their value changes over time. The rates in 1980 were roughly 18 per cent higher in real terms than the rates in 1964, and the more generous the definition of poverty, the more people are likely to fall below the poverty line.

Field pointed out that we need to compare the SB rates with changes in prices to give an idea of whether or not the poor are better off, as the rates have improved. We need also to compare changes in the incomes of the poor with changes in the incomes of the rest of the country.

From 1948 the value of state benefits in general rose faster than price levels. Between 1948 and 1979, the retail prices index (excluding housing costs) rose by 646.6 per cent: benefit scale rates rose over the same period by over 1,300 per cent. So the poor were twice as well off in relation to price levels over that period.

When we compare the scale rates with increases in average earnings over time, we find little change. Field quoted two pieces of evidence. Research carried out at Reading University (1977) shows that between 1953 and 1971 the relative living standards of the poor neither improved nor deteriorated. Also, the Royal Commission's findings show that the poorest three-tenths of family units increased their average real income by 40 per cent during the same period. This compares with a growth in the GNP of 38 per cent.

Hence the apparent prosperity of the poor during this time is little more than a reflection of increased living standards generally. Poverty incomes have risen no faster than the incomes of the rest of the population. The biggest increase in numbers of claimants is accounted for after 1973 as a result of growing industrial collapse and the increases in unemployment. The rest is largely accounted for by demographic change especially increases in the numbers of single-parent families.

WHO ARE THE POOR?

Having defined the poverty line we can now identify those individuals who fall below it. Because we have chosen no single view of poverty as definitive, we shall give a number of answers. In general terms Townsend showed that, according to the State's definition of poverty, about a third of people in poverty belong to income units in which someone is employed, another third belong to units in which someone is disabled, or has been ill for at least five weeks, and another third to units in which someone is of pensionable age. These are the principal groupings from which any description of poverty must proceed. The figures are very rough; Townsend's categories are not mutually exclusive. The figures merely provide an overall picture of the distribution of poverty between different groups of people. As many as 62 per cent of people in a unit with someone sick or disabled were also in a unit where someone was retired. This gives us a broad picture of the groups most likely to be among the poor – the low-paid, the elderly, and the sick and disabled.

SHARE OF POVERTY

Layard (1978) mapped the kinds of people who were poor at different levels of poverty. He provided three levels of poverty, ranging from 100, 120 and 140 per cent of SB (after including housing costs). He looked at the characteristics of the households of people found below these three levels. His analysis was by type of family (it omitted information on handicap or employment characteristics). In order to avoid confusion, we shall call his three levels of poverty the very poor, the poor, and the marginally poor.

Of the very poor, Layard showed that a half were elderly people, mainly women, and a quarter were children (of which two in five were in single-parent families). The rest of the very poor were adults of working age (not necessarily employed). At the next level of poverty (the poor), forty per cent were elderly and a half were families with two parents. There were fewer single-parent families

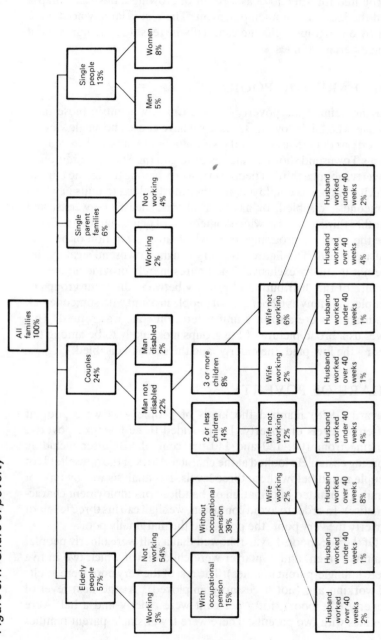

Figure 8.1. Share of poverty

Source: Layard (1978)

among this group than among the very poor. At the margins of poverty, ordinary families predominate (just over a half of this group) and elderly people were relatively less numerous.

But if we lump these three groups together we find the relative importance of different groups of the poor, ranging from the poorest to the marginally poor. Judged at this way, elderly people predominate. They make up about 57 per cent of the poor. The next most important group, two parent families, make up only 24 per cent of the poor. And single-parent families at 6 per cent tail behind single people at 13 per cent (see Figure 8.1).

RISK OF POVERTY

So far we have shown which groups in the population account for the largest share of poverty. Elderly people account for the biggest share of poverty, followed by families with children. But there are other groups that, while they may account for little of the total share of poverty, are at great risk of being poor. For example although the elderly retired accounted for 15 per cent of the population, they accounted for 54 per cent of those in poverty. Single-parent families account for only 3 per cent of the population, but make up 6 per cent of those in poverty. Some groups (e.g. the elderly) have a high share of poverty and are greatly at risk of being poor and other groups (like single-parent families or families with a disabled head of household), while there may be relatively few of them among the poor, are greatly at risk of being poor.

We shall now discuss in more detail each of the groups of people that are prone to poverty, describing them by their particular characteristics. Since poverty is likely to affect all people who are not wage earners at some stage (as well as certain wage earners) there is no one single way of categorizing them except with reference to their exclusion from the labour market (for whatever reason). We can identify five important groups. They are the unemployed, the elderly, single parent families, the sick and disabled, and the low paid. Each of these groups is likely to number among the poor. They are the groups of people that are either unlikely to earn an adequate income or from which the Welfare State fails to provide adequate resources when they are unable to work.

Employment, and property holding, are the two key generators

of incomes in our society. It is not surprising therefore that the poor
are those who do not participate in the labour market. Townsend
pointed out that those who are unemployed are not that distinct
from the low paid. People are differentiated into grades at work
according to their experience and expectations of security and
regularity of work. At one extreme are the continuously unemployed. At the other extreme are those with jobs that are almost
totally secure (they may, like university lectures, have 'tenure' that
entitles them to a job until retirement with little prospect of loss of
earnings even in sickness). In between there are a range of jobs that
offer different kinds of security. Some jobs have high risks of
redundancy and unemployment, others are part-time seasonal jobs,
with poor security. These we call the sub-employed – the unemployed, the discontinuously employed, temporary, seasonal and
marginal (part-time) jobs. Some of the problems of unemployment
are shared with some groups of people who have an insecure
foothold in the labour market.

Also, people in work are not divided sharply into the low paid and
the rest. There are fine gradations of pay for different jobs. Any
definition of the cut-off point between low pay and the rest is bound
to be arbitrary. And since people move into and out of employment,
change jobs and experience fluctuations in earnings, those who are
described as the 'low paid' will change from week to week or year to
year. We need to bear these points in mind when considering the
problems of the unemployed, the sub-employed and the low
paid.

1. The Unemployed
In 1955 the average number of unemployed was around 180,000. By
1965 it had climbed to 306,000. And from then on, the numbers
increased, with the number at the peak of each recovery being
higher than the numbers at the peak of each earlier recovery. By
1975, the numbers had jumped to over a million. At the end of
February 1985 the number of unemployed was put at 3,323,676 – an
unemployment rate of 13.7 per cent.

These official figures do not give the full picture of unemployment. They count only those who are registered for work and
eligible to claim benefit. Typically they are likely to exclude people
who are reaching their retirement who have given up all hope of
finding another job. And they exclude women who want to work but

are pessimistic about finding a job. According to the General Household Survey (GHS) between 300,000 and 350,000 people are unemployed who would like to work and are not on the register of those seeking work. The figures also exclude some people who may have decided that claiming unemployment benefit is too degrading to be worth the money it entails.

This number of unemployed are those without work at any one time. It tells us nothing about the length of time they have been unemployed. In January 1980, male workers had been out of work on average for 21 weeks compared with an average of 17 weeks for female workers. In general young workers are likely to have been unemployed for shorter periods than older workers. Males between fifty and fifty-four had been out of work on average for 35 weeks, and females between forty-five and forty-nine for an average of 23 weeks. Lower paid workers are also likely to experience repeated spells of unemployment. A GHS report showed that, while only 4 per cent of professional workers had been unemployed during the previous twelve months, as many as 15 per cent of semi-skilled and unskilled workers experienced unemployment during the previous twelve months. And the semi-skilled and unskilled workers were more likely to have experienced more than one spell of unemployment.

Also, since low-paid workers were more likely to face unemployment, more often and for longer periods, they were also likely to have exhausted their rights to unemployment benefit and to need supplementary benefit. One of the post-war trends has been the number of the unemployed who are wholly dependant on supplementary benefits. And some of the unemployed receive no benefits at all – because their claims have not yet been processed or because they were not eligible for various reasons.

The differentiation of employment security varies sharply with occupational status. According to Townsend's survey, the unskilled account for 9 per cent of the employed male labour force, 17 per cent of the (nine weeks) unemployed, and 39 per cent of the (ten-plus weeks) unemployed. By contrast, professionals or managers (who are as numerous as the unskilled in the labour force) had experienced very low unemployment.

The differing rates of unemployment for different levels of the occupational structure do not necessarily reflect the personal capacities of people to retain any jobs they have. It reflects the sort of handicaps that exist in the occupational structure to obtain and keep more secure higher status occupations.

2. Low Pay

Any definition of low pay is bound to be arbitrary. The trade unions have traditionally considered anyone earning less than two-thirds of the average male manual wage to be amongst the low paid. In April 1982, this would suggest a figure of around £90 a week. The bottom tenth of the population earns between 66.5 and 70.6 per cent of median earnings and has done so between 1886 and 1970. This suggests that low pay is institutionalized. It shows that the system of free collective bargaining has failed to lift the earnings of the low paid. In fact both unions and management are committed to maintaining the differentials between different occupational groups.

The distribution of low pay shows particular patterns. Low pay is heavily concentrated among women. For every low-paid man there are two low-paid women. Many people find themselves low paid at the beginning and end of their working lives, for low pay is a structural problem. It is heavily concentrated among certain industries, regardless of the age, sex or race of the worker. Low-paid jobs for men are concentrated in agriculture (29 per cent), the professional and scientific services (26 per cent), insurance and banking (23 per cent), as well as public administration (20 per cent). Low-paid jobs for women are concentrated in four manufacturing industries, as well as in distribution and service jobs. Almost three-quarters of

Table 8.1. Average earnings of male manual workers over twenty-one

Date	£ (gross)
1977	69.5
1978	78.4
1979	90.1
1980	108.6
1981	118.4
1982	131.4
1983	140.3

Source: New Earnings Survey, 1984.

all women are concentrated in distribution and service jobs. Four-fifths of all women in distribution are in low-paid jobs.

Low-paid jobs tend to be in small firms, and in firms where unionization is low. For instance, workers covered by collective union agreements earn on average 25 per cent more than non-unionized workers (Layard, 1978). Only 15 per cent of the workforce in retailing is currently unionized: the high turnover due to poor conditions makes it difficult to recruit more to the unions (Pond and Winyard, 1983).

Low pay has both a direct and an indirect effect on the numbers of people near the margins of poverty. We have described the direct effect. Indirectly, low pay may influence a person's future life chances. Low pay in the past can cause indebtedness for years to come, it can prevent the accumulation of assets and reduce the capacity of any family or household to cope with future adversities such as sickness or disability.

3. The Elderly

The poverty of the elderly is a problem that has been recognized for over 100 years. It is a characteristic of all industrialized, market economies as well as developed state socialist societies. Half of the poor who receive incomes near SB level are elderly people. The problem is urgent because the proportion of the elderly in the population has recently grown rapidly. Today, the elderly make up about 16 per cent of the population.

The economic circumstances of the elderly have been well documented. A high proportion of them live in subsistence poverty. A government study in 1965 estimated that 14 per cent of all pensioners would have received SB if they had applied for it. The survey also showed that 78 per cent of all retirement pensioners had pensions no more than 25p higher than the flat rate pension. Not all these would have qualified for SB (some were still working). But among these 78 per cent, any savings they had were relatively meagre. What was most likely to make a difference in living standards among the elderly was whether or not they had an occupational pension.

Poverty among the elderly varies with age. The very old are less likely to have occupational pensions. Even if they do, the value of them is likely to have depreciated through inflation. The very old are also most likely to have used up their sources of savings. The government study showed that, while one in five of all pensioners rely exclusively on their retirement pensions plus supplementary benefits, the same is true of one in two of the over-85 year-olds.

Also, in a male-dominated society, the pensions of women are based on the work histories of husbands (that is, earnings insurance record and retirement age). Yet most old people in retirement are women, especially the very old and the very poor. There is a strong social class bias in the financial resources of the elderly. This is the reality of a stratified society. White-collar workers are more likely to be receiving an occupational pension as well as a pension that is based on their last years of earnings. Blue-collar workers are least likely (three in ten as opposed to six in ten of non-manual workers) to be receiving an occupational pension. If they do receive one, it is most likely to be a fixed rate occupational pension that is, on average, worth about a third of the value of occupational pensions for white-collar workers.

Poverty among the elderly is closely tied up with the relative life chances of people in different parts of the occupational structure. Many working class people face the prospect of poverty in old-age, unlike many middle-class people. Few working-class people can save substantial sums during their working lives. Many of them have to be content merely with help from the State when they reach retirement. The economic insecurity of the elderly is such a long-standing feature of our society that many people accept it without question.

4. Single-Parent Families

Single-parent families have almost twice as high a propensity to be in poverty as do two-parent families. Such families include two-fifths of all children living in poverty, although only 8 per cent of all children live in families with one parent. Along with the unem-ployed, this is the fastest growing group of people in poverty. There are now about 850,000 lone parents, bringing up about 1½ million children.

The Townsend study found this group to be one of the poorest in the entire population. Almost 50 per cent of the families and 60 per cent of the children were in, or at the margin of, poverty, compared with 26 per cent of two-parent families (and 34 per cent of children in those families). Even among single parents who work, they are more likely than two-parent families who work to be in low-paid jobs. And one of the critical problems of many one-parent families is the lack of assets of any kind to help them deal with the sudden financial difficulties of single parenthood. Their low incomes have many outcomes. Fewer own their own homes, fewer own the usual consumer durables enjoyed by many families, fewer take a holiday and fewer have an evening out in the course of a fortnight.

Marsden pointed out that these structural economic disadvantages of the one-parent family stem from the condition of the labour market, where the father is regarded as the breadwinner with the mother a subsidiary earner. Men continue to earn, on average, almost twice what women earn. This crucially affects single-parent families (especially women-headed ones). Single parent families have only one parent's (usually the woman's) earnings. And the earning power of single parents (of both sexes) is curtailed by the obligation to look after the children in the family.

Low pay is a significant contributor to poverty among single-parent families. 85 per cent of single-parent families are headed by women. If they do not work, most of their income comes from the State, apart from allowances from absent fathers (which only half receive). The SB system gives little incentive to go out to work. Earnings in addition to SB payments are severely limited by the State. Single-parent mothers have few options apart from complete reliance on the State, or full-time work. If they work full-time, it is difficult to find employment that pays high enough wages to keep them out of poverty. Nevertheless, a higher proportion of single mothers work full-time than do women from two-parent families. And working single mothers often earn less than other women workers. Working single mothers are doubly disadvantaged. Women are more likely to be low paid than men, and single mothers earn lower pay than other women workers.

The plight of the female-headed, single-parent family highlights many of the disadvantages of being a woman in our society. Marsden pointed out that many resources tend to be channelled to families primarily through the employed male of the household. This applies to property and house-ownership, to credit and mortgage facilities, as well as many housing tenancies.

5. The Sick and Disabled
The permanently disabled are a group with a low share of total poverty but with a high risk of being in poverty. Permanent

disability among those under pensionable age is low. The incidence of poverty among the permanently disabled is high. More than half of the families where the household head was permanently disabled, had incomes below 120 per cent of SB levels (Layard, 1980). He found that a third of households headed by permanently disabled men and two-thirds of households headed by permanently disabled single women, were living below the SB level in 1975.

Townsend argued that government surveys of the disabled in Britain have consistently underestimated the scale of disability. He estimated that 12 per cent of the population have a disability that prevented them from doing things normal for people of their age. Official surveys have shown that between 35 and 40 per cent of the disabled were dependant on SB at any time. And the disabled are, on the whole, poorer than the rest of the community. Increasing incapacity is associated with increasing poverty. More than twice as many incapacitated as non-incapacitated disabled live in households below the poverty line.

Disability is highly skewed in class terms. More working-class people, especially the unskilled, are disabled than middle-class people. The same biases are found with respect to illness. The incidence of chronic sickness is three times more prevalent among the unskilled as it is among professionals and managers. And, since the unskilled are less likely to be covered by sick pay schemes, their financial problems are likely to be compounded. Whereas, for some people, sickness ends with the restoration of full health, for others it results in long-term disability.

Disabilities of all sorts restrict access to employment. Employers are less likely both to employ disabled people and to provide them with a reasonable range of jobs. Employment tends to go to those with the best work record. Disability is usually regarded as a poor work record or as an additional risk that an employer is expected to take. And, once at work, disabled people are likely to be undervalued. They are likely to suffer from lower remuneration, reduced responsibility and lower rewards than their able-bodied counterparts.

They also appear to suffer from handicaps in the distribution of resources from the SB. In November 1974, only 27 per cent of sick and disabled people were receiving exceptional-circumstances additions. Other institutions, too, discriminate against the disabled. Access to life insurance, irrespective of the disability, as well as to sources of credit, may be limited. We have already discussed the difficulties faced by families with handicapped dependants. Other family members may have to sacrifice their earning potential in order to look after their disabled relatives.

THE INSTITUTIONALIZATION OF POVERTY

These five groups of people – the unemployed and sub-employed, the low paid, the elderly, single-parent families, and the sick and disabled – are most likely to be poor. They are the people most likely to be excluded from the labour market. If they do work, their jobs are often insecure or they are found near the bottom of the occupational structure. Consequently they are dependant on welfare benefits provided by the State.

But State benefits are distributed unequally. Those eligible for National Insurance benefits in general receive more than those eligible for SB. And National Insurance benefits are related to a person's work record. Those with an intermittent record are likely to lose out when they apply for benefits.

We have seen that welfare benefits tend to be low in relation to average earnings from work. The long-term benefit for a couple plus 30 per cent (to take account of rent and discretionary allowances) was equivalent in 1970 to about 50 per cent of the median net income.

Identifying the groups in society most likely to be poor tells us little about the causes of poverty. We need to look at the structure of the resource systems in our society to determine why such people are poor.

People are poor either because they are unable to earn an adequate income from work, or because the Welfare State fails to provide them with adequate resources when they cannot work.

We began this chapter by asking how some people can be poor in an affluent society such as ours. Poverty cannot simply be measured in terms of the numbers of calories necessary to keep people alive. It involves a degree of personal judgment. People's lives revolve around social realities which are difficult to cost. Poverty is about achieving a standard of living that allows for self-respect. The poor are those who lack the necessary resources to participate fully in society.

The last section described the characteristics of the poor. They have much in common. They all have limited access to the principal resource systems of the society in which they live. We can group these systems into three. They are the labour market with its wage system: the national insurance system and its associated schemes: and the wealth-accumulating system (especially home ownership, life insurance and occupational pension schemes). The resources in each of these systems are distributed unequally.

We argued in the chapter on class that the rewards of the labour market are allocated unequally. The labour market is highly stratified. We like to believe that wage rates are determined by some sort of consensus in society that agrees to semi-skilled workers and lawyers being paid very different rates of remuneration. We tend to forget that these differences are determined by a complex set of institutions which limit access to certain jobs, keeping their rates of pay correspondingly high. As a result of this differential power within the occupational hierarchy, some sections of the population are denied access to work that is well paid, is secure, and offers good fringe benefits.

Looked at from this point of view, the poor are those who are least secure in the labour market. The value attached to any particular job is determined by negotiations between unions, their members and the owners of production. Those in the strongest bargaining position are likely to get the highest price and the greatest security.

Poverty is not just a question of low incomes. It is also a question of having little or no foothold in the labour market. Poverty is about the unequal distribution of security, primarily in the labour market but also in the other resource systems. Those who are denied access to the labour market are faced with a hierarchy of status groupings within the social security system. National insurance benefits are closely tied to a person's work record. The more fragile the work record, the worse are the benefits that get paid. And many people (for example, housewives, and children) are dependant on the work records of other people (husbands and fathers).

Those who are neither part of the workforce nor members of households of that workforce (for example, elderly people, the disabled and the chronically sick and disabled, as well as single-parent families) get incomes from the state that are similar to those of the worst paid in the labour market. Much of any debate on poverty is about what share of national resources should go to those who have no access to the labour market.

It is important to distinguish between the characteristics of the poor and the causes of poverty. People may be poor, not because they are sick or disabled or unemployed. They are poor because the bulk of the resources in our society is distributed through the productive system. The poor are those who are excluded from this system because of their disabilities. In order to understand poverty in our society, we need to ask why it is that such a large proportion of our resources is distributed through the wage system rather than through the systems of state benefit that so many people are dependant on. We need to look at the institutions that control those resources, rather than the personal characteristics of the poor.

QUESTIONS

1. The poor are always with us.
   Discuss this statement in the light of definitions of poverty.
2. To what extent does the social security system alleviate poverty in Britain?
3. Which are the main groups of people in poverty in Britain today?
4. The risk of poverty is not the same as the share of poverty.
   Explain.
5. Poverty is another way of talking about the distribution of security.
   Explain.
6. In what ways is poverty institutionalized?

FURTHER READING

An interesting and provocative paperback is Frank Field's *Inequality in Britain: Freedom, Welfare and the State*, 1981, Fontana.

The classic study is Peter Townsend's *Poverty in the United Kingdom*, 1979, Allen Lane; very large, it brings together an enormous amount of other work on poverty as well as original research.

A useful discussion of the distribution of security is to be found in Westergaard and Resler's *Class in Capitalist Society*, *A Study of Contemporary Britain*, 1975, Pelican Books.

A good introduction to the problem of low pay and statutory minimum wages is Chris Pond and Steve Winyard's *The case of a national minimum wage*, 1983, Low Pay Unit.

Nine

Racial and sexual inequalities

The last three chapters have described class inequalities. This chapter will discuss important inequalities derived, not from a relationship to the productive resources of a country but from personal characteristics, in particular race and gender. We shall limit our discussion to these two although it is clear there are other – such as age or physical or mental – characteristics that are also the sources of inequalities in the distribution of resources.

There is now a considerable body of material documenting the extent of discrimination that certain ethnic minorities and women experience in most industrially-advanced countries (although, as we shall see later, there are still important gaps in our knowledge). Such discrimination is common to all these countries. In each, women and ethnic minorities are *systematically* denied access to important resources available to others in the society. We emphasise the word 'systematically' since popular conceptions of racial and sexual discrimination usually imply that what discrimination there is is due more to the personal prejudice of a few rather than anything more systematic. We hope to show otherwise in this chapter.

Most industrially-developed countries have a minority of other races living and working in their countries. In Britain 7 per cent of the workforce are immigrants: in Luxembourg it is 35 per cent and in Switzerland it is 25 per cent (Thames Television, 1979).

Immigrants are often employed in these countries to do the menial work that no one else wants to do. They usually work in bad conditions, and in jobs that are insecure and badly paid. Few of them are permitted to rise into better jobs, and most of them live in the worst housing available, often in the run-down parts of the inner cities near where they work.

Women too experience a similar form of discrimination in all industrially developed countries. Their foothold in the job market is usually less secure than men's, their earnings lower and they usually find it more difficult than men to be occupationally mobile. Also, some women are denied the access that men have to housing, unless they take it as dependents of men.

Both forms of inequality are as old as the modern class structure (some people argue that sexual inequalities have a much longer history) but it is only recently that both have been seriously documented. Ever since conflict broke out in 1958 and was taken up by the press as a 'problem' governments have had to tackle racial discrimination in order to avert further trouble. Similarly, the position of women has become a political issue as they, too, began to organize to voice their grievances.

Racial conflict was a new phenomenon although the use of immigrants as a source of cheap labour in Britain has a long history. Large numbers of the Irish, Jews, Poles, Ukranians and Cypriots as well as smaller numbers of Italians, Greeks, Spaniards, Maltese and Chinese all arrived in Britain at one time or another. Usually they managed to achieve some sort of acceptance without much apparent difficulty. But things began to change in the 1950s. Britain turned to its former colonies to meet its labour shortages. London Transport trained drivers and conductors from the West Indies; the Health Service advertized for doctors and nurses in the West Indies as well as India and Pakistan; hotels recruited in Barbados; and other private firms began recruitment drives in New Commonwealth countries.

For convenience of language in this chapter immigrants from African, Caribbean and Asian countries and British people of similar origin are referred to as 'black people'.

Black labour was cheap. Many of the immigrants who first arrived came without their families and could be housed cheaply in hostels. But as some began to settle, they sent for their families to join them and required decent housing as well as education and health facilities. Their demand on these services coincided with the beginning of a recession and made conflict inevitable as they competed for these resources with the existing white population.

Opinions varied as to what exactly was the problem. Some people argued that the immigrants themselves were the cause of the trouble: they regarded black people as inferior, who could never be expected to integrate successfully into a white society. Other people argued that the rate of immigration was the key problem. Britain was a small country and could only assimilate black people successfully if their numbers were carefully controlled.

Whatever the causes, the facts of discrimination against black people are undeniable. A spate of reports since the 1960s has documented the widespread racial inequalities that exist. This discrimination exists despite its proscription by law since the 1968 Race Relations Act outlawing it in employment, housing and the provision of goods and services. The life chances of black people, too, are measurably inferior to white people's. Racial inequalities, in the words of one report (Smith, 1977) range from the substantial to the massive. Another report (Deakin, 1970) argued that the pattern of discrimination against black workers in industry was so widespread and pervasive that an innocent stranger could be forgiven for thinking that it was the result of a central directive, enthusiastically implemented, ordering that the employment of black people be restricted. This state of affairs has persisted with only minor changes, despite its widespread documentation.

In this chapter, we shall outline the broad patterns of racial inequalities in employment and housing: the subject is too big to give a more comprehensive picture. We shall follow this by a similar picture of sexual inequalities before going on to ask what the similarities are between the two forms of discrimination and how it is they persist in spite of the avowed commitment of most governments to eliminate them.

RACIAL DISCRIMINATION IN EMPLOYMENT

Black people have an inferior position in the job market to white people: it is a position that is remarkably stable over time. There are three major characteristics to this inferior position. Although they are found in all parts of the job market, black people tend to be concentrated in particular industries and occupations; they have jobs of a lower social status than white people's jobs; and their position in the labour market is less secure.

Their concentration in a small range of industries is striking. They are more likely to be found in the industries that are declining, where conditions are poor and the wages bad. 47 per cent of black people (compared with 33 per cent of white people) work in manufacturing. While they came in the first place to fill jobs in industries where labour was scarce, they have tended to remain in these jobs even though many of the industries are now in decline.

Within manufacturing, they are over-represented in shipbuilding, vehicle manufacture, textiles and 'other manufacturing industries'. They are particularly concentrated in certain industries. In brick manufacturing, 45 per cent of the hourly paid workers are immigrants. A third of the hourly paid workforce of one large motor manufacturers are black workers. They are concentrated in this way because primarily they do the jobs that white people find unattractive.

They are more likely to be employed directly on the production lines (or in similar work) and less likely to get jobs in manufacturing firms as maintenance workers. They are also more likely to work on shifts, particularly the night shift. A high proportion of black workers are employed permanently on night work. The industries where they are concentrated all have bad conditions in some way. In foundries the work is heavy, hot and dirty; in rubber and plastics it is smelly and hot; in food manufacturing it is low-paid shift work; and in textiles the work is often seasonal, with poor conditions, often night work and badly paid.

Fewer black people are found in the service sector. Those that are work in the low-paid services – transport, communications and professional and scientific services. In transport, the jobs may require split shifts, offer low basic earnings and require unsocial hours. In communications a high proportion of the jobs are unskilled or semi-skilled. The professional and scientific services include many low grade clerical jobs for women. In the health service, a third of the hospital medical staff and a fifth of doctors, student nurses and midwives are black people. Also, a quarter of the workers nationally and a half in Greater London working in restaurants, cafés and snack bars are people born overseas.

Those in manual work find it difficult to get promoted to anything better. When they are offered 'promotion', it tends to be more agreeable work but with a similar status. Few black workers get promoted to jobs that might require them to supervise white workers. One study found that almost twice as many whites as blacks were offered promotion.

The pattern of their employment still reflects the opportunities they had when they first arrived in Britain. They tended to take jobs requiring few skills, that were badly paid, often with unsociable hours and poor work conditions. These were the jobs that others did not want. But they have remained in these jobs even though the employment market has changed and there are now more skilled and better jobs than there were when they first arrived. Black people are stuck in these inferior jobs. According to the 1971 Census, the proportion of black people who have risen to become administrators or managers, or clerical and sales workers is well below the national average.

It is easy to understand the initial disadvantages that all immigrant groups may face in the labour market. Any language difficulties they had on arrival, as well as cultural differences, together with qualifications that British employers did not accept, may all have limited their job opportunities. But it is more than this. The studies of the job market, carried out by PEP, indicate that more than half the firms investigated, practised some form of discrimination against black people. Black people experience considerable difficulty in moving out of the jobs they are in, to something better.

One study found that black applicants in the civil service were considerably less successful than white applicants in both getting jobs and being promoted. More blacks than whites were rejected for the first interview even though they possessed similar minimum qualifications. And, out of a sample of clerical officers, more black people were over-qualified for their current jobs.

Rex (1973) argued that there is a barrier that operates in certain industries and plants as well as in certain occupations and skill levels, making it difficult for black people to move into the jobs usually regarded as jobs for white people. This is true of a large number of jobs at all but the bottom of the job market. Even in unskilled jobs, the PEP study (1977) found that 30 per cent of Indian and West Indian applicants failed to get the jobs because of their colour. The study showed that a black person generally had to make twice as many applications as a white person to finally get a job.

Employers either did not take on blacks at all or, if they did, they reserved the worst jobs for them. Thirty-seven out of 150 firms investigated by PEP refused in principle to employ black, or took them on only if they could not find suitable white people. At plant level, employers who refused to take on black workers were afraid of the possible objections they thought their white workers would make. Many appeared to have mistaken stereotypes about the actual abilities of black workers. The barrier against employing black workers was particularly strong in jobs that involved contact with the public, such as sales and clerical jobs.

The barrier has a cumulative effect for black workers. The process goes as follows. Black people tend to avoid any direct experience of discrimination by applying only to firms known to employ black workers. As they do that, white workers tend to react by moving to other firms. Thus a factory known to take on black workers tends to attract more and it 'tips' to become an all-black factory. This results in some factories employing no blacks at all and others employing nearly all black workers.

The frontier limiting black employment varied: in times of growth black workers get more opportunities. When times are bad, white workers try to restrict the employment of black workers. As unemployment has risen, black immigrants have suffered higher than average rates of unemployment. Department of Employment statistics show that, between 1979 and 1980, registered unemployment among black workers rose by 11.6 per cent compared with a rise of 2.5 per cent for the total workforce. Between November 1973 and February 1980 total unemployment doubled, whereas registered unemployment among black people quadrupled. The 1971 Census showed that almost half of unemployed West Indians were not registered as unemployed, reflecting the widespread disenchantment with the kinds of jobs that were likely to be offered when seeking work. It appears that, in times of unemployment black workers are the first group to experience difficulties in finding work.

The higher rates of unemployment among black workers are not wholly due to discrimination. Their reliance on certain industries, often the ones in decline, as well as the personal disadvantages that newly arrived immigrants face both exacerbate their vulnerability. Unemployment is currently high among young people and this is reflected in the rate among the young black workforce. Black unemployment has been higher than the white rate for the last fifteen years. The incidence of discrimination in employment and the concentration of black workers in insecure jobs account for much of this.

Both blacks and whites have improved their position in the labour market without apparently having come closer together. The gap between the socio-economic status of black and white workers is still wide. A recent study of discrimination against West Indians and Asians in Nottingham (CRE, 1980) found higher levels of discrimination in 1977–1979 than in earlier studies. Certainly the evidence there is pointing to any steady improvement in their position in the job market, is very slight. The pattern of discrimination in employment is very stable, indicating that ethnic minorities are locked in a set of adverse social and economic relationships from which it is very difficult to escape.

RACIAL DISCRIMINATION IN HOUSING

Black people have tended to settle in parts of Britain where other earlier immigrants settled, in areas where there was a demand for labour. They are heavily concentrated in the large conurbations, particularly London and the South-east as well as the Midlands. Smaller concentrations are found centred on the textile industry in Yorkshire as well as in the North-west.

The position of black people in the housing market cannot be separated from their economic roles. Jobs were available in those areas (especially London, the South-east and the Midlands) when housing was in short supply. The disadvantages that they suffer in the housing market are not simply a matter of discrimination. They tend to live in the over-crowded areas of inner cities, in low cost, poor quality housing. According to Glass (1954), immigrants tended to settle in patches of inner London that were neglected or already in the process of decay and social downgrading. They could not afford to do otherwise. This put them in direct competition with other disadvantaged groups whose access to better housing was limited – the poor, the elderly, incomplete families and others who were trapped in the twilight zones.

Black people suffer the disadvantage that they are highly visible. The areas where they live can be easily identified. The possibility that certain areas may be given over to black 'ghettos' has always been a theme of race and immigration debate. This concentration may be produced by market forces limiting the access of black people to certain areas. Nevertheless it is inaccurate to describe any part of Britain as a ghetto. In spite of what many people believe the proportion of black people in any neighbourhood is still very low compared with the rates of concentration in the United States.

Black people have steadily improved their position in the housing market. The early reports on racial inequalities described a number of ways in which immigrants were excluded from certain parts of the housing market. The Milner Holland report (1965) on housing in London showed that ethnic minorities, unable to get local authority housing, were obliged to buy expensive property in poor condition or to live as furnished tenants in equally poor accommodation. The first PEP report (Daniel, 1968) described widespread discrimination by private landlords, accommodation bureaus, estate agents and local authorities. Cullingworth (1969) described how immigrants were largely excluded from public housing and Greve (1964) argued that immigrants were vulnerable to the power of landlords to make them homeless. What improvement there was in their access to better housing at the time was little more than a palliative.

But by 1975 there were signs of improvements. The second PEP study (Smith 1977) showed that overt racial discrimination in rented accommodation and house purchase had decreased and the discrimination that operated in the public sector was de facto rather than intentional. While the situation has improved, it is still true to say that black immigrants live in the worst housing conditions. The quality of their housing is noticeably poorer in all sectors of the housing market including the public sector.

The most striking difference between the pattern of housing among immigrants and the indigenous population is the disparity in the relationship between tenure and socio-economic status. Within the general population, owner-occupation is of course far more common among the higher than the lower socio-economic groups. For example, 77 per cent of professional or managerial households own their own housing, compared with 20 per cent of unskilled manual households. Council housing is far more common among the lower than the higher socio-economic groups. Only 9 per cent of professional or managerial households are council tenants compared with 56 per cent of unskilled manual households.

We would expect to find a high proportion of immigrants in council accommodation since they are concentrated among the lower socio-economic groups. Not only is this not so, but the relationship between tenure and social status is the reverse of that for the rest of the population.

This pattern is most striking among Asians. The rate of owner-occupation rises as social status falls. 58 per cent of professional and managerial Asian households own their houses whereas the rate for unskilled Asian households is 85 per cent. Also, the proportion of Asian households in council accommodation does not vary with socio-economic status. And the proportion of Asians in private rented accommodation is higher among non-manual than among manual households.

Among West Indians the relationship between tenure and socio-economic status is similar to that for Asians except that there are more West Indians in council accommodation. Nevertheless the level of council tenancies among West Indians is much lower than one would expect, given that they are more heavily concentrated among social status groups where council tenancies are usually high. In fact the proportion of West Indians in the council stock is constant for all social status groups at between 20 and 30 per cent.

The level of owner-occupation among West Indians is markedly lower than it is among Asians although a higher proportion of manual workers (of all skill levels) own their housing than among the general population. And it is lower among West Indian non-manual families than it is for the general population. Yet West Indians' level of owner-occupation is surprisingly high, considering their low social status, their low earnings and the fact that so many of them arrived in this country fairly recently and with meagre resources.

These paradoxes become intelligible when we realize that owner-occupation is not synonymous with good quality housing. Asians tend to buy their own homes even if they are poor. For Asians, buying a home is a way of obtaining housing cheaply but the housing they own tends to be of markedly lower quality than that of the rest of the population.

It is also a way of finding housing more suited to their needs (in size and location). Many, particularly those newly arrived who may not speak English, need to live close to other Asians and this usually entails living either in the low-grade rented sector (in the short-term) or buying low-grade housing that is located centrally. Good quality housing for purchase is likely to be too expensive and too far away from other Asians in suburban areas. Suburban housing is likely to be attractive only to the wealthier and more westernized middle-class Asian families. Council accommodation, too, is unsuited to their needs since it is often too small and away from other Asian settlements.

The quality of housing occupied by West Indians and Asians, whether judged by structural measures, the sharing of dwellings, density of occupation or lack of basic amenities, is consistently lower than it is among the general population. It is particularly low among Asians (and lowest of all among Pakistanis) even though this is true for all tenures. It is substantially lower in the public sector. In the private rented sector, the quality is so bad that one report regarded the conditions black tenants had to live in as intolerable. Also, a minority of immigrants live in housing which they own and which is of a poorer quality than the worst housing found in the public sector.

In spite of their greater housing need, Asians and West Indians have penetrated less into the council-owned sector than white people. Even when they do get allocated housing in the public sector, the accommodation they get allocated is usually of inferior quality. A report by the Runnymede Trust (1975) shows that not only were black people underrepresented in council housing, but also black tenants of the GLC were far more likely to be living in pre-war flats in central London whereas white tenants were more likely to be found on the newer cottage estates. The study also found widespread evidence of racial discrimination in the allocation of council dwellings. This was surprising. The GLC had always maintained that it had a policy of equal opportunity in housing, based on clearly defined criteria of housing need. Because of this the Council commissioned its own study. The results (Parker and Dugmore, 1976) were consistent with those produced by the Runnymede Trust. The study assigned eight grades of housing quality to the housing stock (based on the age, type and modernization of dwellings). It found that white tenants tended to get allocated more good quality lettings (mainly houses and post-1964 flats) whereas black tenants got allocated a preponderance of the poorer quality lettings (particularly inter-war and pre-1919 unmodernized flats). Whereas roughly 1,200 out of 8,000 white applicants were given older properties (15 per cent), over 50 per cent of black applicants were given similar. And while the majority of both groups lived in inner city areas before rehousing, white families showed a greater propensity to leave for the suburbs. After rehousing over 70 per cent of black families ended up living in four inner London boroughs.

On the face of it this was not surprising. In fact more black than white families were allocated to the areas of their first choice. But their choices appeared inconsistent and, after rehousing, many ended up dissatisfied with where they were living. On further investigation it appeared that their choices were strongly influenced by housing officials. The study also found that the allocation procedures (especially the way competing needs were given priority) tended to work to the disadvantage of other groups in a low bargaining position. This was particularly so for homeless people of all races. Nevertheless black applicants did relatively worse among all priority groups and especially when they were in the top priority groups (which at the time was rehousing from re-development areas).

Racial discrimination was found in other local authorities (Smith and Whalley, 1975). The London borough of Islington, in a study of the allocation of new properties, found that UK and Irish nationals got 64 per cent of new properties whereas black applicants got only 30 per cent (Taper, 1977).

Locating the source of this kind of discrimination is difficult. Two key elements are choice and discretion. Council housing is allocated in a number of ways according to different levels of priority. Local authorities now own and manage a wide range of properties ranging from near slums to highly desirable houses with gardens. Many reports have pointed out that housing managers tend to develop their own interests in protecting their good properties, ensuring that only carefully chosen tenants (that is, ones that pose no risk of damaging the properties) get the best housing. This means that they offer the better placed tenants a wider range of choices. Tenants who are less well regarded may well get no choice at all. One person's choice is another person's constraint! But discrimination is likely to occur in any system that gives those making decisions any discretion in exercising judgments. Their discretion allows them to favour (often inadvertently) those they regard as nice people. It can mean that they are somewhat more helpful than they need be and that may well increase the effective choice of the person so helped.

Just as in the field of employment, black people are obliged to accept the jobs that white people refuse, so in the field of housing black people are usually obliged to accept housing of a standard and in a location no longer valued by white people. Not only is their choice of alternatives more limited: they may at times experience deliberate attempts to prevent their getting housing for which they are eligible, simply because white people also want it.

One approach towards ensuring that black people get their fair share of good quality council housing has been to set a target for allocating more desirable properties to black people. Lambeth borough announced in 1979 that a target of 30 per cent of all new and modernized properties should go to black people on their waiting lists.

The extent of discrimination against black people in the public housing sector is now well known. The effect of this information, in terms of changes in the allocation procedures, remains to be seen.

SEXUAL DISCRIMINATION IN EMPLOYMENT

The discrimination that woman face in the employment market differs from the discrimination that confronts black people. There are, of course, many more women who work. Traditionally, their position has differed from men's position at work. It is inferior, not merely through direct discrimination but also because their responsibilities within the home handicap their opportunities at work. 62 per cent of women who now work are married, many of them with young children. Employers usually expect women to make their own arrangements for dealing with their family commitments. As a result, women are usually found doing routine, low-skilled work often in part-time jobs which they can fit in with their other commitments.

They tend to be concentrated in certain industries and occupations: their social status is low and the jobs they do are poorly paid: and their position in the job market is less secure than the position of men. Certain forms of the discrimination they suffer is similar to those experienced by racial minorities, but their position is distinct.

Women are highly concentrated in certain industries. More than half of employed women in Britain work in three service industries: the distributive trades (shops, mail order and warehouses); professional and scientific (typists, secretaries, teachers and nurses); and miscellaneous services (laundries, catering, dry cleaning and launderettes). A further quarter are employed in manufacturing industries. Half of these are found in four industries – food, drink and tobacco; clothing and footwear; electrical engineering; and textiles.

Much of their work is badly paid. Department of Employment figures show that in April 1981 average gross weekly earnings for women were £91, compared with £140 for men. This is so because women at each social status level are concentrated in the poorer paid, the less skilled and the auxillary occupations. Even within the same occupations, women still get paid less than men.

Occupationally, women are more likely to be concentrated in semi-skilled jobs (while men are more likely to be in skilled jobs) carrying out routine tasks on production lines, or they are likely to be found in the lower skilled jobs in non-manual work (as shop assistants, typists, punch card operators, as well as teaching, nursing and social work) while men are more likely to hold managerial and supervisory jobs.

An important reason for this is that women are the victims of handicaps associated with their sex. Married working-class women have often taken work of some kind, because they needed to, when and where they could. It has to fit in with their family commitments and needs to supplement the family income. Often, it will be part-time work or work outside normal working hours, and will be located near their homes. Their work will require little or no training since they have neither the time or the money to spare for such luxuries. These factors neatly add up to the main components of a low paid job.

One of the reasons women are in badly paid work is that the jobs they have are less likely to be unionized. Many of them are regulated by wages councils. One-tenth of the labour force is covered by wages councils, but a quarter of all women work in such jobs. This includes hotel and catering, retail and distribution, the clothing trades, as well as hairdressing and laundry work. Jobs covered by wages councils are among the lowest paid of all jobs.

In any case, it is easy for employers to pay less than the minimum statutory rates of pay laid down by wages councils. In 1975 the Department of Employment found that 30 per cent of firms visited by the wages inspectorate were paying less than the minimum rates. Failure to pay the minimum incurs a fine of up to £100. The hotel and catering industry is a good example of the difficulties that women workers face. The industry employs 11 per cent of all women workers and is popular for a number of reasons. There is a lot of part-time work, the work is similar to housework and requires no further training. But 90 per cent of the women employed in the industry earn less than the TUC minimum wage.

About one in every two married women work part-time; work which is closely linked with low pay. A survey by the Low Pay Unit (1978) showed that three-quarters of part-time working women earned rates of pay less than the amount for which full-time employees would qualify for family income supplements. Part-time work is on the increase. Department of Employment forecasts predict that it will increase rapidly. It is a vital feature of the British economy as in all industrially developed countries. In fact the proportion of part-time workers is higher in Britain than in other advanced countries.

It is particularly in part-time work that women are exploited. They are a captive labour force and are not in a position to bargain with employers for better conditions. The International Labour Organization pointed out that part-time work enables employers to refuse vocational training for women and masks unemployment, since part-timers are often regarded as fully employed. In 1973, the OPCS found that women part-timers were eligible for promotion in less than a fifth of the firms surveyed, and had training opportunities in only a quarter. Part-time workers are also likely to lose out on work-related benefits such as sickness and pensions schemes. Part-time work is largely undemanding, ill-paid, and of low social status with no prospects of advancement.

Many of those who work part-time are obliged to work longer hours than they wish and often at times that are inconvenient to them. Mackie and Patullo (1977) pointed out that most managers have only a hazy idea of what family responsibilities their women employees had. 'Too often a firm will announce that it has a shift system to suit women workers without being aware that one end of the shift is as inconvenient for the workforce as any nine-to-five day'.

Employers are not only ignorant of women's particular needs; they often hold discriminatory stereotypes of women. A survey (Hunt, 1978) found that a third of managers believed women were not career conscious: half thought that women belonged at home or regarded them as inferior employees.

Compared with men, women have far fewer chances of occupa-tional mobility. This is due primarily to the enormous concentration of women's jobs at two points in the occupational structure – in semi-skilled manual and lower white-collar work. Women are likely both to get promoted less often than men are and to do less well than men from the same class background. Neither of these sources of inequality is surprising. Few of the women concentrated on production lines in factories are likely to make it to a supervisory job, especially if they would be required to supervise men as well as women. And few women employed as office workers are ever likely to reach the higher echelons of their organizations.

SEXUAL DISCRIMINATION IN HOUSING

The extent to which women are discriminated against in the housing market is not clear. There are few studies of women's access to housing. The law is clear: the 1975 Sex Discrimination Act outlawed discrimination against women in the housing market, in the terms on which housing is offered to them, by refusing their application for housing, or in the way they are treated in relation to men in need of housing. Yet it is not known how often this part of the Act is broken. The lack of information is itself a reflection of the kind of disadvantage that women face in the housing market. Access to housing, independent of men, is not as yet regarded as an important right for women by the organizations that distribute housing resources.

It is ironic that 'a woman's place is in the home' sums up the traditional view about women. Yet any rights they might have to housing is ignored. In spite of many improvements in a woman's legal position in society, women are still regarded as legally dependent on men in certain fields and this still applies to housing rights.

Housing policy is generally based on the notion of the household. With this notion comes certain assumptions. Households are usually assumed to be a collection of people with a household head (usually a husband or a father), typically the nuclear family. Yet many households do not fit this model. About a third of all households are not even nuclear families. And little information exists about the composition of households that are not nuclear families. Men are usually assumed to be the head of any household, even in those where a woman earns more than any man, and could be regarded as the chief breadwinner.

Women's housing needs are fitted into this context. They are assumed to have a different position in any household from the position held by men. Their position in the housing market is still affected by this. Since they are not regarded as household heads, they are assumed not to have housing needs in their own right.

A woman's access to housing is usually determined through her relationship with a man or her housing need is determined in the context of a family. Women who are not part of any nuclear family are usually regarded as living in a state of transition towards such a goal. And their claims for housing will usually be assessed in the light of this. This is true for single women whose future intentions about marriage or family life are not yet clear, women who are experiencing marital breakdown and the dissolution of the family home, and widowed women with insufficient resources to pay off any outstanding debt on their homes.

The facts of a woman's needs for housing differ from these assumptions for a large number of women. One-third of all households are not nuclear families and the majority of these have either not yet had children or no longer have dependent children living with them. Most women do marry at some stage in their lives but at any point in time substantial numbers of them are not married. In 1976, for example, of those aged fifteen to forty-four most were single and of those over forty-five the majority were widowed or divorced. And roughly one in eight of all families have only one parent at any given time, the majority of them women. Many more families now break up at some stage. According to the Family Formation Study (1976) one-tenth of the women who had married between 1966 and 1970 had separated within five years. Of the women who had married between 1966 and 1970 and later separated, just over a half had formed new unions within six years. Of these, two-thirds were legal marriages and one-third were cohabiting. Yet women's housing needs during this period of transition are only recognized if they have young children to care for.

The nub of their disadvantage in the housing market is their assumed dependence of men, even for those that choose to be independent. Some women of course are advantaged through their dependence. Many widows may now be living in housing that is in excess of their housing needs, since they live in houses that were acquired and paid for when their families were still intact.

The extent of disadvantage that women experience in housing varies between the two major sectors. A woman's inferior bargaining position is of particular relevance in the owner-occupied sector. This sector now houses 51.5 per cent of the population of whom 28.5 per cent are buying their houses with mortgages (CSO, 1979). Women tend to earn less than men (women's wages in 1979 were 73.5 per cent of men's) and they tend to be employed in less stable areas of employment. Traditionally, because of a woman's inferior purchasing power, building societies were reluctant to grant mortgages to women on their own, since they were regarded as a bad risk on the grounds of their current and future earnings. Building societies still tend to take the view that women are on their own only until they find a man to support them. Also, one study found that 36 per cent of building societies discriminated in some way against a couple with a higher earning wife (EOC, 1978). Another study (Todd and Jones, 1972) found that, of married couples who owned their homes in 1972, 42 per cent had the home in the husband's name, only 5 per cent in the wife's name and the rest were joint owners.

Divorced women are particularly apt to suffer in the owner-occupied sector. On divorce a woman may apply for a property transfer but there are problems. Courts usually allow a woman one-third of her husband's joint income and capital. In practice this means that a woman who is awarded the family home will find her maintenance reduced. A woman whose family home gets sold will probably end up with insufficient capital to buy another. Women who get the family home often find it difficult to maintain mortage repayments. They will need either to depend on supplementary benefit to pay the interest on the outstanding debt (thereby shifting their economic dependence from a husband to the state) or to find a sufficiently well-paid job to be able to afford the repayments (which is less likely for a woman than a man).

The private housing market thus reinforces women's economic dependence on men within the family and their primary role as wives and mothers. The state offers only minimal support in the repayment of interest charges on mortgages once the marriage relationship has broken down. In general women are likely to find that owner-occupation is too expensive, (not only in terms of the initial and ongoing payments but also the costs of upkeep) for them to purchase easily, bearing in mind their inferior income levels. The notion that owner-occupation offers greater control over one's housing is often a myth for women whose marriages have broken down.

It is often argued that women have greater access to housing than men in the public sector. While it is true that more women than men have tenancies in their own names, Austerberry and Watson (1981) argue that the allocations they receive in the public sector are often inferior to those given to others. Women are given council housing only as mothers: the state provides housing for children and hence for whoever is caring for them. Women also outnumber men in the public sector among the elderly simply because women live longer.

In fact women on their own with children may often be penalized by local authorities. They are most likely to be allocated housing through being homeless or through allocations from the waiting list. If they are homeless they need to prove that they are not intentionally so. Also they tend to be in desperate need at such a time with little bargaining power and are often offered the worst available properties. Even if they obtain housing through the waiting list the system discriminates against them since they lose points compared with two-parent families (Finer, 1974) and they may be expected to share a bedroom with a child. Similarly they are frequently placed in the worst housing since some officials tend to assume that single parents are likely to be unsatisfactory tenants.

Housing in the private rented sector is now in such short supply that, as Austerberry and Watson argue, women are unlikely to be able to afford what decent rented housing is available. Housing associations and co-operatives have more flexible policies and both tend to house people with 'special needs', that is people who cannot be housed within the nuclear family. Housing associations have been important in providing some people with opportunities to live collectively as an alternative to the nuclear family. But the sector is still very small compared with the other sectors and the economic climate makes it doubtful that it will expand much in the future.

Housing policy and building society caution operates in ways that reinforce the nuclear family. The majority of housing is provided for this group. People who wish or need to live outside a nuclear family and notably women whose marriages have broken down, are likely to be discriminated against.

RACISM AND SEXISM

This brief summary of the inequalities that black people and women face in their position in the productive system as well as their roles as consumers of housing resources, suggests that they have much in common.

In the field of employment, there are at least six similarities. Both groups are concentrated in particular sectors of the economy; both experience lower rates of pay than the average; both are required to do work that is unattractive to other workers; both are likely to face barriers to improvements; both lose out with respect to training opportunities; and both are employed for lower social costs than it takes to employ others.

This implies that employers regard both groups as second best labour, useful in certain times or under certain conditions. They are usually taken on as a source of cheap labour to be used when the economy has labour shortages or to carry out work where the profit margins are lower. Both can easily be dispensed with in times of labour surpluses (in bad times, there is usually a call for black people to be repatriated back from where they came and women back to full-time housework).

Black people and women both face discrimination in spite of the avowed intention by the State to outlaw it. The legislation in both cases has little bite; discrimination is assumed not to exist until proven (rather than the other way round which fits the facts more accurately); it has to be fought for on an individual basis (instead of successful cases being applied to all similar instances); and both sets of legislation ignore the initial handicaps each group faces (black people in the educational system, and women in their private relationships with men) in competing for equal opportunities.

The inequalities that both groups face in their position in the productive system handicaps them when they compete with others in the field of consumption. We have outlined the ways this applies in housing but the same is true of other areas – health, credit, education, etc. The summation of these handicaps go to make up inferior life chances for both groups compared with their white or male counterparts. The only edge that women have in their opportunities compared with men is that they live longer!

CONCLUSIONS

These similarities are not merely coincidental. They arise from the supremacy of white people and men in the productive system, in positions where they are entrenched, supported by the institutions of society – trade unions, legal arrangements, and the plethora of other organizations that support the power of white male society.

For sexism and racism to persist, the establishment merely has to sit tight and do nothing. If things were to be changed, those who benefit from the present arrangements would end up losing out substantially. One person's privilege is another person's discrimination. Privilege exists only at the expense of those who lose out.

When we say that black people and women are exploited, it means simply that the productive system gets what profit it can out of them without doing anything to change things. The exploitation is similar to the class exploitation described in Chapter 6. Racism and sexism are similar to social class. All three are systems of inequality: resources are distributed unequally according to a person's relation to the productive system or to a person's race or gender. All three systems persist over time because the institutions that regulate different aspects of society all uphold or take for granted these inequalities. To challenge this would be to promote revolution!

QUESTIONS

1. Describe and account for the employment characteristics of ethnic minority groups in this country.
2. Describe and account for the housing situation of ethnic minorities in Britain.
3. A woman's place is in the home.
   In what ways has this disadvantaged her in the acquisition of housing?
4. The backbone of the class structure, and indeed of the entire reward system of modern western society, is the occupational order. (Parkin)
   How useful is it to regard occupation as the basic economic inequality?
5. Women's equality at work depends on the commitment of the state to intervening in the private relationships between men and women. Explain why you agree or disagree.
6. Legal discrimination against women has virtually disappeared, yet the Women's Movement seems to articulate increasing grievances. Examine the extent to which women still suffer inequalities.
7. Racism is merely a matter of the prejudices of a small and articulate minority. Discuss.
8. In what ways, if any, are women the weaker sex?

FURTHER READING

An excellent introduction to race issues is Moore, R., *Racism and Black Resistance in Britain*, Pluto press, 1975.

A good introduction to issues about women's employment is Mackie, L. and Pattullo, P., *Women at Work*, Tavistock, 1977.

Ten

Deviants in an unequal society

We conclude our review of social inequalities with a discussion of deviance. It may seem strange to include such a chapter in this context. What is the connection between deviance and inequalities? Is it that people at the bottom of the social structure are more prone to committing deviant acts than those higher up? Is it, rather, that they get caught more easily? Or is it that those with the power to make the rules governing society also ensure that people at the bottom get defined as deviants?

One thing is clear: if inequalities are as pervasive as the evidence in the last few chapters suggests, then we cannot assume that justice is given to all equally. The legal processes, applied in such an unequal society as Britain, may well be distorted by the institutions that maintain such inequalities. One obvious way is that the wealthy and most powerful sections of society have access to the best lawyers should they ever need to use them.

When people ordinarily think about deviance they usually focus on those committing deviant acts. They assume that there are particular kinds of people most likely to break the law and do the other misdemeanours that deviants are supposed to carry out. One stereotype is that deviants are often aggressive young men, from a working-class or socially-deprived background, as often as not black young men, and that they indulge in such activities as shop-lifting, taking (cars) and driving away, mugging old ladies or committing other petty crimes. We can add to this stereotype an assumption of trouble at school, and conflict with parents.

Such a stereotype is not easy to verify. Our concern in this chapter is to suggest that a simple answer is that such people get caught more easily than others and to look for some of the reasons why this may be so. We can then use this argument to think more critically about some of the popular beliefs about deviancy in general.

Terms such as drug abuser, glue sniffer, juvenile delinquent, problem family, inadequate mother, alcoholic, rent defaulter, and vandal, all focus on the individual and presuppose that such individuals have particular definable qualities that differ from the rest of society, setting them apart as subjects for scientific study. This view is known as the positivist approach to deviance.

POSITIVISM

This approach concentrates on the search for causes or personal motivations. It is based on the notion of choice: people are assumed to be free to indulge in deviancy or not, as they wish. Social scientists have traditionally adopted this view and applied three assumptions, borrowed from the physical sciences.

First, just as any physical substance can be measured, its properties catalogued and any changes noted, when the substance is subjected to treatment, so this has been applied to deviants. Criminals, alcoholics, mental patients and people living on low incomes have been treated in this way. Deviant acts have been quantified without much regard to the ambiguities involved. The statistics have then been taken at face value. Hence crime has been defined using criminal statistics, juvenile delinquency has been researched, using the data derived from organizations that treat delinquents. Such an approach has to ignore the possibility of definitions of deviance changing over time. Thus, the apparent recent rise in the incidence of mugging or crimes associated with black youth have been treated by positivists at face value as an absolute increase in these forms of deviance.

Second, the positivist approach assumes that any truly scientific explanation of deviance can be found only by focussing on the persons committing deviant acts and ascertaining as objectively as possible in what ways they differ from the rest of the population. The task of the social scientist is then to isolate these differences and ascertain which are necessary and sufficient to explain the deviance. For instance, various attempts have been made to find the ways in which criminals differ crucially from the rest of the population. The variables used have ranged from genetic differences, the early upbringing of criminals, traumatic incidents in childhood, aspects of social deprivation, disfunctional aspects of socialization or intelligence. In spite of the enormous amount of time and resources devoted to this work, the results have so far been disappointing. Very little has been found that clearly discriminates between deviant and non-deviant populations.

Third, the approach assumes that people are bound by immutable laws of behaviour. Once we know what are the variables that distinguish the deviants from the rest of the population, we can then assume that all who possess those attributes will commit deviant acts in the future. As Matza (1969) points out, this often explains too much deviance. Many people who have the necessary attributes do not in fact commit the deviant acts expected of them. The approach also assumes that people's behavioural patterns can be measured without their changing at all.

A social theory of deviance must attempt to deal with people who move (Taylor et al., 1973).

We can easily pick holes in this approach. We have merely to think about a person involved in a car accident or a person who commits suicide, to realize that most events are often quite ambiguous, involving a number of interpretations about what exactly happened. Also, we know that the detection rate for crimes committed is very low. People who are apprehended and incarcerated are few in comparison with the general incidence of crime. We cannot assume that those caught bear much relationship with the wider population of people who commit crimes. Also laws change. Acts defined as criminal at one time can be decriminalized. Furthermore, we know that the police exercise a great deal of discretion in the ways they identify certain forms of deviance. Acts such as delinquency are open to many, different interpretations as we shall see later.

Nevertheless this view of deviance is still widely held and has many attractions. It conveniently ignores a number of difficult issues and focusses instead on the victim. Take the example of drug abuse. Traditionally this is defined as the illicit use of drugs such as heroin, cocaine, LSD or marijuana. But drug use is very widespread in our society. Valium, librium, morphine and many others are prescribed everyday by doctors. Some people would want to argue that these drugs are also abused. They are used to make people docile or to enable people to function in their current situations without thinking much about how acceptable those situations are.

Critics of such practices might want to argue that the drug abusers are those corporations who stand to make enormous profits out of the drug industry, that the illnesses for which such drugs are prescribed ought to be investigated more seriously since they indicate some of the stresses and strains people are expected to put up with in society. Thus, which type of drug one includes in one's notion of drug abuse depends on one's view of society. It is easy to see that the conventional definitions of drug abuse are ones that do not challenge the prevailing social order.

It takes little imagination to realize that many forms of deviance are defined as such because they do challenge the prevailing social order. That order is based on the assumption that the huge disparities in wealth, power and security that we have already outlined are legitimate and acceptable to most people in our society. In general terms, deviance can be defined rather crudely as all activities that question four sets of values – the acceptability of the current distribution of private property, the sanctity of the family and its importance as the main arena for sexual pleasure, the value of hard work as a life goal, and the importance of law and order in maintaining the existing social structure. Anyone wishing to disagree with such values and live their lives differently soon becomes aware of the extent to which many institutions in society buttress these values and sanction people who want to violate them. Deviance is about breaking rules set by powerful institutions in society.

DEVIANCE AS A PROCESS

We can view the definitions of deviants as a process in which some individuals are picked out and their actions defined as deviant and then treated for their deviance. Deviance cannot exist until someone has invoked a rule to be broken. As Becker (1963) puts it:

Social groups create deviance by making the rules whose infraction constitutes deviance, and by applying those rules to particular people and labelling them as outsiders. From this point of view, deviance is not a quality of the act the person commits, but rather a consequence of the application by others of rules and sanctions to an offender.

So deviance is not so much a particular quality that some people have because they are bad or mad: it is a process whereby some people get identified and treated as deviants. Thus, alcoholics are not merely all people who drink heavily: they are people who drink *and* have been identified as a 'threat to themselves and others' and consequently treated in a mental hospital. Most people drink, some do so to excess; some cannot control their drinking yet are still not identified as alcoholics. Some people act bizarrely, many people appear to be quite peculiar at times, yet they do not all get incarcerated in a mental hospital. Many young people act defiantly, anti-socially and quite destructively at times. Some are permitted to do so. They are allowed that freedom at certain times and in certain social situations. Other young people are likely to be caught and treated as delinquents.

RULES AND RULE BREAKING

Rules may define deviance, but not all rule breakers are defined as deviants. Rules are not always invoked, even though they are clear. Stealing stationery from work, tax evasion, jay walking, speeding, cheque frauds, fare dodging, certain unpaid debts: these are all activities that are publicly frowned on but widely practised. Also there are other situations where no one may have set out to break the rules but where the results can be interpreted in that way. Suicide, family violence, deaths in a riot, are all situations where it is difficult to know what was intended by the parties concerned. Similarly, there are situations where a certain amount of disruption may be tolerated but, at some stage, the activity may be defined as deviant. Football hooliganism, riotous assembly, rowdy behaviour in the streets or causing an affray are all examples. There are other situations where the rules are not at all clear and may get defined arbitrarily. Those with the power to invoke the rules are afforded considerable discretion at times in defining what the rules are. School children know this very well. So do young people who spend a lot of their time on the streets.

What is deviant for one person may be normal for another. 'The act of injecting heroin into a vein is not inherently deviant. If a nurse gives a patient drugs under a doctor's orders, it is perfectly proper. It is when it is done in a way that is not publicly defined as proper that it becomes deviant' (Becker, 1971). Some writers argue that the apparently arbitrary invoking of rules in some situations and not in others is closely connected with the social class of the persons concerned. People at the top of the social structure are often afforded more freedom to indulge in behaviour that would be defined as deviant if displayed by people lower down the social structure.

Invoking the Rules

Rules are in fact so widely broken that it is more fruitful to concentrate on the instances when they are invoked and the behaviour defined as deviant. We run our lives in society by taking calculated risks most of the time. These risks range from the trivial to the hazardous. Each time we step in the road in front of oncoming traffic we take a risk that the vehicles will knock us down. But we become skilled at judging the extent of the risk. Most of the behaviour is based on a personal morality that is at variance to some extent with public morality or the rules that define it. Risk-taking is not only part of life: it is an exciting aspect of living. Getting away with things both trivial and serious is part of most people's social repertoire of living. Rules in school may be widely broken. A teacher may suddenly choose to enforce a rule in order to 'make an example of' a student. What the teacher may forget is that many school students have quite a sophisticated appreciation of how and when a teacher is likely to invoke a rule. The risk of such a game of bluff and counter bluff is knowing when to stop the game!

People in authority can always claim – 'this is the rule and everyone knows it' – but still exercise their discretion of when and whether to invoke the rule. That is partly what authority is about. It is the legitimacy to use one's powers in making decisions affecting others. That applies to rules. Social workers invoke the legislation affecting children, the police invoke rules on street behaviour, wages inspectors invoke rules about the minimum wages in certain industries, and factory inspectors do something similar. Our interest at present is not whether or not they should do this in any instance, but the fact that a large amount of behaviour is permitted that contravenes rules and those with the power to invoke the rules do not take any action.

It is not only professionals who invoke the rules. Others, moral entrepreneurs go around looking for an appropriate rule they can apply. Mary Whitehouse took *Gay News* to court in 1977, invoking blasphemy laws that had never before been used this century. She was successful: the rule was still on the statute book and was applied in the circumstances. Council tenants are surrounded by rules that many would regard as extreme. For instance, one authority has a rule – 'no weeds will be allowed' (National Consumer Council, 1976). They are formulated with some notion of the perfect tenant and how such a person might behave. The rules are widely disregarded but they remain there, to be invoked when it suits the interest of someone to do so.

For our purposes this is the key. Rules are often invoked, not for the purposes of helping a possible deviant but because it serves the interests of some powerful group or institution. We shall look at how this happens in more detail in the rest of this chapter.

DEVIANCE AND INEQUALITIES

This emphasis on the social nature of rules is especially important to the context of inequalities. It enables us to see that deviance is not primarily about people who break rules. It is about people and institutions who make as well as enforce those rules. It is also about how people react when rules are broken, sometimes with apparent indifference and sometimes apprehending and incarcerating the deviants.

> Whether a given act is deviant or not depends in part on the nature of the act (that is, whether or not it violates some rule) and in part on what other people do about it. (Becker, 1963)

The contribution of this approach to deviance has been its focus on the significance of the agents of social control as the independent variable in the creation of deviance. That is not to say that people blindly indulge in certain behaviour only to find out later that these acts are deviant. Rather many people indulge in similar behaviour and do not get apprehended or incarcerated.

In considering the relationship between deviance and inequalities, we should bear in mind the following. First, if rules are invoked in such a way that they tend to identify some deviants while ignoring others, this has the effect of associating deviance with certain kinds of people. Deviants are those so defined. Thus, if the definitions of deviants are selective, then people's beliefs about who are the deviants will also be selective. The process becomes self-reinforcing. Second, if the same kinds of people persistently appear in court charged with deviant acts, this tends to confirm the legitimacy of the law enforcement agencies. After all, they always seem to find the same kind of people guilty: that must mean they are guilty! Third, each time the system of justice focuses on an individual deviant, it avoids any questioning of inequalities or the legitimacy of the existing pattern of inequalities. This serves to reinforce those inequalities and to make them legitimate. If instead, it was legitimate to say in court 'everyone knows the police pick up the most defenceless groups in society when they go about getting arrests, and that there are just as many deviants in other sections of society', this would imply a completely different ball game when it came to the police's arguments! Fourth, deviance and criminality are both shaped by society's larger institutions of power, that determine the rules and how they should be invoked. This is a fairly complex relationship, but we shall look at aspects of this in the next section.

'To him who has will more be given, and he will have abundance: but from him who has not, even what he has will be taken away' (Matthew 13 v 12). This applies not only to wealth but also to the distribution of power and its legitimacy! We shall consider what evidence there is for the analysis that we have offered so far.

Justice is Selective
We shall begin by asking what is meant by justice. That it includes a notion that equal treatment is given to equals is taken for granted generally. But in the context of this chapter, that notion becomes problematic.

> In the administration of justice, inconsistencies in police decisions to make arrests and prosecute are too systematic and frequent, court decisions of guilt and innocence are too incommensurate. The result is that in more than a few people's minds there is a persistent and discomforting nag that the ideal is one thing, but the practice is 'something else again'. (Box, 1971)

Although our system of justice is based on the notion of equality, many people with experience of the system do not believe this.

The Police Pick the Easiest

The detection rate for crimes is low. For Greater London in 1982 it was around 25 per cent. Many crimes go undetected and the perpetrators are not caught. We cannot assume that those who are apprehended are very typical of all lawbreakers. Those who appear in the official statistics are only a small minority.

Many of those who pass through the legal system are released at various stages within the system. They may be taken to a police station for questioning and later released for lack of evidence; they may be charged and processed through the courts but later released or judged not guilty for a variety of reasons.

The process is selective; the selections are carried out not only or primarily in terms of whether a person is guilty. Many other criteria come into the decisions.

Our interest is in asking to what extent such criteria as social class, race and gender are significant. If justice entails equal treatment then those finally apprehended and processed through the legal system would reflect the same mix on these criteria of those who break the law overall. If not, we would have grounds for believing that justice was biased in some ways.

Of course, we cannot know with any accuracy whether or not this is the case. We have very little information about the social characteristics of the entire population of law breakers. We shall argue that, although the evidence available is sketchy, the bias in terms of the criteria mentioned is striking.

POLICE CONSTRAINTS

One of the principles that determines who gets arrested and processed, and who gets let off concerns the maintenance of the system itself. The legal system can only operate smoothly by processing a similar number of people over time. Given that there are more unsolved crimes than there are arrests, the police are likely to fill up the available time in the courts with cases where there is a good chance of those apprehended being found guilty.

Put another way, the police, like people working in any organization, are likely to use the techniques they already know and that have produced the results they want in the past, to produce the same results in the future. They are unlikely to fill up court time with cases that are unlikely to get guilty verdicts or where the evidence they produce is likely to be strongly challenged. They have to be sure that the arrests they make stand a reasonable chance of resulting in guilty verdicts. Otherwise they would lose their credibility as effective police.

Hence the concern of the police is not primarily with justice or equality of treatment. It is with achieving enough success (judged by verdicts of guilt) to be permitted to continue doing their job. Thus, when they arrest someone, they are not interested in how representative this particular person is of those who commit crime, but whether the evidence they present is convincing enough to get a guilty verdict. The police are likely to present cases to the courts that will cause the least amount of trouble in obtaining a guilty plea.

> Those persons are arrested, tried and sentenced . . . who can be processed without creating any undue strain for the organizations which comprise the legal system (Chambliss, 1969).

This means that they must deploy their resources carefully to achieve the best possible results they can. To do their job at all, the police have to take short cuts at times. They depend on a set of conflicting expectations and have to balance these conflicts so that they both uphold the law, apprehend people who break the law, but also do it in a way that does not violate the public's civil rights and respects their needs for privacy.

> In England, for example, police are entitled to question people but have no power to detain them short of arresting them for a specific offence. Moreover, far from being able to insist on answers, they must tell a suspect of his right to silence, must allow him, within reason, private interviews with his solicitor, and must not search his premises without either his consent or a warrant. Since in many cases they neither catch an offender red-handed nor can produce willing and reliable witnesses, their best hope is to obtain a confession at his home or workplace. But how are they to get an admission if they cannot hold for questioning, or have to punctuate it with a warning as soon as they see they are getting near the mark? And how are they to get the evidence needed for a search warrant if they believe it is to be found on the premises they want to search?' (Radzinowicz and King, 1977).

So they may be tempted to bend the rules.

The police are also constrained by public opinion. They depend for their operations on a great deal of support and co-operation from the public. They can only operate with the consent of the public and opinion makers. The public are not, of course, the 'people in the street': they are those with the power (and access) to express their opinions. Their criticism and praise buttress the operations of law enforcement agencies. As a result, the police are under pressure to secure 'sufficient convictions of the right kind to allay community fears that crime is getting out of hand, and avoiding over-enforcement, particularly of some offences, so as to avoid giving the impression, at least to the influential sections of the community, that the police are getting out of hand' (Box, 1971). This does not mean that the police are the culprits for any bias in the selection of criminals: they are merely the public face to the power structure.

We must not over-emphasize these constraints, however. Most people have very little idea of exactly how the police go about their job and are probably not particularly interested, unless they themselves get apprehended. The police will in general be able to rely on co-operation from the public at large as they go about their job. But they must be careful when making arrests to ensure that they do not lightly arrest someone with the power to make a great deal of trouble for them if they have made a mistake. This means that they are likely to be more cautious in making an arrest of a person with the power to make trouble.

Discretion

Although they are subject to constraints, the police have a great deal of discretion in how they go about their work. There are four stages at which this discretion could be significant in determining who gets arrested. Given that they cannot follow up every possible criminal action, they need to decide first which complaints that come in from the public should be followed up; second, who are those most likely to commit an offence; third, in which situations there is likely to be an offence committed; and fourth, where it is politic not to look for an offence. We shall deal with each in turn.

In the detection of crime, the initial stage is often carried out by a member of the public. The police depend on the public to report any events where they believe a crime has been committed. This often happens where the member of the public is himself or herself the victim of the crime.

There is considerable bias in the kinds of crime that are reported in this way. Generally, it is more likely that such crimes will consist of actions such as larceny, robbery, assault, breaking and entering premises, and car theft. This is because the victims of these crimes invariably know that they have been victimized. The typical crime reported by citizens to the police is usually a crime against property, often committed in a public place. In 1965, 96 per cent of all crimes known to the police were property offences and, of these, a majority were reported by the public (McClintock and Avison, 1968). What may be regarded as the more 'respectable' crimes such as embezzlement, fraud, forgery, tax evasion, corporate crime, and shoplifting, are less likely to be reported by members of the public since the victims are less likely to know what has occurred. A good example of this comes from a study of store detectives by Cameron (1964). She found that shop detectives had particular theories about who was likely to engage in shoplifting and, as a consequence, monitored adolescents and black people rather than white, middle-class shoppers. Even when the shopwalkers apprehended culprits, they were far more likely to press charges on black than white people. It has been noted in studies of the public's willingness to report crimes committed that they are more likely to do so where the suspect is of a lower social status than the person making the complaint (Box, 1971).

Furthermore, this kind of crime is more likely to be committed by a person from a less powerful section of society. Respectable crimes are more likely to be committed by the middle classes, people with access to the necessary documents to commit such crimes. Thus, even if the public were not selective in who they pressed charges against, it is still the case that such complaints are more likely to be against people at the lower end of the class structure.

Also, Box (1971) suggests that the police are selective in which complaints they follow up from the public. He argues that the police pay more attention to those complainants that want to press for prosecution. He suggests that they are likely to be influenced in this by whether or not the complainant is civil in demeanour and whether or not he or she is from a white-collar occupation. A study by Reiss (1970) gives some evidence that the complainant was more in favour of pressing charges when the police had apprehended a suspect from an underprivileged background. The evidence for this is patchy but it is sufficient for the reader to bear in mind the possibility that the complaints that come to the attention of the police, in their dealings with the public, is itself selective of a certain section of society.

In order to reduce their detection work to a manageable task, the police exercise a good deal of discretion in who they look at. As a matter of routine necessity they eradicate large sections of the population from any hint of suspicion. In the eyes of the police, most people are respectable citizens unlikely to commit any crimes. That may or may not be true. It means that the police concentrate their efforts on a small part of the population who they believe are more likely to commit crimes. In doing so, they are guided by their own stereotypes of who they believe criminals are most likely to be, where they operate and what they are most likely to be doing that may warrant the police's attempts to make an arrest. The police tend to believe that crimes emanate from the disadvantaged more than from members of the well-to-do sections of the community (Bayley and Mendelsohn, 1969), and they are often particularly suspicious of racial minorities. The police, in their work on the streets, are often on the lookout for people who confirm their stereotypes of a typical criminal. They look for people they believe are about to commit an offence.

The police are apt to ask themselves such questions as – does this person look like a delinquent? Is the person's behaviour, demeanour, deportment, or manner of dress such that it signifies a typical law breaker? If so, given behaviour that could be construed as law breaking (such as loitering with intent), the police are likely to make an arrest. Robins and Cohen (1978) point out that working-class youths walking in a middle-class area are more likely to be arrested for suspicious behaviour than if they were walking in a working-class area.

In dealing with such suspects, the police are likely to interpret disrespect and hostility towards them as signs of criminality. Piliavin and Briar (1968) point out that police tended to assess a boy's character from his demeanour, in their encounters with juveniles. Those boys who were co-operative were fourteen times less likely to be apprehended than those whose demeanour was aggressive. Black youths were more likely to be accosted by the police and to be required to explain themselves and what they were doing at the time, than white youths.

The police also exercise their discretion in which areas they look for crime. Box (1971) points out that it is when the policeman is in the community that his discretion is widest. The infiltration of bias in police detection work is greatest at the point the police use their discretion in choosing particular parts of the city in preference to other areas. Their routine suspicion falls on those areas most associated in their minds with criminial activity and areas where they believe criminals are likely to live.

According to Cicourel (1968) the police partition off the city into different areas, each with their own expectations of types and levels of crime. A study by Hardt (1968) suggests that the police are likely to apprehend more people in low income areas than in higher income areas, even when the incidence of crime in both areas is similar. It means that the police make their decisions on how much resources to deploy in surveillance work in any area on the basis of their beliefs about the areas.

In any case, the police are more likely to find crime happening on the streets in certain areas merely because the inhabitants (or the people who use those areas) are more likely to be spending their time on the streets or in public places, than the inhabitants of other areas. Many crimes are committed in public, often on the streets. Thefts, drunkenness, aggressive behaviour between people, vandalism to property, are all committed in places where the police are likely to patrol. Even though much of this behaviour is ambiguous and entails the police in interpreting the behaviour as criminal or not, similar ambiguous behaviour happening in private would obviously not come to the attention of the police.

All minority groups likely to be using public places are open to police suspicion at times. Drunks, ethnic minorities, self-disclosed gay people, street traders and juveniles are all the stock-in-trade for the policeman on patrol. Arresting such people is comparatively easy. They often offer little resistance and, when they come before the courts, the police accounts of what actually happened during the encounter is likely to be believed.

People in low-income areas are more prepared to believe that the police are biased and to act accordingly. A study in the USA indicated the people living in certain ghetto areas are twice as likely to have such beliefs, compared with white areas. The study also suggests that black people in low-income neighbourhoods are likely to be taken into custody on less evidence than white people (Radzinowicz and King, 1977).

Finally, the police have considerable discretion in their choice of who not to arrest in situations where they could have taken action. There is the issue of the under-enforcement of the law against the respectable and well-to-do. Middle class delinquents have traditionally been allowed to get away with damage to property as long as someone could pay for the damage. This has always been true for undergraduates from Oxbridge.

Middle-class adults who commit crime are often immune. The police have little access to their strongholds: few officers are trained to find their way through the labyrinths of frauds. Many other white-collar crimes need lengthy investigations of complex records if the police are to make arrests. Such detection work is costly. These crimes are usually committed in private places. Gaining legal access to private areas is a cost to the plice. While the police may not always be constrained by such legal niceties they are likely to be cautious in attempting to gain access to property belonging to middle-class people because of the possible repercussions if they make mistakes. The police respect differentially people's right to privacy.

The police are likely to use their discretion in 'saving their skins' by keeping out of trouble with anyone possessing sufficient political clout to cause trouble if necessary. This may appear to run counter to what is published in the press. We need to remember that reports of influential people being arrested and later released for, say, lack of sufficient evidence is itself newsworthy because it is not routine.

We should also not underestimate the importance of manipulative skills used by middle-class people in situations where they might get arrested. Some suspects are able to convince the police that they are not really criminals even though the evidence that they have broken the law is considerable. 'Interpersonal skills enable them to control their social environments to a much greater degree than is possible for lower class (people) who have not had the opportunity to acquire and perfect these techniques' (Myerhoff and Myerhoff, 1964).

We are not suggesting that the use of discretion by the police in these ways is a deliberate attempt on their part to subvert the legal process: it is merely a necessary way of getting as many arrests as possible in the least troublesome way. That the result may be to act in a biased way and to concentrate their detection work on members of lower income groups is an unintended outcome that is significant for the purpose of this chapter.

CONCLUSIONS

We need to take crime statistics with a pinch of salt if we think they are an accurate measure of criminal behaviour. We have drawn on them in this chapter to make connections between deviance and inequalities.

We have argued that people picked out by the judicial system are not necessarily representative of all criminals. In fact, they tell us more about the distribution of political clout than they do about crime. Those selected through the processes are likely to be people least able to cause trouble in challenging the judicial process.

We picked out crime to illustrate these processes of deviance because more was written on crime than other forms of deviance. We should not assume that it is only in the area of criminal behaviour that the least powerful get selected for treatment. We could equally have chosen to look at 'trouble makers' in schools, 'problem families' processed by local authority departments, juvenile delinquents, vagrants, etc.

Equally it is not only those agencies in society that process people (like schools, hospitals, local authorities, prisons) that select out certain groups of people and stereotypes as deviants. The press has a powerful role in the identification of deviants. For example, when the Metropolitan Police first reported an ethnic breakdown of crime in London, the popular press seized on the figures of street crime (2 per cent of all London crime) to produce alarmist headlines on the extent of crime committed by black people. Yet, when the Home Office produced figures showing that, for every one racial attack on a white person, there were thirty-six on Afro-Caribbeans and fifty on Asians, only one popular paper carried the figures.

One of the surprising aspects of law and order issues is that the resources devoted to maintaining them are so low. Only about 3 per cent of all government expenditure in 1971 went to supporting the police, the prisons, etc. But, as Westergaard and Resler (1976) argue, that is not an indication of the low priority given to these services. Rather, it is a measure of the wide support the public gives to these services and the routine acceptance of the way things are. People treated by the system of British justice, although they may personally feel aggrieved, do not complain. Westergaard and Resler argue that the biases that we have touched on in this chapter are, in fact, rather more systematic than what we have described here.

Much of the evidence we have offered in this chapter is circumstantial, and we could certainly not prove that the system of justice is as heavily weighted as we have suggested in favour of the wealthy and powerful and against the favour of those with few resources and little power. One of the reasons for this is that few writers attempt to make any connection between deviance and inequalities.

The evidence that the incidence of crime stretches widely across social classes, whereas the prosecutions that are the result of police activity and the co-operation of the public produces far more officially-defined lawbreakers from the lower social class groupings leads us to question how far the system of justice offers equal treatment for equal people before the law.

What appears to happen, rather, is that there is a vicious circle based in part of the beliefs of the public as well as law-enforcement organizations. These beliefs in large part determine who the public as well as the police believe are the real culprits. Accordingly those culprits are produced by the routines and techniques of law enforcement organizations. The people selected by the systems reinforce these stereotypes of who commits crimes. They become the official statistics on which further studies of crimes are based.

We have suggested that at every stage of this process, certain people are let out of the process. The reasons for their being let off are often less to do with whether or not they have committed a crime. Rather it has more to do with the way the system operates to ensure a smooth flow of suspects being brought before the courts. Those with an ability to cause trouble because of their social status, their negotiating skills, where they live, what they look like, or what power and influence they have with the people who run the court procedures are more likely to be let off than those with little power, influence, wealth or political clout.

QUESTIONS

1. How could the thesis that deviants tend to be the least powerful groups in society be applied to mental patients?
2. In what ways can the police use their discretion in the detection of criminals?
3. Once a criminal always a criminal.
   In what ways might this be so?
4. Not all rule breakers are deviants, although rules define deviance. Suggest ways in which this is the case.
5. Outline the positivist approach in criminology and suggest some of its weaknesses.
6. In what ways does the identification of shoplifters depend on self-fulfilling prophecies?
7. Middle-class people commit their crimes in private: working class people commit their crimes in public.
   Discuss.
8. Justice is selective.
   Discuss.

FURTHER READING

An excellent book discussing issues on deviance and inequality is Box, S., *Deviance, Reality and Society*, Holt, Rinehart, Winston, 1971.

See also Cain, M., *Society and the Policeman's Role*, Routledge and Kegan Paul, 1973.

A rather more detailed review of these issues is contained in Taylor, L., Walton, P. and Young, J., *The New Criminology. For a Social Theory of Deviance*, Routledge and Kegan Paul, 1973.

The classic introduction to deviance is Becker, H., *Outsiders: Studies in the Sociology of Deviance*, Free Press, 1963.

Eleven

Choices in an unequal society

Students on professional courses usually encounter two difficulties as they attempt to come to grips with the social structure of their own society.

In the first place, they find difficulty in dealing with 'facts'. What should they do with them, and how do they judge what significance particular facts may have? They may be confronted with the kind of social statistics that are available in the Social Trends reports. And they may believe that these statistics have a reality in themselves. People, on average, drink so many gallons of beer each year: this is such and such a rise over what they drank last year. The average size of family in Britain is smaller than it used to be. The rainfall has increased very slightly this century. It is expected to decrease throughout the 1980s. 'So what?' is likely to be what students say!

Facts can only have any meaning or significance when they are placed in a context. That context will provide some sort of explanation of the real world. And any explanatory context will be limited in what it is trying to explain. Each explanatory framework is a device for being disciplined about what facts to select out of a plethora of statistics, all of which may be interesting, but only certain of which will be relevant to a particular framework.

In the second place, students have unrealistic ideas about the extent to which ordinary people are free to choose how to run their lives. They usually bring to their courses a set of prejudices about various social groups and how they behave. And they use their own moral values to judge the behaviour of these other people, without understanding the limits of their own morality or on what it is based.

Their own prejudices, drawn from their experience, are given shape and meaning from their own families and social-class background. It is usually extremely difficult for students to distance themselves from their social positions and to appreciate how other backgrounds mould the lives of other social groups.

Usually students have very little appreciation of the extent to which they themselves are privileged. They have usually imbibed the dominant notions of free enterprise society, that people are free to achieve whatever goals they have a mind to pursue. And that those who fail in such a land of opportunities are not well motivated. These notions may be buttressed by their own educational experiences. They may have found easy access to educational opportunities, commensurate with their own attainment levels. And they may have deduced from this that education is the key that will open up all avenues to those who want to pursue them. They may have little idea of the barriers experienced by others who come from less privileged backgrounds. They will probably have no realistic idea at all of the difficulties faced by people who are clearly discriminated against in a racist and sexist society such as Britain.

To deal with these difficulties, we have attempted to offer an explanation of most of the social phenomena discussed in this book that is simple, easily understandable and fairly consistent. We believe it confuses most students to be offered a number of competing explanations in one book. They ha· ˄ enough difficulty thinking about which facts to use and how to use them, let alone to deal with alternative explanations that may require different kinds of facts. One explanation throughout enables students to pit their own experience against it and challenges their own sets of explanations of the everyday world.

One of the purposes of sociology is to provide a critical explanatory framework. It should be critical in the sense that it does not allow students to take the explanation for granted. Nor should it allow them merely to apply their common-sense explanations to behaviour. It should also be critical in the sense that it does not merely confirm the explanations provided by the institutions it is attempting to describe. This includes the institutions that employ the students to carry out professional work.

This implies that sociology does not necessarily accept the con-sensus among society's institutions. It should look for explanations beyond any consensus. We hope that the accounts we have given have done this. By questioning the ideological frameworks current in society, we have sought to make connections between the control of the means of production and the ensuing social structure.

In particular, we have tried to show that people are not free to behave as they might wish but are bound by a web of constraints. Choices are made only by reference to those constraints. This is why we began with demographic data. Initially, demography may appear to be about the choices that individuals make in such matters as when to marry or when to start a family.

One of the facts that arose from our demographic analysis was the ageing of the population. The relative increase in the numbers of the aged, compared with the young, pointed to the growing import-ance of the social problems of dependency in old-age. And we highlighted this in our discussion of dependency ratios.

But the trouble with these facts is that, by themselves, they do this rather too powerfully. It is difficult to see the wood of social processes for the trees of statistics. They suggest, without any explantory context, that the social problems spring simply from the biological characteristics (the infirmity of the aged) and the demo-graphic changes (increases in life expectancies and decreases in the birth rate). What is obscured by these simple statistics is that the problem of dependency in old age is also a socially-created one.

The social problem of old-age is created not by the sheer numbers of the aged. It is created by the institutions: the family as a domestic institution, dominated by the demands made on it from outside; retirement as an economic institution; and the role of pensions as a political institution. But in particular, those who own capital and control labour can determine the value attached to wage labour and the relative low value attached to anyone outside the labour force and socially dependent. Each of these forces, together, combines to produce the 'problem' of old age in our society.

Thus facts by themselves can be misleading. They are given a significance only when they are used in context. The problem is which framework to use and what sets of explanations to look for. We chose a framework that highlights the power of the ruling class in determining many of the social relationships because that lies furthest from most students' own explanations of the everyday world.

Similarly, with our description of the family, we chose to highlight the forces at work outside the family that directly impinge on what happens within families. We argued that, contrary to popular beliefs, families are not just private spheres of activity where people are free to treat each other as they would like to. Parents cannot mould their children as they wish. They are themselves constrained by wider forces at work in society. Whether or not women are free to choose to participate in the workforce depends, not on what they or their spouses wish, but on the decisions of those who own capital and make decisions affecting the relative demand for capital and labour.

The family of today, a small nuclear unit with its intense emotional ties to each member, cut off from the wider kinship structure and only tenuously connected to the local neighbourhood, is the product of these industrial forces.

Men, too, are constrained in what they can do in families by these wider industrial processes. They may have a certain amount of space within their own families to choose to operate as they wish. But how much responsibility they can take for some of the central activities of the family – especially childcare – will depend on the constraints imposed on them in their jobs. Whether or not they can take time off to care for their children when they are ill depends mainly on their own career structures, the degree of competition in the workforce for their type of jobs, and how these caring demands may jeopardize their chances of promotion and better incomes.

We argued, too, that the relationships between spouses within the home – domestic politics – is partly determined by the amount of power they bring to those relationships from outside the family. Men get a great deal of their power in the family from their position in the workforce, often as the principal (that is, better paid) breadwinner for the family. That power is often buttressed within the family by their superior physical strength as well as by the ideological notions of what is expected of men and women.

Even with the conflicts that go on in all families, their resolution is determined in part by forces outside the family. Men, women and children may try to negotiate these conflicts in a civilized and caring way. But in the final analysis, those negotiations will depend on the distribution of power within each family. Men start with two advantages. They are more powerful, and they have been taught a series of strategies aimed at winning battles. Women are taught to defer, thereby being at a disadvantage. This may be seen at its crudest with family violence. We suggested that violence happens very widely in families. An explanation that some families are 'pathological' is not sufficient to account for such a high level of violence. The preconditions of violence exists in most marriages and are based on notions of property and ownership that are widespread in society.

Often women and children remain in violent families, not because they are pathologically incapable of resisting, but because they are not free to walk out of the situation. For working-class girls, pregnancy may still be the only avenue to moving out because of housing shortages and the difficulty of competing with better paid house renters. Women in general are not free to leave a violent marriage. Their low foothold in the job market puts them in a much weaker bargaining position if they ever contemplate leaving their husbands to try to set up separate households.

Students may feel comfortable with a view of families as private domains over which the members have control. But such a view is clouded by appearances and does not take into account forces that are not easy to see so clearly. But their invisibility makes them no less real. The individual choices that people make may seem to be far removed from the wider social structure. And people may wish to take responsibility for their own lives in spite of the pressures of the wider ideolocal forces that are derived from the economic structure. These ideological forces are reinforced by the actions of the State. We argued that the State continues to preserve the illusion of the family as a private domain even though it intrudes in certain families quite ruthlessly. The State polices the behaviour of some parents towards their children. The difficulty that some lesbian mothers find in trying to get custody of their own children is but one example. And families still risk break-up if they do not conform to certain rules laid down by local authorities.

But the State also buttresses the patriarchy by imposing one set of standards for men and another set for women. According to the State, breadwinners are still male and women are still expected to take responsibility for childcare, the sick members and the aged within their families. People do not have the choice to make whatever domestic arrangements they may wish to within their own families.

Social policy is made in an ideological context. By accepting the notion that families are private domains, the State can avoid taking responsibility for the full costs of having the labour force reproduced in the family. Whether or not people believe that a woman's place is in the home looking after children depends on the ideological consensus achieved by the alliances between capital and the state. We saw that, when capital needs the participation of women in the labour force, the State is prepared to change its notions of what the place of women is and offer subsidized childcare arrangements for women who work.

There are many, different ways of organizing society. Each way will benefit certain people at the cost of others. We have argued that our society benefits the rich and the powerful at the cost of those with a smaller stake. We have highlighted the prevailing pattern of inequalities, not only because the inequalities are so pervasive, but also because they are so widely taken for granted. And anything that is taken for granted on so big a scale is difficult to appreciate clearly. There is a massive consensus that this is the way things are, there is no other way of organizing our affairs. The mass media supports the consensus and few people challenge these assumptions.

Of course, many books are written that discuss other ways of organizing our affairs. Sociology does not have the monopoly of critical theory. But for the average person in the street it is extremely difficult to know where to find alternative notions about the organization of society. They are rarely given much credence in the newspapers or on television. An odd programme or two on Channel Four may seriously consider alternatives. But the very fact of where such a programme appears makes a statement about how seriously such ideas should be viewed. Programmes at peak viewing times, on popular channels will be far more cautious of their criticisms of the status quo.

This is not to suggest that there is a conspiracy under capitalism to eradicate all critical ideas. But we tend to underestimate the enormous ideological support that is given to those in power. Their easy access to the mass media ensures that, in any struggle between capital and labour, their case is put for them. In writing this book, we could have chosen to ignore these 'facts' and presented a very different description of the way society is.

Instead of pointing out that some people (mainly men) are still born with silver spoons in their mouths, and that sons of bank directors still have a 300 to 1 chance of themselves becoming bank directors, we could have highlighted more clearly the fluidity of the social structure. We could have concentrated much more on the ease with which some people change their socio-economic position, moving up and down the class structure.

We could have taken for granted the competition in our society and focussed more readily on those who do not succeed, looking at their personal characteristics. And we might have concluded that those who fail are poorly motivated. We could have looked at the personal characteristics of the unemployed and again concluded that they do not seem to be achievement-orientated.

We argued in Chapter 10 against taking this approach in looking at deviants. Such a positivist approach has the disadvantage that it focusses too much on the deviants who are caught and processed through the courts. Detection statistics tell us about those caught. It tells us nothing about crime. We tried to show how people who are picked up by the police tend to be certain kinds of people. And the processes of selection tend to amplify the existing inequalities in society.

No textbook can give the 'whole story'. The value of providing one broadly consistent explanation is that it enables the student to make connections between one set of data (for example, demography) and another set (for example, conflict in families). Sociology has to account for an awful lot of facts. All we can hope to do in one textbook is to present a few of the facts and fit them together into a framework.

Students may not necessarily agree with the emphasis we have given to certain aspects and the way we have treated topics. It is up to each reader to decide whether our explanations are convincing. Facts are used selectively to strengthen particular arguments. They present the evidence for a particular viewpoint. The social sciences are not value free. All social science writing is in some way ideological. It has a particular political perspective.

We have tried to be as objective as possible by offering only one framework and making links through to each of the topics discussed. It is a framework that is sufficiently different from the usual set of explanations that students have to make them think quite hard about their everyday notions of how people take decisions in their lives. Whether or not our explanation of the data is convincing is up to each student to decide.

Bibliography

Abrams, P., 'Age and Generation' in Barker (1972).

Anderson, M., *Sociology of the Family*, Penguin, 1971.

Aries, P., *Centuries of Childhood*, Jonathan Cape, 1962.

Austerberry, H. and Watson, S., 'A Woman's Place: A Feminist Approach to Housing in Britain', *Feminist Review*, Summer 1981.

Bacon, R. and Eltis, W., *Britain's Economic Problem – The Few Producers*, Macmillan, 1976.

Banks, J. A., *Prosperity and Parenthood: A Study of Family Planning among the Victorian Middle Classes*, Routledge and Kegan Paul, 1954.

Banks, J. A. and Banks, O., *Feminism and Family Planning in Victorian England*, Liverpool University Press, 1964.

Barker, D. L. and Allen, S., *Dependence and Exploitation in Work and Marriage*, Longman, 1976.

Barker, D. L. and Allen, S., *Sexual Divisions and Society: Process and Change*, Tavistock, 1976.

Barker, P., *A Sociological Portrait*, Penguin, 1972.

Bayley, D. and Mendelsohn, H., *Minorities and the Police*, Free Press, 1969.

Becker, H., *Outsiders: Studies in the Sociology of Deviance*, Free Press, 1963.

Becker, H., *Sociological Work*, Allen Lane, 1971.

Blood, R. O. and Wolfe, D. M., *Husbands and Wives*, Free Press, 1960.

Blythe, R., *The View in Winter*, Allen Lane, 1979.

Bosanquet, R., *A Future for Old Age*, Temple Smith, 1978.

Bott, E., *Family and Social Network*, Tavistock, 1957.

Bowlby, J., *Child Care and the Growth of Love*, Penguin, 1953.

Box, S., *Deviance, Reality and Society*, Holt, Reinhart, Winston. 1971.

Boyd, D., *Elites and their Education*, National Federation for Educational Research, 1973.

Brooke, R., *Law, Justice and Social Policy*, Croom Helm, 1979.

Brown, M., 'Priorities for Health and Personal Social Services' in Jones (1977).

Brown, M., *The Yearbook of Social Policy in Britain*, Routledge and Kegan Paul, 1980.

Burr, W. R., *Theory Construction and the Sociology of the Family*, Wiley, 1973.

Cameron, M. O., *The Booster and the Snitch: Department Store Shoplifting*, Free Press, 1964.

Cicourel, A. V., *The Social Organisation of Juvenile Justice*, Wiley, 1968.

Chambliss, W. J., *Crime and the Legal Process*, McGraw-Hill, 1969.

Chester, R., *Equalities and Inequalities in Family Life*, Academic Press, 1977.

Cooper, D., *The Death of the Family*, Allen Lane, 1971.

Cox, P., *Demography*, Cambridge University Press, 1976.

Central Policy Review Staff, *Population and the Social Services*, HMSO, 1977.

Commission for Racial Equality, *Half a Chance*, 1980.

Cromwell, R. E. and Olson, D. H., *Power in Families*, Wiley, 1975.

Central Statistical Office, *Social Trends No. 9*, HMSO, 1979.

Cullingworth, J. B., *Council Housing Purposes, Procedures and Priorities*, HMSO, 1969.

Daniel, W. W., *Racial Discrimination in England*, Penguin, 1968.

Davidson, T., *Conjugal Crime: Understanding and Changing the Wife-beating Problem*, Hawthorn, 1978.

Deakin, N., *Colour, Citizenship and British Society*, Panther, 1970.

Delphy, C., *The Main Enemy: A Material Analysis of Women's Oppression*, Women's Research Resource Centre Publications, 1977.

Dobash, R. and Dobash, R., *Violence against wives*, Open Books, 1980.

Donnison, D., *The Government of Housing*, Penguin, 1967.

Dreitzel, H. P., *Recent Sociology No. 1*, Macmillan, 1969.

Equal Opportunities Commission, *It's not your business: It's how the Society works*, EOC, 1978.

Farmer, M., *The Family*, Longmans, 1979.

Fiegehen, G. C., Lansley, P. S., and Smith, A. D., *Poverty and Progress in Great Britain 1953-73*, CUP, 1977.

Field, F., *Inequality in Britain*, Fontana, 1981.

Finer, M., *Report of the Committee on One-parent Families*, HMSO, 1974.

Fletcher, R., *The Family and Marriage in Britain*, Penguin, 1966.

Frankenberg, F., *Communities in Britain*, Penguin, 1966.

Frankenberg, F., 'In the Production of their lives, Men (?) . . . Sex and Gender in British Community Studies, in Barker and Allen (1976).

French, M., *The Women's Room*, Sphere, 1978.

Gans, H. J., 'The Negro Family: Reflections on the Moynihan Report', in Rainwater and Yancey (1967).

Gavron, H., *The Captive Wife*, Penguin, 1966.

George, V., *Social Security: Beveridge and After*, Routledge and Kegan Paul, 1968.

George V. and Wilding P., *Ideology and Social Welfare*, Routledge and Kegan Paul, 1976.

Glass, D. V., *Social Mobility in Britain*, Routledge and Kegan Paul, 1954.

Glass, R., *London: Aspects of Change*, McGibbon and Kee, 1964.

Glennester, H., 'The Year of the Cuts', in Jones (1977).

Glennester, H., 'Public Spending and the Social Services', in Brown (1979).

Glyn, A. and Sutcliffe, B., *British Capitalism, Workers and the Profits Squeeze*, Penguin, 1972.

Goldthorpe, J. H., *Social Mobility and Class Structure in Modern Britain*, Clarendon Press, 1980.

Goode, W. J., 'Force and Violence in the Family', in *Journal of Marriage and the Family*, 1971.

Greve, J., *London's Homeless*, Codicote, 1964.

Halsey, A. H., *Change in British Society*, OUP, 1978.

Hammerman, S. B., and Kahn, A. J., *Family Policy: Government and Families in Fourteen Countries*, Columbia, 1978.

Hanmer, J., 'Violence and the social control of women' in Littlejohn (1978).

Hardt, R. H., 'Delinquency and social class: bad kids or good cops', in Deutscher, I. and Thompson, E. J., *Among the people*, Basic Books, 1968.

Harris, A., *Labour Mobility in Great Britain*, HMSO, 1967.

Harris, C. C., *The Family*, Allen and Unwin, 1969.

Harris, A., *Handicapped and Impaired in Great Britain*, HMSO, 1971.

Heath, A. H., *Social Mobility*, Fontana, 1981.

Hunt, A., *The Home Help Service in England and Wales*, HMSO, 1970.

Hunt, A., *Families and their needs*, HMSO, 1973.

Jackson, B. & Jackson, S., *Child minder: A study in Action Research*, Penguin, 1981.

Jones, K., *The Yearbook of Social Policy in Britain 1976*, Routledge and Kegan Paul, 1977.

Kelsall, R. K., *Population*, Longman, 1975.

Laing, R. D., *The Divided Self*, Penguin, 1970.

Lambert, P., 'Perinatal mortality: social and environmental factors', *Population Trends 4*, Summer 1976.

Land, H., 'Women: supporters or supported?', in Barker and Allen (1976).

Land, H., 'The myth of motherhood' in *New Society*, Feb 26 1976.

Lansley, S., 'What Hope for the Poor?' in *Lloyds Bank Review*, April, 1979.

Leach, E. R., *A Runaway World?*, BBC, 1968.

Littlejohn, G., *Power and the State*, Croom Helm, 1978.

Llewellyn-Jones, D., *Human Reproduction and Society*, Faber and Faber, 1974.

Low Pay Unit, *Sweated Labour*, LPU, 1974.

Layard, R., Piachaud and Stewart, M., *The Causes of Poverty*, RCDIW Report, Background Paper No. 6, HMSO, 1978.
Lupton, C. and Wilson, C. S., 'The social background and connections of top decision makers' in *The Manchester School 27*, 1959.
Lydall, H. F., *The Structure of Earnings*, OUP, 1959.
Mackie, L. & Pattullo P., *Women at Work*, Tavistock, 1977.
Malos, E., *The Politics of Housework*, Allison & Busby, 1980.
Marriott, O., *The Property Boom*, Hamilton, 1967.
Marsden, D., 'Sociological Perspectives on Family Violence' in Martin (1978).
Marsden, D., *Mothers Alone*, Routledge and Kegan Paul, 1973.
Martin, J. P., *Violence and the Family*, Wiley, 1978.
Matza, D., *Delinquency and Drift*, Wiley, 1964.
Meade, J. E., *Efficiency, equality and the ownership of property*, Allen and Unwin, 1964.
Milner-Holland, *Report of the Committee on Housing in Greater London*, HMSO, 1965.
Morgan, D. H., *Social Theory and the Family*, Routledge and Kegan Paul, 1975.
Moroney, R., *The Family and the State*, Longman, 1976.
Moss, P. and Fonda, N., *Work, the Family and Equal Opportunities*, Temple Smith, 1980.
Murdock, G. P., *Social Structure*, Macmillan, 1949.
Myerhoff, H. and Myerhoff, B., 'Field observations of middle class gangs', *Social Forces*, 42, 1964.
McClintock, F. H. and Avison, N. H., *Crime in England and Wales*, Heinemann, 1968.
McGregor, O. R., *Divorce in England*, Heinemann, 1957.
National Consumer Council, *Tenancy Agreements*, NCC, 1976.
Nixon, J., *Fatherless Families on Family Income Support*, HMSO, 1979.
Oakley, A., *The Sociology of Housework*, Martin Robertson, 1974.
Oakley, A., *Housewife*, Penguin, 1976.
Oakley, A., *Becoming a Mother*, OUP, 1978.
Oakley, A., *Subject: Women*, Martin Robertson, 1980.
Oakley, A., *From Here to Maternity*, Penguin, 1982.
OPCS, *General Household Survey*, HMSO, 1973.
OPCS, *Family Formation Study*, HMSO, 1978.
Pahl, J., 'Patterns of Money Management within Marriage', in *Journal of Social Policy*, Vol. 9, 1980.
Pahl, R., *Patterns of Urban Life*, Longman, 1970.
Parker, J. and Dugmore, K., *Colour and the allocation of GLC housing*, GLC Research Reports 21, 1976.
Parsons, T., *The Social System*, Tavistock, 1952.
Piliavin, S. and Briar S., 'Police encounters with juveniles', in *American Journal of Sociology 52*, 1964.
Pond, C. and Winyard, S., *The case for a national minimum wage*, Low Pay Unit, 1983.

Radzinowicz, L. and King, L., *The growth of Crime and the international experience*, Hamilton, 1977.

Reiss, A. J., *The Police and the Public*, Yale University Press, 1971.

Reiss, A. J. and Rhodes, A. L., 'The distribution of juvenile delinquency in the social structure, *American Sociological Review 26*, 1961.

Rainwater, L. and Yancey, W. L., (eds), *The Moynihan Report and the Politics of Controversy*, MIT Press 1967.

Rex, J., 'Racialism and the urban crisis', in Kuper, L., *Race Science and Society*, Allen and Unwin, 1975.

Robins, D. and Cohen, P., *Knuckle Sandwich*, Penguin, 1978.

Rock, P. and McIntosh, M., *Deviance and Social Control*, Tavistock, 1973.

Rosser, C. and Harris, C. C., *The Family and Social Change*, Routledge and Kegan Paul, 1965.

Royal Commission on the Distribution of Income and Wealth, *The Causes of Poverty, Background Paper 6*, HMSO, 1978.

Royal Commission on the Distribution of Income and Wealth, *The A–Z of Income and Wealth*, HMSO, 1980.

Royal Commission on Population, *Report*, HMSO, 1949.

Rustin, M., 'Social Work and the Family' in Parry, N., Rustin, M., *Social Work, Welfare and the State*, Edward Arnold, 1979.

Runnymede Trust, *The Coloured Population of Great Britain*, Runnymede, 1975.

Rutter, M., *Maternal Deprivation Reassessed*, Penguin, 1972.

Rutter, M. & Madge, N., *Cycles of Disadvantage: a review of research*, Heinemann, 1976.

Scanzoni, J., *Sex Roles, Women's Work and Marital Conflict*, Lexington, 1978.

Seebohm, F., *Report of the Committee on Local Authority and Personal Social Services*, HMSO, 1968.

Schumpeter, J. A., *Capitalism, Socialism and Democracy*, Allen and Unwin, 1977.

Select Committee on Violence in the Family, *First Report*, HMSO, 1977.

Slater, P., *The Pursuit of Loneliness*, Penguin, 1971.

Smith, C., *Adolescence*, Longmans, 1968.

Smith, D., *Racial Disadvantage in Britain*, Penguin, 1977.

Smith, D., and Whalley, A., *Racial Minorities and Public Housing*, PEP Broadsheet 556, 1975.

Strauss, M. A., *Behind closed doors: violence in the American family*, Doubleday, 1980.

Strauss, M. A. and Hotaling, G. T., *The social causes of husband–wife violence*, University of Minnesota Press, 1980.

Study Commission on the Family, *Happy Families?*, 1980.

Taper, T., *Allocation of Islington Housing to Ethnic Minorities*, Research report 12, 1977.

Tawney, R. H., *Equality* . . . (4th Edition), Allen and Unwin, 1964.

Taylor, G. and Ayres, N., *Born and Bred Unequal*, Longman, 1969.

Taylor, I., Walton, P. and Young, J., *The New Criminology: for a social theory of deviance*, Routledge and Kegan Paul, 1973.

Tilley, L. A. & Scott, J. W., *Women, Work and Family*, 1978.
Titmuss, R. M., *Essays on the Welfare State*, Allen and Unwin, 1958.
Thames Television, *Our people*, Thames Television, 1979.
Todd, J. and Jones, L., *Matrimonial property*, HMSO, 1972.
Townsend, P., *Poverty in the United Kingdom*, Allen Lane, 1979.
Tutt, N., *Violence*, DHSS, 1976.
Weightman, G., 'Health Strategy', in *New Society*, Mar. 2nd, 1978.
Wells, H. G., *Experiment in autobiography: discources and conclusions of a very ordinary brain since 1866*, London 1966.
Westergaard, J. and Resler, H., *Class in a capitalist society*, Penguin, 1976.
Wilson, E., *Women and the Welfare State*, Tavistock, 1977.
Wynn, M., *Family Policy*, London 1970.
Young, J., 'Wife beating in Britain: a Socio-historical analysis', in Littlejohn, G., (1978).
Young, M. and Willmott, P., *Family and Kinship in East London*, Penguin, 1962.
Young, M. and Willmott, P., *The Symmetrical Family*, Penguin, 1973.

Index